P9-DGT-130

Attention-Deficit/ Hyperactivity Disorder

This book is printed on recycled paper.

Attention-Deficit/ Hyperactivity Disorder

What Every Parent Wants to Know

Second Edition

by

David L. Wodrich, Ph.D., ABPP
Phoenix Children's Hospital
Phoenix, Arizona

Baltimore • London • Toronto • Sydney

Paul H. Brookes Publishing Co.
Post Office Box 10624
Baltimore, Maryland 21285-0624

www.brookespublishing.com

Typeset by A.W. Bennett, Inc., Hartland, Vermont.
Manufactured in the United States of America by
The Maple Press Company, York, Pennsylvania.

The people described in the examples in this book are derived from composite case studies. The names of individuals are pseudonyms. Any similarity to actual individuals or circumstances is coincidental, and no implications should be inferred.

The reader is advised that this volume is not to be considered a substitute for the professional judgment of a psychologist or a physician.

Library of Congress Cataloging-in-Publication Data

Wodrich, David L., 1948–
Attention-deficit/hyperactivity disorder : what every parent wants to know / by David L. Wodrich. —2nd ed.
p. cm.
Includes bibliographical references and index.
ISBN 1-55766-398-X (alk. paper)
1. Attention-deficit/hyperactivity disorder. 2. Hyperactive children—Family relationships. I. Title
RJ506.H9 W63 2000
618.92'8589—dc21

99-32070
CIP

British Library Cataloguing in Publication data are available from the British Library.

Contents

About the Author

David L. Wodrich, Ph.D., ABPP, is Director of Psychological Assessment Services at Phoenix Children's Hospital in Phoenix, Arizona. He helped organize the multidisciplinary ADHD Clinic at Phoenix Children's Hospital in 1987 and has conducted research on this topic there and at Illinois State University as a member of the school psychology training faculty. His interest in children with ADHD includes diagnosis, objective monitoring of behavior change associated with medication usage, educational programming, and social skills training. After receiving his doctoral degree from Arizona State University in 1975, Dr. Wodrich served as a school psychologist and consultant to school districts, private treatment facilities, and federal programs before joining the staff at Phoenix Children's Hospital. In addition to training school psychologists in Illinois, he has taught in hospital-based pediatric, psychiatry, child psychiatry, and clinical psychology programs. He is a diplomate of the American Board of Professional Psychology, President of the American Board of School Psychology, and a past president of the Arizona Psychological Association. He is also the 1992 recipient of the award for "Distinguished Contribution to the Practice of Psychology" from the Arizona Psychological Association.

Also Contributing to this Book

Eric Benjamin, M.D., is Section Chief, Division of Behavior/Development, at Phoenix Children's Hospital in Phoenix, Arizona, and Associate Clinical Professor of Psychiatry at the University of Arizona. His interests in children with ADHD include the effective use of medication by children with complex and co-morbid disorders and child advocacy. He has participated in the outpatient multidisciplinary ADHD clinic and is Medical Director of the Pediatric Biobehavioral Program for inpatient treatment of children with severe or complex disorders at Phoenix Children's Hospital. Dr. Benjamin holds a medical degree from Mt. Sinai School of Medicine in New York City and a master's degree in nutritional sciences from the University of Wisconsin–Madison. He is board certified in both adult and child psychiatry by the American Board of Psychiatry and Neurology. Dr. Benjamin has published basic research on biochemistry and nutrition as well as clinically related articles for child psychiatrists and pediatricians. He teaches medical residents in psychiatry and pediatrics and is a regular presenter at national conferences on childhood psychopathology. He is a consultant to several treatment programs and is a frequent contributor to government panels concerned with children's mental health needs.

Foreword

For many children and adults, it is easy to concentrate on reading or to complete a project in a single sitting. For others, however, focusing on details or keeping still for a period of time is the hardest thing in the world to do. Attention-deficit/hyperactivity disorder (ADHD) is a very real burden for children and adults to bear and can present a very difficult situation with which many parents must cope. Understanding how ADHD affects our children, the ways in which we should parent and teach our children through behavioral management skills, and whether medication treatment is an appropriate option are very important issues to be considered when a loved one has ADHD. *Attention-Deficit/Hyperactivity Disorder: What Every Parent Wants to Know, Second Edition,* takes a systematic approach to examining the needs of children with ADHD and guiding parents in the decision-making process that will affect their children's entire lives. Identifying ADHD and addressing these issues early can enable individuals with ADHD to move forward with their lives—to do better in school; succeed in their adult professional lives; and yes, even become a member of Congress!

Any adult with ADHD will remember the trauma of attending school. In the past, students with ADHD were labeled as troublemakers—unable to sit at their desks for long periods of time, full of excess energy that they could not control—and punished for uncontrollable outbursts. Today, more information about ADHD is available, but some parents and teachers are still unable to identify ADHD and cope with the special difficulties, such as learning disabilities, that often accompany ADHD. *Attention-Deficit/Hyperactivity Disorder* will help parents and educators understand what to look for in making a diagnosis and how to treat the child with ADHD while nurturing the child's ability to be expressive.

As a mother of six children, I know that every child is not the same and that the education process of a child with ADHD may be different from that of a child who is not affected by ADHD. School placement, appropriate classroom techniques, and a commitment from the school are essential to the future success of your child with ADHD. Right now, the federal government provides millions of dollars to fund education programs, but many of these programs "miss the mark" at the school level when it comes to children with ADHD and learning disabilities. Fortunately, research by the National Institute of Child Health and Human Development (NICHD) has demonstrated which teaching techniques reach children who are having problems with learning to read. For students with ADHD, this is particularly important because their ability to focus their attention is limited. The problem is that this type of instruction is not yet practiced in many classrooms.

We all know of the link between literacy and future success for individuals. If a child does not learn to read, he or she will not "open the door" to other subjects such as science and history. Unfortunately, about 60% of U.S. children experience difficulty with learning to read. For at least 20%–30% of these children, reading is one of the most difficult tasks that they are asked to accomplish. If children with ADHD do not have the best, most appropriate education possible using the latest research-based instruction methods, then they may be unable to pursue important opportunities available to them. *Attention-Deficit/Hyperactivity Disorder* addresses the options available to parents when seeking the best education and accommodations for their children with ADHD.

This book also challenges the myths that exist about ADHD. Too many times, parents have been told simply,

"ADHD only affects boys," or, "Boys will be boys." The myths that are perpetuated have harmed progress in understanding children with ADHD. I remember the day when our physician told my husband and me that ADHD came through my husband's side of the family. As our doctor told us this myth, I silently recalled that it was *my* father who had tried endlessly to get me to stop swinging my feet or to convince me to finally settle down for the evening. These myths are not only inaccurate but also fail families in so many ways. Understanding that a family member has ADHD is the first step toward proper management of the disorder by the parents and a positive response from the child with ADHD, as well as the first step toward achieving positive outcomes for *all* children with ADHD.

ADHD is something that many of us must face, whether as a parent or as an individual with a diagnosis of ADHD. But it is something that can be *controlled*—so that life may go on in the most positive sense. Every child deserves a chance to fulfill his or her dreams. With a little bit of assistance and a nudge in the right direction, individuals with ADHD can be well on their way to a successful and fulfilling life.

U.S. Congresswoman Anne M. Northup
Third Congressional District of Kentucky
Washington, D.C.

Preface

A great deal about ADHD has changed since publication of the first edition of this book in 1992; a great deal also remains the same, however. Regarding science and practice, a new set of diagnostic criteria presented in DSM-IV defines ADHD. Practices necessary to make an accurate diagnosis and to fully understand each child, however, remain largely unchanged. Theoretical advancements offer hope for better understanding of ADHD's core and related elements. These considerations may lead to better diagnosis and treatment. Incremental advancements in behavioral and educational treatments have occurred, although their application still requires forging an alliance between parents and teachers (and other school professionals). New medications are available that offer the hope of enhanced symptom reduction and the possibility of diminished inconvenience and side effects.

Regarding the social and cultural aspects of ADHD, even more has changed. The diagnosis of ADHD and its treatment is the subject of wide-ranging public conversation. Dramatic increases in the number of children who have been diagnosed and treated for ADHD have fueled debates about over- and underdiagnosis and treatment and even about the very existence of the disorder. Parent advocacy and support groups are common. Internet sources providing facts and opinions about ADHD abound. School districts, responding to public awareness and often to parent advocacy, have delineated their positions regarding ADHD and its treatment.

It is understandable for parents to feel confused or overwhelmed.

Like the first edition of this book, this edition attempts to answer parents' most common questions: What is ADHD? How is it diagnosed? How is it treated? This edition also highlights common myths that parents may encounter. To promote better understanding, these myths are conspicuously placed at the beginning of each chapter. Like the first edition, this edition is intended to speak forthrightly, clearly, and honestly, as if you—as a parent—were meeting face-to-face with the author.

Although it was written with parents in mind, this book may also address concerns of teachers. Parents often request that information be shared with their son's or daughter's teacher(s). Generally, much of the information that parents find useful in understanding and living with their child proves valuable for classroom teachers, too. Teachers who are seeking information about this condition may thus benefit from reading any or all of this book, although Chapters 10–12, which deal directly with educational issues, are probably most useful for them. It would certainly be appropriate for parents who have found helpful information in this book to pass it along to their child's teacher. The book may also be a valuable supplement to teachers in training because it contains classroom suggestions. Also reviewed are eligibility requirements for special school services.

Although this book is valuable for parents, it has limitations by its very nature. First, the information provided is general. Direct application for your child should not necessarily be assumed. Nonetheless, the information in this book may constitute an initial knowledge base that enables you to work more effectively with your child's professional caregivers, be they physicians, psychologists, or educators. You are strongly encouraged to identify a qualified professional who can perform a detailed evaluation and assist you in all aspects of intervention. With regard to issues of medication, of course, it is essential that you work under the direct supervision of your child's physician. Only he or she knows your child's health status and history well enough to render care appropriately. Second, this book is intended for parents. It is not a scholarly treatise on ADHD that practicing professionals or students in psychology or medicine might require. Those seeking more in-depth and critical information are encouraged to seek one of the many excellent sources that exist in the professional literature.

I also point out that the case examples contained in this book are fictitious as to the precise details presented. They are invented examples designed to depict important points. While the details of the examples are contrived, the general points reflect essential information that the author has gained from working with many children and families.

Finally, with regard to the format of this book, I have elected to list the references separately at the end of the book in order to be less disruptive for the reader. It is hoped that this consolidation augments the usefulness and enhances the accessibility of this book for professional and lay readers alike.

To those who first encouraged me to seek a higher education:

Lawrence R. Wodrich
Louise Davisson Leonhardt
Paul H. Davisson
Eunice M. Davisson
Dr. Delbert L. Patty

Section I

What Is ADHD and What Causes It?

Chapter 1

Definition and Characteristics of ADHD

ADHD Myths

ADHD is a single disorder that appears with nearly identical symptoms among all affected children.

Inattention is the primary problem experienced by most children with ADHD.

ADHD is equally common at all ages and among boys and girls.

ADHD is usually outgrown.

ADHD is a learning disability.

Exactly what is attention-deficit/hyperactivity disorder (ADHD)? If your child has been diagnosed as having ADHD or you suspect that he or she demonstrates symptoms of the disorder, the answer to this question is crucial. Given an understanding of the disorder's characteristics, a plan to help your child can be devised. Without this understanding, you and your child are likely to experience unnecessary frustration. If you are unsure whether your child is affected by ADHD, familiarizing yourself with its definition and characteristics may help you decide to either seek professional diagnostic assistance or conclude that your child does not have ADHD.

DEFINING ADHD

Understanding today's definition of ADHD is easier if we first review the history of ADHD and how terminology has changed over time. A brief digression is called for.

Among the early labels used to describe children now referred to as having ADHD was *minimal brain dysfunction.* An epidemic of encephalitis (inflammation of the brain) early in this century left many with problems of inattention, impulsivity, and hyperactivity. Thereafter, these problems were thought to be neurological because they were seen as clear consequences of brain injury among epidemic survivors. When the same set of problems (inattention, impulsivity, hyperactivity) was noted among children without known brain injury, it was assumed that some unidentified brain injury must be present, but that it must be extremely subtle, hard to detect, or "minimal." This minimal brain injury, or minimal brain dysfunction, was believed to be the root of all inattention, impulsivity, and hyperactivity for which no clear history of brain injury existed. As a result, hyperactive or inattentive children were often referred to as having minimal brain damage or dysfunction. This label continued through the 1950s and 1960s.

With publication of the *Diagnostic and Statistical Manual of Mental Disorders, Second Edition* (DSM-II)[1], in 1968, reference was made to children with these problems, but "hyperactivity" was singled out as the predominant element. DSM-II thus included "Hyperkinetic [meaning hyper motoric movement] Reaction of Childhood" among its childhood disorders. During the 1960s and 1970s, children with ADHD were often referred to as *hyperkinetic* or more simply as *hyperactive.*

With the publication of DSM-III in 1980, *attention-deficit disorder* (ADD) became the new title because some researchers had come to believe that inattention was the central deficiency. Symptoms for ADD were listed under three broad clusters: *Inattention, Impulsivity,* and *Hyperactivity.* It should be noted that at that time it was possible to assign either a diagnosis of attention-deficit disorder with hyperactivity or attention-deficit disorder without hyperactivity, depending on whether hyperactivity accompanied inattention and impulsivity.

The term ADD was changed to ADHD in the late 1980s. DSM-IV upheld the change in terminology, but grouped the symptoms of ADHD under the heading of either *Inattention* or *Hyperactivity-Impulsivity.* DSM-IV—a standard and authoritative source for U.S. practitioners, researchers, and others in the field of mental disorders—contains formal definitions of virtually every conceivable emotional, learning, or behavior problem ranging from reading disorders to severe depression and is the source from which the definition of ADHD is derived for use in this book.

Table 1.1 outlines the criteria for defining ADHD. You are encouraged to study these criteria closely in determining whether your child may have ADHD. In giving a positive diagnosis for ADHD, the following four conditions must be met:

---

[1]For ease of reading this book, specific reference citations do not appear in the text. The interested reader should refer to the reference list at the end of this book.

1. Presence of a minimum number of symptoms (six or more) of either inattention or hyperactivity-impulsivity or both (see symptom list in Table 1.1)
2. Presence of symptoms for 6 months or longer
3. Presence of symptoms before 7 years of age
4. Impaired functioning in two or more settings caused by ADHD symptoms

It is also assumed that no other DSM-IV disorder accounts for these symptoms as readily as ADHD. A child is diagnosed as having ADHD only after data have been compiled from several sources, such as observations, interviews, and rating forms. The focus of this chapter, however, is understanding precisely what these symptoms are.

SYMPTOMS OF ADHD

It is difficult for most parents to remember each of the symptoms outlined in Table 1.1, much less comprehend precisely what each encompasses. To better understand the nature of ADHD, consider the distinct facets of ADHD separately—inattention and hyperactivity-impulsivity. By examining the DSM-IV symptoms in Table 1.1, you may appreciate how these primary deficits cause problems.

Inattention

Inattention refers to errors either in selecting what to attend to or in keeping attention focused for as long as necessary to perform a task. DSM-IV symptoms, for example, that exemplify these problems are

- "Often fails to give close attention to details or makes careless mistakes in schoolwork, work, or other activities" ("a," Table 1.1)
- "Often has difficulty sustaining attention in task or play activities" ("b," Table 1.1)

Table 1.1. DSM-IV definition of *attention-deficit/hyperactivity disorder*

A. Either (1) or (2):

(1) Six (or more) of the following symptoms of inattention have persisted for at least 6 months to a degree that is maladaptive and inconsistent with developmental level:

Inattention

(a) often fails to give close attention to details or makes careless mistakes in schoolwork, work, or other activities
(b) often has difficulty sustaining attention in tasks or play activities
(c) often does not seem to listen when spoken to directly
(d) often does not follow through on instructions and fails to finish schoolwork, chores, or duties in the workplace (not due to oppositional behavior or failure to understand instructions)
(e) often has difficulty organizing tasks and activities
(f) often avoids, dislikes, or is reluctant to engage in tasks that require sustained mental effort (such as schoolwork or homework)
(g) often loses things necessary for tasks or activities (e.g., toys, school assignments, pencils, books, tools)
(h) is often easily distracted by extraneous stimuli
(i) is often forgetful in daily activities

(2) Six (or more) of the following symptoms of hyperactivity-impulsivity have persisted for at least 6 months to a degree that is maladaptive and inconsistent with developmental level:

Hyperactivity

(a) often fidgets with hands or feet or squirms in seat
(b) often leaves seat in classroom or in other situations in which remaining seated is expected
(c) often runs about or climbs excessively in situations in which it is inappropriate (in adolescents or adults, may be limited to subjective feelings of restlessness)
(d) often has difficulty playing or engaging in leisure activities quietly
(e) is often "on the go" or often acts as if "driven by a motor"
(f) often talks excessively

Impulsivity

(g) often blurts out answers before questions have been completed

(continued)

Table 1.1. *(continued)*

(h) often has difficulty awaiting turn

(i) often interrupts or intrudes on others (e.g., butts into conversations or games)

B. Some hyperactive-impulsive symptoms that caused impairment were present before age 7 years.

C. Some impairment from the symptoms is present in two or more settings (e.g., at school [or work] and at home).

D. There must be clear evidence of clinically significant impairment in social, academic, or occupational functioning.

E. The symptoms do not occur exclusively during the course of a Pervasive Developmental Disorder, Schizophrenia, or other Psychotic Disorder and are not better accounted for by another mental disorder (e.g., Mood Disorder, Anxiety Disorder, Dissociative Disorder, or a Personality Disorder).

Code based on type:

Attention-deficit/hyperactivity disorder, combined type: If both Criteria A1 and A2 are met for the past 6 months

Attention-deficit/hyperactivity disorder, predominantly inattentive type: If Criterion A1 is met but Criterion A2 is not met for the past 6 months

Attention-deficit/hyperactivity disorder, predominantly hyperactive-impulsive type: If Criterion A2 is met but Criterion A1 is not met for the past 6 months

These symptoms can be recognized readily by parents. What is surprising to parents, however, is that children with ADHD are extremely variable in exhibiting their attention problems. On the one hand, a child with ADHD may have no problem concentrating on highly stimulating activities or on ones that the child selects for him- or herself. A child with even fairly severe ADHD may show no difficulties in these situations. On the other hand, he or she may appear distractible, inattentive, or may give up quickly when confronted with repetitive or tedious tasks. Thus, an 8-year-old boy with ADHD may work for hours without interruption while playing a video game but may sustain attention for only a few minutes during monotonous arithmetic drills at school. A 5-year-old girl with ADHD may organize and reorganize dolls provided that playmates are present but may wander from activity to activity during solitary play. In other words, the demands of the situation may determine the severity of symptoms that are evident.

The pervasiveness of these problems across situations and their ongoing nature is the key to deciding whether your child is genuinely inattentive. It is not fair to evaluate only the best or worst instances of inattention; however, if adult direction, close supervision, high levels of rewards, or high-interest activities are required to sustain a child's attention, then a genuine problem may exist. In the final analysis, someone must make a judgment about whether each of the individual symptoms related to inattention is present. Again, as emphasized in Chapters 3–7, multiple data sources can aid this process.

Hyperactivity and Impulsivity

Although the terms *hyperactivity* and *impulsivity* imply two distinct problems, in reality the two symptom clusters occur together so consistently, and their basic characters are so similar, that it is now concluded that they represent one dimension of ADHD.

Hyperactivity *Hyperactivity* relates to excesses in physical movement, especially excesses that have a purposeless, poorly directed, or driven quality. Examples of symptoms related to hyperactivity are

- "Often fidgets with hands or feet or squirms in seat" ("a," Table 1.1)
- "Often leaves seat in classroom or in other situations in which remaining seated is expected" ("b," Table 1.1)

Children with ADHD are more restless, fidgety, and on the go than children without ADHD. Situations requiring quiet, focused, and controlled behavior seem to present special problems for children with ADHD, whereas more open settings may be no problem. This is because a child who races about the playground may trouble no one; but teachers and peers find it troublesome when a boy gets up repeatedly to sharpen an already-sharp pencil, a girl persists in leaving her bus seat to visit with friends despite warnings from the driver, or a teenager cannot sit through an entire movie without multiple trips to the snack bar or the rest room. With the hyperactivity dimension, too, a judgment must be made about the appropriateness of the behavior for the situation and the age of the child. The requirement of judgment makes diagnosis of ADHD less simple than it appears on the surface. Later chapters describe how the information necessary for an ADHD diagnosis is collected.

Impulsivity *Impulsivity* means that the individual has difficulty properly controlling or regulating impulses. The urge to act is expressed too readily in behavior; the typical controls that are expected of a child of a given age simply fail. Examples of symptoms include

- "Often blurts out answers before questions have been completed" ("g," Table 1.1)
- "Often has difficulty awaiting turn" ("h," Table 1.1)

For instance, a child with ADHD may not be able to control his or her impulses during a simple board game. The exuberance to make a quick deal, to roll the dice, or to comment on others' play is often expressed unchecked. This makes the child apt to play out of turn, to grab the dice before another player has finished, or to make too many careless or inappropriate comments about the play of others.

Social difficulties seem to spring from impulse control deficits. Impulsive behavior is apt to annoy other children. It can also frustrate parents. Virtually any situation involving rules or expectations can result in adult–child conflict. For example, children with ADHD often fail to recognize obligatory classroom behavior such as keeping their hands to themselves, talking quietly, or remaining seated. The child with ADHD may require constant reminders, reprimands, and redirection to control impulses. Teachers and parents often complain of exhaustion after caring for a child with ADHD. Because the child's internal controls of behavior are so deficient, parents complain that they must constantly restate expectations and enforce rules with yelling or threats of heavy-handed punishment. Chapter 8 shares ways in which parents can manage the behavior of a child with ADHD most effectively.

ADHD: MORE THAN ONE PROBLEM?

As the previous discussion of deficits implies, ADHD may be several interrelated problems rather than a single problem. In fact, analysis of parent and teacher questionnaires completed on hundreds of children has led researchers to conclude that ADHD is not a single condition that appears equivalently in all individuals. Rather, two main underlying problems seem present among the many individuals studied: inattention and hyperactivity-impulsivity.

It is important to point out, however, that both inattention and hyperactivity-impulsivity may not be present in all children with ADHD. It appears that some children have predominantly attentional deficits but no hyperactivity, whereas others have both attentional and hyperactivity problems. Some, especially as preschoolers, may have hyperactive-impulsive behavior but may not appear inattentive. These children seem to differ from each other in important ways. Children who are both inattentive and hyperactive-impulsive, for instance, are apt to have more social difficulties and a harder time with following rules. Russell Barkley at the University of Massachusetts Medical Center has advanced a detailed theory of ADHD that identifies failures in inhibition as the central deficit. Unable to inhibit their actions, stop what they are doing, or delay responding, children with ADHD experience a variety of related problems. They are, for example, less able to plan ahead, to use internal controls and working memory to guide their actions, or to control their emotions. According to Barkley's theory, the lack of behavioral inhibition, rather than inattention, is the primary problem with ADHD.

Research has shown, in contrast to hyperactive-impulsive children, that inattentive children tend to be more anxious and shy. Research has also suggested that these children may respond somewhat differently to the most frequently used type of medication, stimulants. The following table lists characteristics that seem to distinguish these two groups of children:

With hyperactivity	Without hyperactivity
Conduct problems	Sluggish, drowsy
Impulsive	Daydreaming
Distractible	Anxious, shy
Rejected by peers	Learning disabilities
Higher-dose stimulants	Lower-dose stimulants

Note: The differences listed here are generally true. Individual children, however, may or may not show any or all of these differences.

DSM-IV provides an easy, if wordy, means of denoting the exact type of ADHD that is diagnosed. DSM-IV identifies three subgroupings of ADHD:

- *Combined type*—Characterized by both inattention and hyperactivity-impulsivity
- *Predominately inattentive type*—Characterized mostly by inattention with little hyperactivity or impulsivity
- *Predominately hyperactive-impulsive type*—Characterized mostly by hyperactivity and impulsivity but few attentional problems

It was once thought that most children with ADHD would be classified as combined types, but research of the late 1990s suggested that there may be as many children with the predominately inattentive type as those whose disorder includes obvious features of hyperactivity-impulsivity.

ONSET OF SYMPTOMS

The DSM-IV definition of ADHD requires that symptoms appear before the child is 7 years old. This requirement is seldom a problem. In fact, the average age at which symptoms first become evident is 3–4 years. Many parents report that their child was hyperactive, restless, driven, and constantly on the go since he or she was a toddler or even before. Others recall brief attention, lack of inhibition in social situations, and poor appreciation of danger among their 2- or 3-year-olds. Some researchers have even suggested that infants differ in the characteristics of attention span and activity level.

Although many children are recognized as having ADHD when they are preschoolers, many are not. Not surprisingly, for many children, being in the school environment is the challenge that causes their inattention, overactivity, or self-control problems to become manifest in behavior. For these children, the demand to cope with a new situation means that a previously underlying but undetected deficit becomes unmistakably present in day-to-day behavior. Some parents are confused that a child who seemed fine as a preschooler suddenly has ADHD as a kindergartner. It is usually true that the deficit did not emerge for the first time at age 5 (on beginning kindergarten); rather, the school requirements of, for example, lining up quietly, refraining from talking, and staying on task, culminated in symptoms unmistakable to a classroom teacher. When symptoms of ADHD are not pronounced or do not cause impaired functioning until later (i.e., after age 7 years), clinicians may still use flexibility in recognizing and formally diagnosing ADHD.

DURATION OF SYMPTOMS

DSM-IV also stipulates that maladaptive symptoms of inattention or hyperactivity-impulsivity must have been present for 6 months. This criterion is reasonable in that assigning important and potentially stigmatizing diagnoses should not be done unless the problem is longstanding.

Furthermore, this criterion is designed to help eliminate the tendency for diagnosticians to misinterpret temporary or transient reactive problems as ADHD. For example, a child who is reacting to a family move or to an assignment from an unfavorable teacher may have temporary problems with inattention or overactivity. He or she should not be diagnosed with ADHD; a thorough evaluation can determine the true nature of the child's problem and the 6-month duration criterion can help keep diagnosticians vigilant to other causes of problems.

SYMPTOMS MUST CAUSE IMPAIRMENT

In the same vein of diagnosing only significant conditions, DSM-IV also stipulates that the symptoms of ADHD must cause impairment in two or more settings and that there must be clear evidence of negative impact in an important aspect of life, such as social or academic environments. This, too, is a protection against overdiagnosis and inconsequential labeling. The logic here is that individual differences are to be tolerated (if not celebrated) as long as they do not cause problems. If a child is active, impulsive, or spacey, but these characteristics do not cause impaired functioning, then it is extremist and inappropriate to label him or her as having ADHD. Only when symptoms of inattention or hyperactivity-impulsivity begin to prevent school success, limit friendships, or, for older individuals, impair job success should a label be affixed. Moreover, the impairments caused by these symptoms should be evident across situations rather than in one setting only. To require impairment in more than one setting helps guarantee that diagnoses are made based on inattentive or hyperactive-impulsive characteristics inherent in the child rather than on poor management or inappropriate adult expectations.

PREVALENCE OF ADHD

It is estimated that 3%–5% of U.S. school-age children are affected by ADHD. Precise estimates of the percentage of affected children, however, are virtually impossible because of the changing definition of the disorder and the nature of the way in which children are identified. Definitions in DSM-IV were formulated by a committee of experts who were obliged to set standards, which are often arbitrary. For example, the current definition of ADHD calls for six symptoms of either inattention or hyperactivity-impulsivity. If the committee had selected an eight-symptom cutoff, then fewer children would be identifiable; if they had selected a four-symptom cutoff, then more would be identifiable. Chapter 6 points out that rating instruments allow researchers and clinicians to remove some of the imprecision of diagnosing ADHD.

In whichever way ADHD is defined, it is clear that far more boys than girls are affected, by ratios estimated at 2:1 to 10:1. Why this maldistribution? Many researchers believe that a greater inherent risk, perhaps related to brain biochemistry or structure, exists for males. Others have pointed to the school-related demand to sit quietly and attend, which may be relatively harder for boys because of the manner in which they are socialized. Still others have wondered about subtle discrimination occurring among elementary teachers, who are predominantly female. No clear answer is available.

ASSOCIATED PROBLEMS

A major advance in recent research has revealed a number of problems that can accompany ADHD. Children, teenagers, and even adults are at risk for a variety of these associated problems. Although ADHD's symptoms can be troubling in their own right for parents, teachers, peers, and the individuals themselves, often coexisting problems with behavior control, school learning, and social relationships can be even more disturbing. Many parents and a surprising number of professionals mistakenly assume that ADHD is a harmless disorder characterized by too much busy activity but few other negatives. This assumption is wrong, as careful studies have shown.

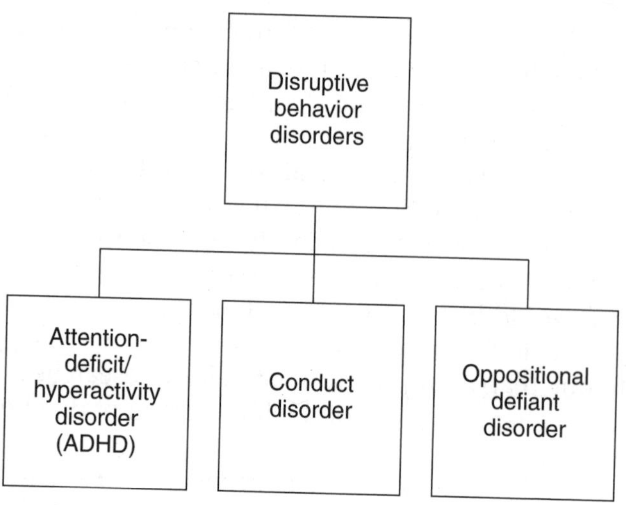

Figure 1.1. DSM-IV categorization of ADHD as disruptive behavior disorders (see text for description).

Behavior Problems

Figure 1.1 depicts ADHD as one of three disruptive behavior disorders, as it has been historically classified. The three disorders in this category—ADHD, conduct disorder, and oppositional defiant disorder—occur together frequently, although the disorders also frequently exist alone, without the presence of the others. In many instances, these are not benign disorders. Each is often socially disruptive or distressing, and each can have a significant negative impact on the child's life. Because it is important for you as a parent to understand ADHD's relationship to these other disorders, brief descriptions of conduct disorder and oppositional defiant disorder are included next.

Conduct disorder, as described by DSM-IV, is "a persistent pattern of conduct in which the basic rights of others and major age-appropriate societal norms or rules are violated" (p. 85). Table 1.2 contains a complete set of diagnostic criteria for conduct disorder. Briefly, the symptoms relate to breaking rules and participating in antisocial behavior, such as stealing, running away from home, lying, and skipping

Table 1.2. DSM-IV definition of *conduct disorder*

A. A repetitive and persistent pattern of behavior in which the basic rights of others or major age-appropriate societal norms or rules are violated, as manifested by the presence of three (or more) of the following criteria in the past 12 months, with at least one criterion present in the past 6 months.

Aggression to people and animals

(1) Often bullies, threatens, or intimidates others

(2) Often initiates physical fights

(3) Has used a weapon that can cause serious physical harm to others (e.g., a bat, brick, broken bottle, knife, gun)

(4) Has been physically cruel to people

(5) Has been physically cruel to animals

(6) Has stolen while confronting a victim (e.g., mugging, purse snatching, extortion, armed robbery)

(7) Has forced someone into sexual activity

Destruction of property

(8) Has deliberately engaged in fire setting with the intention of causing serious damage

(9) Has deliberately destroyed others' property (other than by fire setting)

Deceitfulness or theft

(10) Has broken into someone else's house, building, or car

(11) Often lies to obtain goods or favors or to avoid obligations (i.e., "cons" others)

(12) Has stolen items of nontrivial value without confronting a victim (e.g., shoplifting, but without breaking and entering; forgery)

Serious violations of rules

(13) Often stays out at night despite parental prohibitions, beginning before age 13 years

(14) Has run away from home overnight at least twice while living in parental or parental surrogate's home (or once without returning for a lengthy period)

(15) Is often truant from school, beginning before age 13 years

B. The disturbance in behavior causes clinically significant impairment in social, academic, or occupational functioning.

C. If the individual is age 18 years or older, criteria are not met for Antisocial Personality Disorder.

Specify type based on age at onset:

Childhood-onset type: Onset of at least one criterion characteristic of Conduct Disorder prior to age 10 years

(continued)

Table 1.2. *(continued)*

Adolescent-onset type:	Absence of any criteria characteristic of Conduct Disorder prior to age 10 years
Specify severity:	
Mild:	Few if any conduct problems in excess of those required to make the diagnosis and conduct problems cause only minor harm to others
Moderate:	Number of conduct problems and effect on others intermediate between "mild" and "severe"
Severe:	Many conduct problems in excess of those required to make the diagnosis or conduct problems cause considerable harm to others

From American Psychiatric Association (APA). (1994). *Diagnostic and statistical manual of mental disorders* (4th ed., pp. 90–91). Washington, DC: Author. Reprinted with permission from the *Diagnostic and Statistical Manual of Mental Disorders, Fourth Edition.*

school. It is estimated that 30%–50% of children with ADHD between the ages of 7 and 10 years are likely to show antisocial symptoms and symptoms of conduct disorder. These symptoms may bring children with ADHD into conflict with authority and lead to severe problems unless they are corrected by the late teenage or adult years.

Oppositional defiant disorder is defined by DSM-IV as "a pattern of negativistic, hostile, and defiant behavior toward authority figures" (p. 91). The more serious violation of others' rights seen in conduct disorder is generally assumed to be absent among children with this disorder. The complete criteria for oppositional defiant disorder are listed in Table 1.3. The symptoms cover excesses of behaviors such as temper outbursts, arguing with and defying adults, blaming others, and responding vindictively. Although encompassing symptoms less severe than conduct disorder, oppositional defiant disorder embraces behaviors that can nonetheless produce severe strains at home and at school, although some children are much less asymptomatic outside their own homes. In a study at the University of Massachusetts Medical Center, Russell Barkley and colleagues found that when rating forms were used to identify the most ADHD-symptomatic 3% of a group of children, 59% of those chil-

Table 1.3. DSM-IV definition of *oppositional defiant disorder*

A. A pattern of negativistic, hostile, and defiant behavior lasting at least 6 months, during which four (or more) of the following are present:
   1. Often loses temper
   2. Often argues with adults
   3. Often actively defies or refuses to comply with adults' requests or rules
   4. Often deliberately annoys people
   5. Often blames others for his or her mistakes or misbehavior
   6. Is often touchy or easily annoyed
   7. Is often angry and resentful
   8. Is often spiteful or vindictive

B. The disturbance in behavior causes clinically significant impairment in social, academic, or occupational functioning.

C. The behaviors do not occur exclusively during the course of a Psychotic or Mood Disorder.

D. The criteria are not met for Conduct Disorder, and, if the individual is age 18 years or older, criteria are not met for Antisocial Personality Disorder.

From American Psychiatric Association (APA). (1994). *Diagnostic and statistical manual of mental disorders* (4th ed., pp. 93–94). Washington, DC: Author. Reprinted with permission from the *Diagnostic and Statistical Manual of Mental Disorders, Fourth Edition.*

dren also met the criteria for oppositional defiant disorder. This is an enormous overlap; it implies, as have other studies, that approximately half of the children with ADHD also have severe problems with compliance, temper control, and cooperation. As shown in Chapters 3–7, a thorough evaluation does not stop once a diagnosis of ADHD has been established; a full accounting of the child's problems (including possible conduct or oppositional aspects) and strengths must be made.

Why do conduct and oppositional disorders and attentional and impulse disorders occur together so often? Several answers have been postulated. It may be that the deficits associated with ADHD, such as poor regulation of impulses and difficulty in sustaining attention, prime the child for behavior problems. If this is so, it is easy to see how arguing, losing one's temper, or even stealing may be a consequence of deficient impulse control or of poor attention to rewards and punishments. Another explanation suggests a single common cause for ADHD, oppositional defiant disorder, and conduct disorder. Whichever malfunction exists in the child's nervous system or in his or her personal history, it causes multiple problems to eventuate, with ADHD being just one of them and behavior and conduct problems being others. Feelings of frustration and anger resulting from chronic failure may also be implicated. Children with ADHD often feel as though they can do little right. After failing at school or receiving repeated negative parental and peer feedback, anger accrues. Too often it may boil over into unacceptable conduct. Likewise, the child with ADHD who has experienced little success in socially accepted endeavors, such as school, clubs, or family, may turn elsewhere in search of success. Success sometimes occurs only in unacceptable, antisocial activities. When this happens repeatedly, a pattern of breaking rules and affiliating with other children or teenagers who do the same may occur, and conduct disorder may ensue. As a parent, it is important for you to recognize the risk for these types of problems without forgetting that they occur only among *some* children with ADHD.

Emotional Problems

ADHD is often accompanied by emotional problems in addition to those already mentioned. Given all of the negatives associated with the disorder, it is not surprising to learn that children with ADHD are more subject to poor self-esteem than are children who are developing typically. As adults, they have more depression-related problems, such as severe discouragement and demoralization; yet, clear evidence is lacking that children with ADHD are more likely than children without ADHD to have severe depression.

Two other DSM-IV conditions, tic disorder and Tourette syndrome, occur more often among children with ADHD, albeit only in a small minority. Tics are repetitive twitches or movements, usually around the eye or other parts of the face but sometimes involving vocal noises. Although many tics are mild and may be virtually unnoticeable to the untrained observer, some tics are severe and chronic. Many times, parents and even professionals overlook the presence of tics, writing them off as mere "nervous habits," and vocal tics are thought to be throat clearing or sniffing as a result of allergies. One reason why it is important to recognize tics is that their presence may suggest that stimulant medications (e.g., class stimulants) require cautious use with this child by a knowledgeable physician (see Chapter 9). The rarer Tourette syndrome involves both motor and vocal tics that extend over a long time (i.e., longer than 1 year) and may involve other problems, such as self-injurious behavior or an irresistible urge to swear.

Interpersonal Problems

Following rules, dressing and grooming oneself, completing homework, and cooperating are among the many tasks that parents must teach their children. Impaired by difficulty in attending and by poor impulse modulation, the child with ADHD is bound to struggle with these responsibilities. All too often, the parent–child relationship is strained as a result. Many parents find that they must repeat directions; use immediate, potent, and frequent consequences; or constantly organize their child's life. If they do not do these things, they have tenuous control over their child's behavior or their child seems to fail constantly. It is little wonder that parents experience frustration and fatigue. Perhaps it is because of these factors that much more self-blame and depression are found among mothers of children with ADHD. These factors may cause stresses throughout the family—parents of children with ADHD are three times more likely to divorce than are parents of unaffected children.

Research has shown that parents of children with ADHD use more commands to direct their children and are more negative toward them. Such parents often comment that without loud commands or threats of punishment, there would be little cooperation. Not surprisingly, families often find that one of the most valuable services professionals can offer is to teach alternative methods to govern these difficult-to-discipline children. (For a detailed discussion, see Chapter 8.)

For some children with ADHD, winning and maintaining friends is a special challenge. The core deficits of inattention, impulsivity, and hyperactivity once again prevent success, this time in the social realm. If other 7-year-olds regularly spend 40 minutes sitting attentively and organizing their baseball cards, the 7-year-old with ADHD whose attention span for this activity is 5 minutes may fail to fit in. Similarly, if the social expectation is to speak quietly at a party and contribute to but not dominate a conversation, the 14-year-old who impulsively interrupts to speak loudly and incessantly about himself is apt to be rejected. So, too, is the child who plays so actively, roughly, and with such exuberance as to imperil playmates' safety. It is for these reasons that children with ADHD are often rated as unpopular (i.e., nonpreferred as playmates) in research studies. It is also why children with ADHD often try to find a niche with children who are far younger or far older than themselves.

School Learning Problems

A strong association exists between ADHD and school problems. The ADHD symptom list (Table 1.1) itself seems to revolve around problems with school origins. After all, it is in the classroom where one is expected to remain seated, refrain from answering until the question is completed, and see a task through to completion.

Children with ADHD may experience several types of trouble at school. First, they may be underproductive—for example, by failing to complete assignments or by losing their work—or disorganized; therefore, they may risk failure because their work is not done. Parents may be told their child cannot be awarded passing grades even though he or she seems knowledgeable about the subjects taught, because the child is not completing enough work.

Second, children with ADHD may have learning disabilities. Disorders of memory, language, visual perception, or the like that are severe enough to prevent the child from achieving up to potential are more common among children with ADHD. Reading problems, for example, are common among children with ADHD. Unlike the underproductive child who knows how to read but fails to complete his worksheets, the child with learning disabilities has not learned to read (or do mathematics, spelling, or other academics) at a level commensurate with his or her intellectual ability. It is estimated that approximately 3% of children in the United States without ADHD have learning disabilities. Among children with ADHD, the percentage jumps to as high as 35% by some estimates. It may be factors closely related to ADHD, such as problems with working memory, linguistic and phonological processing, or fine motor output, or general problems with attention and impulse control that explain this high rate of learning disabilities. In this vein, it appears that even children with mild ADHD symptoms have more academic problems than classmates who are symptom-free.

ADHD symptoms and learning disabilities, however, are often distinct problems that unfortunately co-occur in the same child. For example, it is well established among children without ADHD that errors in sound discrimination, memory for sound sequences, and the ability to blend sounds (together these are referred to as *phonological process deficits*) result in reading problems. When children with ADHD have reading problems, it appears that these phonological deficits rather than the inattention and impulsivity of ADHD cause them to be poor readers. Of course, wise management of a child with ADHD who has reading problems requires a thorough examination so that all problems can be addressed in order for comprehensive planning to occur. Unfortunately, diagnosticians sometimes stop their assessment once they establish the presence of ADHD. This practice often leads to students who are underserved by overly simple, single-focus treatments (e.g., use of medication alone). Learning disabilities are particularly devastating for children with ADHD because they already struggle to learn and to produce work in class.

Finally, behavior and conduct problems may be evident at school just as they may be at home. Unfortunately, the typical public school classroom has too many students and too little teacher time to allow easy individualization of instruction and discipline. Many children with ADHD are expelled from school or are labeled as being severe disciplinary problems, often without the understanding that they are affected by a disorder that contributes to their behavior. Other children with ADHD merit and receive special school services (related either to their behavioral or emotional status or to their learning disabilities). Chapters 10–12 provide information about how children with ADHD may be helped in school.

WILL MY CHILD OUTGROW ADHD?

"It's too bad my son has this hyperactivity problem, but he *will* outgrow it, won't he?" Many parents have heard that ADHD is confined to the childhood years; they expect the disorder to disappear by the teenage years and certainly by adulthood. The answer to this concerned parent's question is, "Yes and no."

If 100 eight-year-olds who are highly symptomatic with ADHD were followed until they reached 16 years of age, certainly fewer than 100 of them would still be found to be symptomatic. Those who were would probably behave much differently from the way they did as 8-year-olds. Most would have slowed motorically, would attend better to repetitive tasks, and would regulate their impulses better. Physiologic maturation and the myriad of learning experiences encountered in growing up would guarantee this outcome.

Sadly, approximately 75% would continue to have problems at school, with their families, or with authorities.

Although their behavior may appear to be more mature than it did when they were 8 years old, the same underlying deficits may remain. For example, impulsivity now may interfere with responsible completion of chores or homework, or with following community rules, such as curfew. As teens, the ADHD group may exercise poor judgment when they are unsupervised and with peers. Twenty-five percent or more might exhibit antisocial or conduct-disordered behavior (e.g., stealing, running away, truancy). Almost 60% would be anticipated to have failed one grade in school. Thus, although as teenagers many of these children would appear less conspicuously inattentive or hyperactive, many nonetheless would continue to struggle in life.

Several factors seem to lessen the risk of teen problems: high IQ score, high social status of the family, good peer relationships, few aggressive and conduct problems as children, parents without emotional problems, and a relatively problem-free history of interactions with parents. The more of these factors that are present in the child's favor, the better the chances of good long-term adjustment. The presence of co-existing diagnoses predicts other problems. For example, ADHD plus conduct disorder is associated with especially high risk of injurious or fatal driving accidents; ADHD plus mood disorder or conduct disorder is associated with especially high risk of substance abuse.

If we followed the same set of individuals even further forward in time, a surprising prevalence of problems would yet be found. As adults, as many as 50%–65% would still be symptomatic for ADHD. As many as 25% might have actual antisocial personalities as adults, with accompanying problems—for example, court involvement, most often for problems such as traffic violations; physical aggression toward others; and theft. This group of adults would also be expected to change jobs more frequently, to work less well independently, and to be less likely to get along well with their supervisors. They would have completed few years of formal education and be more prone to abuse psychoactive substances, such as street drugs. Although clear evidence of greater prevalence of mood disorders is lacking, rates of attempted and successfully completed suicides are higher among adults who had ADHD as children than among adults without this history. This fact may be due to these individuals' years of frustration and discouragement.

CONCLUSIONS

ADHD represents a set of interrelated deficiencies in attention, activity level, and impulse control that often results in educational, social, parent–child, and vocational problems, some of which continue into adulthood. As demonstrated in subsequent chapters, comprehensive assessment and intervention are essential for maximizing the individual's adjustment and for promoting long-term happiness.

Chapter 2

Causes of ADHD

ADHD Myths

ADHD is caused primarily by faulty parenting.

There is no evidence of physiological differences between individuals with and without ADHD.

Sugar ingestion is a primary cause of ADHD.

Scientists and parents share an equal interest in determining the causes of ADHD—scientists because they want to find better ways to treat or prevent ADHD, and parents because, although they seek modes of treatment or prevention, they are also eager for an answer to their personal dilemma of "why my child?" Considerable research has been devoted to the search for ADHD's causes. Although a precise understanding of ADHD's causes remains elusive, a general understanding of the origins of the disorder has emerged. In addition, we now know much more about what does *not* cause ADHD. Such findings have allowed several myths about ADHD's causes to be dispelled.

INHERITANCE

The current scientific consensus, which was reached by studying the characteristics of biological relatives of individuals with ADHD, is that ADHD is principally an inherited condition. This is known by studying the characteristics of biological relatives of individuals with ADHD. Using this strategy, Dennis Cantwell at the University of California at Los Angeles observed that children with ADHD were far more likely to have relatives, especially fathers and uncles, with ADHD than were children without ADHD. It has also been found that between 20% and 32% of children with ADHD have a parent or a sibling with ADHD. Clearly, for many individuals, a genetic factor must cause or at least contribute to the emergence of ADHD. Several additional studies have examined families of children with ADHD, not only for the disorder itself but also for associated problems. These studies have generally found that ADHD is associated with family members who have histories of aggression, legal difficulties, and mood problems. Speculation that a common underlying deficit may be present in the brain's operation or biochemistry has subsequently arisen. Of course, because biological relatives also may share a common environment (i.e., live in the same household), learned behavior, in addition to inherited characteristics, may contribute to the family-related patterns of symptoms.

Some small-scale but interesting studies have addressed this last point. Identical twins (genetically the same) and fraternal twins (genetically no more alike than siblings) have been examined closely. In one study in which the identical-twin siblings of four children with ADHD were assessed, all of them also had ADHD. When fraternal-twin siblings of children with ADHD were examined, however, only about 17% had ADHD. Subsequent studies, some using much larger numbers of twins, have produced findings that continue to show much greater co-occurrence of ADHD when twins are genetically identical. Since identical and fraternal twins share the same social environment and differ only in their genetic similarity, scientists are offered a unique chance to study the effects of inheritance. The strikingly greater similarity of identical twins over fraternal twins must be due to their common genes.

Experts who have examined all of the inheritance studies have offered their conclusions. Research shows that ADHD can be understood as being between 30% and 50% inherited, with the child's social environment playing a much smaller causative role than previously believed. Still, scientific knowledge is insufficient to explain a large portion of the causes of ADHD. Moreover, although inheritance explains much, a great deal remains to be discovered about precisely how inheritance works. Why some individuals are affected and others are not, or why males are more affected than females, is not entirely clear.

In the real world of the individual child with ADHD, many family patterns may be found: Some individuals with ADHD have ADHD-diagnosed relatives, some have ADHD-suspected relatives, and some have entirely ADHD-free relatives. Even for the child with ADHD who has no relatives with ADHD-related problems, the disorder may be inherited. Just as families composed of short- or average-stature individuals occasionally produce a very tall child, so too may the family with no history of ADHD produce a child who is symptomatic for ADHD.

BRAIN DIFFERENCES

Scientists are now seeking the brain site(s) and the nature of the brain's imperfection that may underlie ADHD. Some of their findings have been reported in the popular press, such as an investigation by Zametkin and colleagues at the National Institutes of Health. Using a scanning technique called *positron emission tomography* (PET), which allows study of the brain's use of glucose, these researchers found differing use of glucose between individuals with a history of ADHD and those without such a history. More interesting, they found that areas of the brain involved in motor planning and control and those that control arousal and attention used less glucose or were underactive in individuals with a history of ADHD. Of further importance is that this study, by identifying a physical-biomedical difference in individuals with ADHD symptoms, helps refute the claims of those who have contended that ADHD merely represents a nonphysical behavioral style or that the disorder itself is a myth.

Although Zametkin and colleagues' study involved only a few participants and its conclusions must be viewed tentatively, its findings agree with other exploratory studies. Other small-scale studies of individuals with ADHD have found decreased blood flow and less electrical activity in brain centers related to planning and control. Psychological tests designed to measure the performance of specific sites in the brain have also found that centers that govern regulation of impulse suppression work poorly among individuals with ADHD. Additional studies have also found differing levels of chemicals involved in nerve transmission between individuals with and without ADHD. These crucial chemicals, called *neurotransmitters,* appear to be deficient in individuals with ADHD in a portion of the brain believed to be related to rewards and punishment.

Collectively, these studies imply that deficient functioning in those areas of the brain that involve response inhibition, attention, and sensitivity to rewards and punishment may characterize at least some individuals with ADHD. This research offers hope for advancing treatment. Perhaps medications' action could be better understood if the actual brain deficits underlying ADHD were identified and their function in producing symptoms were elucidated. As of the late 1990s, however, these findings had no direct impact on ADHD treatment. By the same token, the sophisticated laboratory techniques used in these studies have no clear role as yet in the routine clinical assessment of individual children with ADHD (see Chapter 9).

BRAIN INJURY

As indicated in Chapter 1, early in the 20th century, many clinicians assumed that ADHD symptoms were manifestations of brain injury. Not surprisingly, the connection between ADHD and brain injury has been extensively researched.

Children with ADHD have had their histories scrutinized for evidence of brain injury, yet less than 5% of those studied had evidence of actual brain damage. That is, events such as head trauma, brain infection, and stroke simply failed to account for many cases of ADHD. Although brain injury is not a common cause of ADHD, it may indeed cause symptoms of inattention, hyperactivity, and impulsivity. For example, children who have sustained severe head traumas often manifest conspicuous ADHD symptoms but generally as part of a multifaceted clinical picture. In instances of clear-cut brain injury, the child's physician typically recognizes the unique causative factors so that the child's condition is distinguished from ADHD.

Subtle, difficult-to-detect brain injury, as well as possible birth-related brain injury, has also been investigated extensively. Events surrounding birth, such as lack of oxygen or prematurity, have shown only a weak association with later development of ADHD. Other factors that may affect the fetus before birth, such as maternal smoking or alcohol use, have also been investigated. Some of these studies did not show clear evidence that these factors play a causative role in ADHD, whereas others suggested that chronic conditions (i.e., mother's heavy smoking, drug abuse by the mother) do indicate some association with ADHD. Among those children who do have ADHD as a result of pregnancy- or birth-related problems, other evidence of brain injury may also be present that can be detected by a health care professional.

GENETIC ANOMALIES

Rare genetic disorders can be associated with ADHD symptoms. Children with, for example, neurofibromatosis, Turner syndrome, or fragile X syndrome are known to experience high rates of ADHD. They usually have other obvious problems as well. For instance, children with neurofibromatosis have multiple skin lesions and may experience other health problems; the disorder often runs in families—thus, its manifestation is generally noted before the onset of ADHD symptoms. As another example, children with fragile X syndrome often experience a variety of physical and learning problems in addition to ADHD symptoms. If your child has a complicated history that includes physical differences, delayed development, or behavioral peculiarities, then his or her ADHD symptoms may represent something other than the common ADHD discussed in this book, in which case a thorough evaluation is obviously essential.

FOOD ADDITIVES, SUGAR, AND ENVIRONMENTAL TOXINS

Since Benjamin Feingold proposed food coloring and additives as possible causes of ADHD in 1973, the notion of environmental substances as a cause of ADHD has drawn wide attention. Articles in the popular press have claimed that dyes and preservatives can somehow alter the brain's chemical balance and induce ADHD symptoms. The apparent explosion in the occurrence of ADHD during the 20th century is attributed by some to the increased use of such additives and dyes.

Concern has also been expressed about the role that sugar plays in producing symptoms of ADHD. Because sugar (i.e., glucose) is the energy source used by the brain, there has been broad speculation that sugar ingestion could stimulate the brain, perhaps leading to hyperactive behavior. Many parents and teachers alike report symptom exacerbation in children with increased sugar intake.

Although intuitively plausible, several carefully controlled empirical studies have not found food additives or sugar to be a cause of ADHD. Moreover, despite Feingold's reports that an additive-free diet reduced ADHD symptoms, subsequent and more carefully controlled studies by independent researchers failed to replicate these findings. At present, most experts conclude that there is little reason to advocate an altered diet for most children with ADHD. The same is true with regard to sugar. Studies that have used placebos and independent observers have failed to note behavioral differences between those who ingested sugar and those who took neutral substances.

Environmental lead may be a different matter. Recent reports suggest that lead deposited in the soil from long-term use of leaded gasolines may exist in many cities, and that children may be contaminated when they play in urban dirt. Lead-based paints, especially as they age and flake, represent another source of potential lead ingestion. It is assumed that if these substances are inhaled or ingested orally, they ultimately are transported via the bloodstream to the brain, where they are deposited and cause damage. Empirical studies to date have shown generally weak associations between the levels of lead found in the bloodstream and

ADHD symptoms. More research is sure to be conducted; but, as of yet, it cannot be assumed that lead ingestion is a primary cause of ADHD.

HEALTH PROBLEMS

In rare instances, physical or health problems may produce symptoms that mimic ADHD. For instance, case reports of cysts on the brain's surface have been associated with three cases of ADHD. Likewise, in some instances, thyroid abnormalities may be associated with symptoms that seem to indicate ADHD, and among individuals with specific thyroid problems (those resistant to thyroid hormone), an association between various hormone levels and symptoms of ADHD may exist. For these reasons, it is wise to have children being assessed for ADHD or undergoing treatment to be assessed by a physician.

SIDE EFFECTS OF MEDICATION

Some prescription medications can have side effects that mimic ADHD. For example, two antiseizure medications (i.e., those taken for epilepsy), phenobarbitol and Dilantin, can produce symptoms of hyperactivity and irritability. An asthma medication, theophylline (appearing also with names such as TheoDur and Slobid) can also cause ADHD-like symptoms. Because these medicines are often used for extended time periods (6 months or longer), it can be difficult to distinguish whether symptoms are a result of medication or ADHD. It is important, therefore, that a diagnostician knowledgeable about both ADHD and the side effects of commonly used pediatric medicines participate in your child's evaluation.

FAMILIAL AND SOCIAL INFLUENCES

Inevitably, parents wonder about their own role in their child's ADHD condition. Many parents have been accused by relatives and friends of causing the problem by virtue of poor parenting. As a society, we often assume that children's behavior mirrors the parents' approaches to child rearing. According to this line of thinking, a direct line of cause and effect exists between parents' actions and children's behavior—lenient, inconsistent, or hostile parenting, the thinking goes, leads to problem behavior in children. Objective studies of families with children with ADHD, however, have helped to correct some erroneous thinking.

Russell Barkley has cited studies of interactions between children with ADHD and their parents. Parents of children with ADHD have been found to be negative and to use excessive commands and directions. By contrast, parents of children without ADHD are more likely to allow their children to direct themselves without frequent commands and without obvious signs of negative parental attitude. On the surface, this would seem to imply that parents of children with ADHD are doing a poor job—that their inept parenting style has led to problem behavior in their children. Barkley, however, goes on to describe the same parent–child interactions after the children with ADHD are treated with Ritalin (methylphenidate), a medication known to reduce ADHD symptoms. After treatment, the rate of commands and directions decreases, and the parents' previously negative attitude improves. Rather than parents' child-rearing style causing their child's problem behavior, the opposite may be true. When forced to discipline inherently difficult children, parents resort to frequent commands: They become overly directive, and their attitude and patience suffer. These reactions occur as a result of the extraordinary demands of living with a child with ADHD; they do not cause ADHD.

Research reflects the view that most children with ADHD have an inherent, biologically determined temperament that strongly predisposes them to ADHD symptoms. Some related problems, such as conduct or oppositional defiant disorder, however, may be influenced more directly by child rearing. This is easy enough to understand. Conduct problems such as stealing and lying may be encouraged by parents' lenience or by the influence of peers. Noncompliance may similarly develop if parents or teachers fail to exercise control. Of course, the child with ADHD is predisposed to these problems because of the inattention and impulsivity that define ADHD. Even when conduct problems occur in conjunction with ineffective parental discipline, the ADHD symptoms probably still have a primarily biological cause.

There are a few dissenting voices to this aforementioned view. Alan Sroufe at the University of Minnesota has argued that ADHD may occasionally be caused, or at least aggravated, inadvertently by parenting practices. In some cases, parents have been shown to interact with their children in ways that interfere with task completion (e.g., completing a building activity for the child during play). These parents may distract their children in the midst of activities, thus short-circuiting the development of their children's ability to stay focused and attentive. In addition, a child who is already aroused or stimulated to a high level may be further overstimulated by a parent's influence. Such actions, of course, hamper a child's budding competence in self-control.

Although the role of parenting in causing ADHD may be limited, help for parents is often recommended as part of a comprehensive intervention plan (see Chapter 8). By working with a knowledgeable professional, parents may find it easier to live with their child (and vice versa). At the same time, strategies to improve the child's conduct can be developed, and any inadvertent parental contribution to the child's problem can also be addressed.

CONCLUSIONS

Although the exact causes of ADHD are not fully known, some facts are evident. ADHD is at least partially inherited and is not generally caused by brain injury or external factors such as sugar ingestion. Furthermore, it is generally assumed that ADHD is caused by factors in the central nervous system that are different from those existent in the central nervous systems of individuals without ADHD, although the exact nature of these differences has yet to be determined. The manner in which parents raise their children, however, is not generally considered a chief cause.

Section II

How Is ADHD Diagnosed?

Chapter 3

Diagnosing ADHD by Observing Behavior

ADHD Myths

A child must undergo careful and sustained direct observation before ADHD can be established.

Clinic-based observations are just as good as school-based observations.

If your child doesn't demonstrate ADHD symptoms during an office examination, then he or she doesn't have ADHD.

Observation techniques are too crude to measure progress during treatment.

so is adaptive. It is best to scan the environment, size up the situation, and then determine the advisability of proceeding. The behavior just described is, in many ways, the opposite of a cautious approach. It is characterized by such an intense desire to explore and a correspondingly low regard for danger, that the child tends to react with a "full speed ahead" approach. Although an undercontrolled approach may be acceptable in some situations (e.g., on a playground), in many situations it is neither appropriate nor adaptive.

An office, however, is only one such setting. The way in which the child behaves in other settings can be inferred based on behavior seen in the office, or, more important, may be determined by more-structured observations in the classroom (discussed later in this chapter) or by interviews with parents and teachers (see Chapter 4).

Settling in and Signs of Inattention

How a child warms up to a stranger's office and how long he or she takes to warm up are two observations worthy of noting. Much more is revealed as time elapses. A typical assessment practice of including both parent and child in the office during history taking offers opportunities for such ongoing observation. Because history taking may require 45 minutes or more, an extended time is available during which to observe the child. Some children select a toy from among the objects kept in the diagnostician's office, such as blocks, and they stick with that toy for a reasonable interval. Other children play only briefly at one activity, then find another, and so forth. At the conclusion of a 45-minute interview, the child may have tried many activities without adhering to any. Children of different ages, of course, are expected to be able to sustain attention for different time intervals. Older children who have been to school are expected to remain with a self-selected activity longer than younger children who have not yet attended school. The diagnostician watches for problems with inattention relative to age expectations. Such observations provide one source of information when reaching conclusions about your child.

Activity Level and Rule Following

The child's motor activity and ability to follow rules are similarly of interest. Some children are quite restless even if they are able to maintain interest in an activity. For example, many children with ADHD, especially school-age children, may sit and listen as their parents talk. Still, the child may change sitting positions frequently; may rest his or her head intermittently on the parent's lap; or may recline, tap repetitively at the furniture, or fidget with his or her foot. Obviously, a few of these behaviors are of no significance; however, frequent and intense behavior of this type, particularly after the child is directed to behave otherwise, is of importance.

Inability both to adhere to a rule immediately after it has been stated (i.e., basic "compliance") and to keep track of a rule over time (called "tracking" by some experts) is exhibited by many children with ADHD. Examples seen during an extended observation may include obvious failure to abide by simple directions, such as, "Please keep your hands off the books in the bookcase." The child who continues to grab books from the shelf may have failed to keep track of the rule; thus, his or her behavior was not influenced by the directive. If the child intentionally looks at a parent and does the opposite of what has just been requested, then a compliance problem is probably being observed. Much more is discussed in other chapters of this book about how to manage rule violation problems.

Coping with Distractions

Compared with most environments, the office setting contains relatively few distractions. Nevertheless, some children cannot ignore even minimal distractions in an age-appropriate manner. Hallway noises, movement outside the window, a parent opening or closing a purse, and the temperature control system starting or stopping are all examples of environmental changes that may challenge the child's ability to sustain attention. The same child who interrupts parents to report a bird flying by the window may have problems with avoiding similar kinds of distractions at school. In addition, the child who stops in the midst of telling the diagnostician about home behavior to ask, "Is someone talking in the next office?" may be unable to complete desired activities in other areas of life. As mentioned previously, it is an accumulation of these observations that form a pattern of inattention of diagnostic significance. These and countless other instances of an inability to focus or sustain attention are seen in the office.

Talkativeness

Many children with ADHD are extremely talkative during history taking (recall that "Often talks excessively" is one of the symptoms of ADHD; see Table 1.1, Chapter 1). Clinicians may refer to this behavior as *hyperverbal.* Empirical studies have shown that in social situations, children with ADHD are more likely than others to start conversations. This, no doubt, is often seen in office settings. Unfortunately, the same research shows that children with ADHD are more likely than children without ADHD to ignore conversation initiated by others. That is, children with ADHD are more likely to initiate social interaction, but are less responsive to social give and take. In the office setting, children with ADHD often interrupt, dominate conversations with little recognition of their dominance, or ramble excessively on irrelevant topics. Although often seen as mere friendliness by nonprofessionals, this type of behavior may actually underlie the social problems experienced by many children with ADHD. Children who are too talkative or too intrusive tend to alienate peers. Through careful observation, professionals can learn much about the child's ability to focus and maintain attention, control activity, and inhibit impulses and may draw tentative conclusions about social behavior as well.

Parents also can observe their child's behavior for this same array of symptoms. In most instances, however, objective rating forms (see Chapter 5) and a detailed history of symptoms recounted to a professional (see Chapter 4) are better ways for parents to provide input than are informal, self-interpreted observations.

STRUCTURED OBSERVATION TECHNIQUES

Unfortunately, not all professionals are equally informed and experienced, and some may fail to obtain valuable information from their informal observation. Such differences in the skills of professionals are among the drawbacks of informal office observations. Another drawback of such observations is that office settings are artificial in that they differ from most of the real-life settings where children play, attend class, or interact with their families. In addition, informal observations make it very difficult to evaluate the child's current behavior precisely enough to know for certain whether the child's behavior is improving once treatment begins. Structured observation techniques can overcome one or both of these shortcomings.

Simple, Structured Office Technique

The following is a description of a simple, structured observation procedure similar to that used in some office or specialty clinic settings. Techniques such as this can be used to supplement the less-structured, informal techniques just described. According to this structured technique, a child accompanies his or her parents to an observation room and is presented with a task that requires concentration. For school-age children, this consists of working simple addition and subtraction problems; for preschoolers, a simple, repetitive coloring task is presented. Children are instructed as follows: "Work as many problems [or color as many shapes] as you can, keep working without looking up, and do not talk to your parent(s)."

Each child is also told that he or she will be observed by a staff member in an adjacent observation room. An observer is positioned within this room behind a one-way mirror. The child is then given a predetermined time interval during which to work (in our case, 10 minutes). Meanwhile, the observer completes an observation form, recording whether the child is paying attention and working or looking around, talking, or in any other way not attending (i.e., whether the child is "on task" or "off task"). To enhance the chances of two observers' ratings agreeing, clear and specific definitions of "on task" and "off task" must exist. The 10-minute observation period is divided into segments, each of which is 15 seconds long. Thus, 40 such 15-second segments occur during the 10-minute observation. For the first 10 seconds of each 15-second segment, the child is watched closely. Only if the child remains continuously attentive is "on task" (+) credited. If the child is off task for any part of this 10-second interval, even if he or she merely glances around momentarily, an "off task" (0) is recorded for that segment. The last 5 seconds of each interval are to be used by the observer to mark the form. A new 10-second observation interval then begins, followed by 5 seconds for the rater to mark the form. This sequence continues until the entire 10 minutes have elapsed.

Because each child has a potential of 40 segments during which he or she can be credited with being either "on task" or "off task," it is easy to calculate the percentage of either type of behavior. For example, if John earns 30 "+" marks out of the possible 40, his percentage of on-task behavior is calculated as 30/40, or 75% (see Figure 3.1). Similarly, if Mary is on task 39 out of 40 times, her percentage is calculated as 39/40, or 97.5%.

Because of the brevity of the task and the absence of distractions in this setting, staying on task is relatively easy for most children. Most children's on-task percentage is far higher in this setting than in others, such as school. Nonetheless, because the technique is objective (i.e., it does not rely on the observer's judgment or impressions), it serves to sup-

Name: John Doe
Date: 3-23-99
Observer: mm
Method: _____ Point _X_ Interval

Minutes	Seconds 15	30	45	60
0	+	+	0	+
1	0	+	+	+
2	+	+	+	+
3	+	+	+	+
4	+	+	+	+
5	+	0	+	+
6	+	+	+	+
7	0	+	0	+
8	+	0	+	0
9	0	+	0	0

Number of observations off task [0]: 10
Percentage off task [0]: 25
Percentage on task [+]: 75

Figure 3.1. Observation form for simple, structured observation.

plement an informal office observation. Moreover, the technique results in a numerical index (i.e., the percentage of on-task behavior) that can be used to help determine whether the child is progressing once treatment begins. Behavior changes can be monitored easily over time if observations are repeated, perhaps after a specific treatment such as medication is started.

Structured School Observations

Of course, the same observation technique as that described in the previous subsection can be used in the child's classroom. Techniques similar to this one are often used by school psychologists, counselors, and teachers trained in behavior management. School-based observations are generally far more comprehensive and detailed than those used in professionals' offices. Behaviors such as attending to directions, talking with classmates, completing seatwork, leaving one's seat, aggression, and so forth may be observed, and their rate of occurrence may be recorded. A popular and well-organized observation system (the Student Observation System from the Behavior Assessment System for Children—often referred to as *SOS*) has been produced commercially and appears to be used widely by school personnel. Individualizing a behavior observation system may be even more helpful. By tailoring observations to students' unique problems, structured observations can be extremely valuable data sources. For instance, Wally has many ADHD symptoms, but his repeated talking out in class is the most disturbing to classmates. If school staff were to establish his rate of "inappropriate talking out" by using objective observation techniques prior to beginning treatment, progress could be monitored. The effects of a behavior modification program (discussed in Chapter 8) or of medication (discussed in Chapter 9) could then be examined objectively and accurately. It is extremely helpful to be able to rely on knowledgeable school personnel who can adapt observations to the individual child's characteristics. Even though children with ADHD have many symptoms in common, each child is nonetheless unique. Individualization of assessment, and later of treatment, is important.

In-class observations have enormous advantages over office observations. Foremost among these is that the child is being observed in his or her real world. When observed in everyday settings, the child's typical behavior is far more likely to occur. With other "typical" classmates available, developing a frame of reference is feasible. This can be accomplished by comparing the child with ADHD with one or two other classmates. This child-to-child comparison is important because, despite objectivity, there are as yet no standards or norms regarding how much "off-task" or "talking-out" behavior might typically be expected. For example, Zeke was noted to look around the room 12 times and to shout

out unsolicited answers 4 times during a 20-minute social studies assignment. Although these rates seem excessive, without a standard against which to compare them, it is impossible to be certain whether Zeke's scores are truly rare or atypical. By watching Bill and Larry, two classmates the teacher has identified as typical, Zeke's rate of distractibility and impulsive talking out can be appraised fairly. If Bill and Larry's 20-minute observation segments each produce only one or two episodes of looking around, and if neither boy shouted out in class, then Zeke's problems are clearly and objectively evident. Parents may wish to ask diagnosing professionals or school staff about the availability of objective observation techniques, both to help determine their child's current status and in order to monitor his or her progress over time.

CONCLUSIONS

There is no substitute for the observations of a trained professional. It is one thing for a parent to read or be told that ADHD is characterized by excessive inattention, hyperactivity, and impulsivity; but it is quite another to know what these symptoms look like as expressed in their child's behavior. An experienced professional diagnostician offers the ability to observe and interpret as few others can. Chances are that if a trained professional confirms the existence of severe ADHD symptoms during extended or repeated office observations, the same symptoms are present elsewhere, too. The more demanding nature of the child's home, neighborhood, and school environments virtually guarantees that ADHD-related problems will occur in these settings if the underlying attention and self-control deficits exist. A rule of thumb is that if ADHD is clearly and definitively seen in the office, it probably exists in other settings as well. No one observation, or even series of observations, however, can prove that a child should not be diagnosed as having ADHD. Many children control themselves well for brief or even for extended time intervals but cannot duplicate that behavior day in and day out. Merely because a child sits still for his or her pediatrician or during a classroom visit by the school psychologist does not mean that the child does not have ADHD. A child who attends well in one instance may have severe problems in another instance when different and perhaps greater demands to inhibit impulses, pay attention, and slow down exist. As discussed in Chapter 4, only by tapping parents' intimate knowledge of their child's behavior as it occurs in many settings is it possible to conclusively diagnose ADHD.

Chapter 4

Diagnosing ADHD by Interviewing

ADHD Myths

Parents should expect to hear only questions about ADHD when they take their child for an ADHD evaluation.

Parent interviews are unnecessary to determine whether ADHD is present.

A good way to determine whether a child has ADHD is to interview him or her.

Parents who suspect that their child may have ADHD are frequently a diagnostician's most valuable resource in attempting to establish a diagnosis. The child, too, has a story to tell, although his or her self-descriptions and firsthand narrative may be less valuable than one might suspect. The job of the professional diagnostician is to elicit proper information from parents, teachers, and the child so that 1) an accurate diagnosis can be established, and 2) the child, educational settings, and family can be understood well enough to formulate a treatment plan. Here is how the process might work.

PARENTAL INTERVIEW

As a parent, your interview with the diagnostician is your chance to tell the diagnostician what concerns you about your child's behavior. Parents should be as candid as possible, revealing everything worrisome, puzzling, or troublesome. Often a pattern begins to emerge, and this is what the professional will be listening for. He or she will be knowledgeable about the DSM-IV criteria for ADHD (see Table 1.1, Chapter 1). The diagnostician, by virtue of his or her experience, evaluates whether the characteristics identified by the parent in descriptions of the child's day-to-day home behavior can be matched to the ADHD symptom list. This is a crucial task. Although parents know their child, often they don't know what symptoms the ADHD syndrome causes. Even when parents are familiar with the symptoms, they may not fully comprehend them. For example, a mother may comment that her preschool son seems to have an inconsistent appetite because he frequently leaves the table at mealtime, only to return later to nibble. The same child may be described as disinterested in puzzles and coloring and unresponsive to frequent attempts to draw him into simple games such as Candyland. Although the parent may see little in common among these behaviors and may fail to attach significance to any of them, an experienced diagnostician may see things differently. He or she may interpret these behaviors as evidence of the ADHD symptom "Often avoids, dislikes, or is reluctant to engage in tasks that require sustained mental effort" (Table 1.1).

As helpful as this open-ended conversational approach with parents may be, it is seldom sufficient. Professionals often want to inquire more systematically into many crucial areas of the child's life. Following is a list of topics frequently addressed during a parent interview:

I. Health and developmental data
    A. Pregnancy and birth
    B. Early temperament and development
    C. Current health
    D. Hearing and vision status

II. Family
    A. Current living arrangement
    B. Child's role in family
    C. History of ADHD and learning or mental disorders among other family members

III. Education
    A. School history, year by year
    B. Presence of ADHD problems
    C. Review of any prior psychoeducational evaluations
    D. Review of special services (if any)

IV. Interpersonal development
    A. Relationships with peers
    B. Relationships with family
    C. Success in sports, organizations, and so forth

V. Home status
    A. ADHD symptoms reviewed
    B. Conduct and compliance

C. Mood quality, control, and self-esteem

D. Anxiety and phobias

E. Strengths and special interests

A full and detailed interview touching on these areas is often quite helpful. Besides detecting ADHD symptoms with this approach, the diagnostician may gain a comprehensive view of your child and family.

Consider, for example, information that may arise during a discussion of the child's preschool years. Parents may recall that the child was "constantly on the go and into everything." The diagnostician may ask whether the child was a climber or was careless around dangerous objects. The ensuing discussion not only may help establish the presence of the symptom "Often runs about or climbs excessively in situations in which it is inappropriate" (Table 1.1) but also may lead to revelations about parents' longstanding concern about their child's safety or disagreements between parents about how to discipline their child. This information assists in developing a plan to help the child and the child's family. Likewise, questions about how the child gets along with other children may expose the symptom "Often interrupts or intrudes on others" (Table 1.1) and may also point out the need to include work on social skills development as part of the child's treatment plan.

Sometimes parents and experienced diagnosticians interpret the same behavior differently. Parents who raise difficult children may develop extreme levels of tolerance for their child's actions. They may lose awareness of what typical behavior is really like. Once a couple brought their 5-year-old son in for counseling in the hope of developing a better relationship between him and his younger sister. During the standard intake process, the child damaged several items in the office, repeatedly tripped his 3-year-old sister, attacked his parents as he became bored with the intake process, and then had a tantrum when his parents refused to terminate the session prematurely. When asked how they evaluated their child's behavior at home, the parents stated that he was "pretty easy to manage." When further quizzed about whether the child's office conduct was typical of that seen at home, the parents calmly stated that "what we're seeing right now is quite typical for him." Much of a professional's value to you is his or her experience and judgment. It is important that parents recognize this aspect of assessment and proceed with an open mind when parents' and diagnosticians' interpretations differ.

By proceeding in the listening and interpreting fashion just described, the diagnostician may mentally check off the necessary symptoms to establish the ADHD diagnosis. Of course, additional questions may be necessary to help determine if, in fact, each symptom is present. Questions about the onset of symptoms may also be asked (recall from Chapter 1 that the necessary symptoms must have a 6-month duration and must have been evident before 7 years of age).

Because children with ADHD are so much more likely than other children to be affected by conduct disorders or learning disabilities or to become discouraged or depressed, the thorough diagnostician scrutinizes parents' comments about these considerations as well as those about ADHD. Thus, if information about adhering to household rules, controlling aggression, stealing, and lying is not volunteered by the parents, then the diagnostician will probably probe these areas through direct questioning. The same is true with regard to the child's mood state and his or her self-concept. As shown in previous chapters, this information is important in predicting problems that the child might encounter later as well as in planning how best to proceed with treatment.

Of course, parents should be questioned about their child's school status. Parents' unique ability to summarize their child's school experiences over several years is particularly helpful. For instance, knowing that a child has always had trouble with pencil-and-paper seatwork is a perspective that no one teacher can provide. Still, direct input from current teacher(s) is also important.

A strong working relationship with your child's physician or psychologist is essential. The assessment phase may be the beginning of a long-term relationship, and you are strongly encouraged to start by being completely open as you describe your child. The need to be candid and to trust the diagnostician is especially important during one aspect of the parent interview: questions about the family. Family stresses related to finances, marital problems, disagreements about discipline, health of the parents, parent vocational problems, and the like can all affect the functioning of a household. Although such problems by themselves seldom cause the symptoms that may appear as ADHD, stresses of these types can contribute to children's adjustment problems. The diagnostician may be able to offer direct help for such problems or may make a referral to other professionals who may assist you.

The diagnostician is likely to ask probing questions about the child's biological relatives, too (i.e., whether such relatives have had problems with ADHD, learning disabilities, psychiatric disorders [e.g., mood or affective disorders], juvenile neurological problems [e.g., epilepsy, tics], juvenile delinquency, alcohol or drug problems). Many parents regard such questions as frankly intrusive or irrelevant. Yet, because ADHD is at least partially inherited, these questions may help determine whether your child is at heightened risk for ADHD or another related disorder besides ADHD. The information may also help determine whether, and if so, which, medication is appropriate (see Chapter 9). In addition, questions about the mother's pregnancy and delivery, the rate of the child's development, and the child's health may be asked. Comprehensiveness rather than personal curiosity is the motive behind these questions.

TEACHER INTERVIEW

Research shows that many children with ADHD manifest their symptoms most dramatically in the classroom; thus, an interview between your child's diagnostician and the classroom teacher can be of enormous value. Unfortunately, however, both for logistical and financial reasons, such an interview often does not occur. Just as few doctors today find it financially feasible to make house calls, few professionals can afford to visit schools. Even telephone contact can be tricky, given teachers' busy schedules and the demands of in-office patient contact that most diagnosticians face.

Consequently, most professionals begin the assessment process by using general questionnaires to be completed by classroom teachers. These questionnaires can elicit information that might come from a teacher interview, including the following:

- Academic skill level in each subject
- Work habits and productiveness in class
- Ability to sustain attention (especially on monotonous work)
- Activity level in class and on the playground
- Degree of emotional control
- Presence of conduct problems
- Social skills and acceptance by classmates
- Special or remedial services now provided or contemplated

Rating forms (see Chapter 5) to determine more precisely the presence of ADHD symptoms and/or multidimensional rating forms are generally used as well (see Chapter 5). Some type of reporting form completed by a classroom teacher (in lieu of direct teacher contact) is usually required before a comprehensive assessment of your child can be considered complete. Sometimes a report card or notes from the classroom teacher to the parent can suffice. If a professional attempts to proceed with an ADHD diagnosis without any information from the child's classroom teacher (assuming that the child is of school age and the child is not, e.g., on summer vacation), then parents may want to request that this information be included.

Depending on the style of your child's diagnostician, telephone conversations may either follow the review of completed rating forms and questionnaires or occur only if clarification is required. Frequently, however, direct teacher contact may await the beginning of treatment. At that point, the physician or psychologist may contact your child's teacher(s) to explain the nature of the problem and to propose a unified approach at home and in school.

A comment about teacher reports of ADHD is in order here. Most teachers are excellent observers of behavior, and they provide indispensable information about your child. Two extreme attitudes among teachers in their reporting about ADHD are worth noting, however, although these attitudes are uncommon. One attitude is typified by the teacher who contends that there are many students with ADHD and that they should be identified promptly and started on Ritalin. Teachers with such an attitude are probably rarer than many parents believe. A thorough and professional assessment can prevent the kind of incorrect mislabeling that results from exaggerated symptom reporting and leads to overuse of medication.

The second attitude is expressed by the teacher who claims to have never seen a child with ADHD. These teachers, most of whom are well intentioned, do exist. Bias against the perceived overuse of the ADHD diagnosis probably motivates many teachers in this group. They contend that too many children are being identified as having ADHD and that they want to slow or perhaps even stem the tide of ADHD labeling. Other teachers underreport symptoms in response to pressures exerted by school administrators to minimize identification of children with problems. (Such administrators fear that local school districts will be held responsible for supplemental and expensive services for children identified as having ADHD [see Chapter 10].) Other teachers believe that an ADHD diagnosis is a sentence to a life of Ritalin and that Ritalin is an unqualified evil. Such teachers are thus loath to acknowledge symptoms of restlessness or inattention during a telephone interview with a diagnostician.

The experienced diagnostician recognizes that these extremes in attitude do occasionally occur and can factor them into the equation when deciding on an ADHD diagnosis. More important in the long run, however, is securing teachers' cooperation in the event that a classroom modification is later required. Providing knowledge about ADHD and offering support and encouragement rather than confrontation is the best way to begin the diagnostic process with a classroom teacher. Parents are strongly encouraged to avoid confrontations with teachers who initially may appear either ignorant about ADHD or inclined to obstruct an accurate assessment.

CHILD INTERVIEW

As stated at the beginning of this chapter, interviewing a child is a relatively poor method for determining whether he or she is affected by ADHD. Even so, there are structured ADHD interviews for children. The following example of such an interview format is completed by the interviewer:

1. Some kids find it hard to sit through something when they are supposed to. Is that hard for you?
   0 1 2
2. Do you often find that you fidget with your hands?
   0 1 2
3. Sometimes kids are supposed to play quietly. Do you find that difficult?
   0 1 2
4. Do grown-ups tell you that you talk too much?
   0 1 2
5. Sometimes kids don't finish a game or something but start something else instead. Do you do that a lot?
   0 1 2
6. Do you sometimes do dangerous things?
   0 1 2

Key: 0, No or never; 1, Maybe sometimes, a little; 2, Yes, a lot. (*Source:* Selected items from Garfinkel, B.D. [n.d.]. *Structured ADHD Interview: Child Version.* Unpublished manuscript; reprinted by permission of Barry D. Garfinkel, M.D.)

Research on these interviews continues, but the interview technique has yet to be proved very effective in discriminating children with ADHD from those without ADHD. The techniques may be more helpful in adolescents and adults with ADHD.

Does this mean that interviewing the child has no role in the diagnostic process? The answer is no. The interview is helpful with the broad task of assessment, even if it is not effective in detecting ADHD. Parents seldom appreciate that the diagnostician must not only determine whether a child might have ADHD but also whether he or she might have any of a variety of other disorders that might accompany ADHD or even be mistaken for it. A detailed interview of the child can be particularly enlightening when other information is ambiguous.

Rather than discuss the specifics of the interview, some examples of the kind of information that might emerge from this process are in order. Children who are anxious may be mistakenly labeled as having ADHD, as may children with mood instability characterized by symptoms such as irritability, poor self-esteem, and lack of motivation to perform in school. Although some of the external manifestations of these disorders may mimic ADHD, unique and important internal feelings and subjective emotional states are associated with these disorders. The interview with the child is designed to assess these internal emotional elements.

Contrast, for example, the hypothetical responses of a child with ADHD with those of a child with overanxious disorder during the clinical interview. When asked to describe classmates, a child with ADHD might say, "They're alright. We have a lot of fun on the playground, but sometimes they get mad at me in class." To the same question, the child with overanxious disorder might respond, "I don't really like them too much. Most of the kids call me names, and the teachers don't do anything about it." When asked to enumerate his or her three fondest wishes, the child with ADHD might answer, "A million dollars, a party with my friends, and a Lamborghini," whereas the overanxious child might respond, "To mess up less in school, to have lots of friends, and to have the police catch all burglars." Information about the child's internal feelings and perceptions may thus offer helpful hints for the diagnostician. The anxious child may be restless and frequently off task, but the child's underlying problems differ from those of his or her less anxious but equally inattentive and restless counterpart with ADHD. Of course, some children have both ADHD and anxiety symptoms, and there are special considerations for treating these children. Efforts to differentiate children with ADHD from those with mood disorders are likewise aided by interviewing the child. Here, as with anxiety disorders, objective personality questionnaires (discussed in Chapter 5) are often invaluable.

A few children with ADHD, as well as some teenagers and many adults, are insightful and verbal enough to describe their own problems. Questions related to their abilities to control their activity level, to work without being distracted, and to avoid the impact of impulsive behavior may be telling. Of course, recognizing the subjective aspects of each individual's disorder—whether child, teenager, or adult—often helps in planning ways to circumvent these difficulties once treatment begins. Understanding of the discouragement and frustration experienced by the individual living with ADHD is best conveyed through open conversation. For many individuals, a chance to tell their own story is an important element in devising a plan to help.

CONCLUSIONS

The popular clinical technique of interviewing parents is indispensable in conducting a thorough evaluation of a child or a teenager. Even though a direct interview with a child seldom influences the final decision regarding the presence of ADHD, such an interview can help determine the presence of co-existing problems. Moreover, only through direct discussion is the child's unique viewpoint apparent so that it can be considered in intervention planning.

Chapter 5

Diagnosing ADHD by Using Parent and Teacher Ratings

ADHD Myths

ADHD rating scales apply the same standards for boys and girls.

Rating scales have no role in treatment.

Scores from rating forms alone are sufficient to establish an ADHD diagnosis.

In an effort to objectify and quantify their subject of study, ADHD researchers and clinicians have developed a variety of parent- and teacher-completed rating forms and personality questionnaires. These rating forms are straightforward and generally consist of a brief list of symptoms, each of which is rated for severity by parents or teachers. The forms contain items primarily or exclusively related to ADHD symptoms.

In addition, multidimensional personality questionnaires and rating forms have been developed. These longer and more complex scales are typically designed to measure a variety of symptoms, including those for ADHD as well as those for anxiety and depression. Research into the presence, severity, and changes in ADHD symptoms during treatment spurred the development of some of the popular rating techniques discussed in this chapter. The more sophisticated of these scales were constructed by using elements of the logic outlined in the following section. These techniques have gained wide acceptance because of their objective numerical aspects and are an important part of ADHD evaluations. Parents should expect to encounter them during the assessment process. If techniques such as those discussed here are not included in your child's evaluations, you may want to ask the diagnostician why they are absent.

LOGIC OF RATING FORMS

Rating forms frequently contain questions that are similar to those a parent might be asked orally (e.g., "Is your child overexcitable and does he or she fly off the handle easily?"). A diagnostician conducting an interview may vary the questions slightly. For instance, one parent may be asked, "Is your child easily excitable and prone to overreacting?" whereas another may be asked, "Does your child become so excited that he or she reacts too strongly and quickly at times?"

Objectivity

The relatively minor differences between rating form questions and questions that are asked orally probably matter little if the goal of the interview is to obtain a general impression of the child. If the intent is to fix precisely the presence and severity of ADHD symptoms, however, this inconsistency may be a problem. Each of the three variations of the question in the previous section may be interpreted differently by the same parent! Thus, merely because of the fashion in which the question is posed, the same parent may hypothetically respond "Yes" to the first question, "No" to the second, and be undecided about the third. Rating forms are objective and thus avoid this problem. Hence, on a rating form, everyone is asked exactly the same questions. The questions (called *items* in objective assessment techniques) are also presented in written form so that they can be read and considered carefully.

Item Selection Process

Instead of containing just one item, of course, ratings contain many. This fact allows for fuller investigation of disorders such as ADHD. Scale developers are confronted with a formidable task: to decide which items should be included in a rating scale.

One method is to ask experts, perhaps experienced clinicians, to recommend items for inclusion in a scale. This pool of items may then be sent to a committee or a panel that decides which items are to be retained in the final rating scale. Some scales thus represent nothing more scientific than a consensus of opinion by expert diagnosticians.

A second method is more favorable to scientists. Rather than rely on items that merely appear to measure ADHD (or any other disorder), researchers empirically investigate each item's effectiveness. Plausible items such as, "At times, does your child become so excited that he reacts too strongly and quickly?" could be tested. Two groups of parents would assist in this item tryout: one group of parents whose children have been diagnosed as having ADHD and a second group whose children do not have ADHD. For an item to have value, parents of ADHD children should, in general, respond with a "yes" more frequently than parents whose children do not have ADHD. Items that help discriminate children with ADHD from those without ADHD are thus retained as part of the scale, and those that do not are rejected. This method of objective, scientific item development (together with expert input about item type) has led to the creation of rating tools of great clinical merit.

Quantifying Data

Scientists are not content with imprecision. They would not, for instance, be satisfied with the statement, "Mrs. Smith agreed with a lot of the ADHD items," when obtaining a more precise statement such as, "Mrs. Smith agreed with 17 of the 22 ADHD items when describing her daughter," is possible.

As helpful as it is, simply tallying endorsed items is by itself insufficient. An even more important task is to determine which numerical values represent typical (or average) and atypical (or abnormal) ratings. It is simple to calculate the average on a rating scale. If a 22-item true-or-false ADHD questionnaire were developed, all that would be necessary would be to study the ratings of a representative group (i.e., from the general population) of parents (and their children) and average their scores (of course, finding enough "representative" parents would be far from easy). Perhaps an average of 5.1 items would be agreed to by this representative group. Such a value would reflect the number of ADHD symptoms present among children in general. That's fine, but how is an atypically high amount of ADHD symptoms identified?

Often researchers take the extreme 2%–3% of a representative group and assume that they are unusual or abnormal. For instance, only 2 of 100 parents would agree with as many as 13 of the items, whereas the average parent would agree that only approximately 5 of the ADHD items described their child. This rare score (the 98th percentile) could then be considered to be a cutoff. Any child whose parents agreed with 13 of the items would receive a rating above this cutoff; that is, his or her child would be placed in the highly symptomatic range. Diagnosticians would use this finding, together with observation and interview information, to establish a diagnosis.

Not surprisingly, different rating forms use slightly different methods. Some forms employ ratings on a continuum (rather than employing true-or-false questions), so that parents rate symptoms on a range, for example, from "Totally absent" to "Present to a severe degree." This method is equally easy to handle mathematically because numerical values can be attached to each rating so that average and cutoff scores can be calculated (see examples later in this chapter). In addition, different standards must be calculated for different ages (the presence and severity of symptoms change with age) and for each of the sexes (boys are generally rated as more symptomatic than girls). It is also true that other methods of establishing cutoff scores exist and that scales may include many characteristics besides ADHD; however, the essential logic of rating scales remains as outlined previously.

RATING FORMS FOR ADHD

It is impossible in a brief book such as this one to discuss all of the rating forms and questionnaires available for assessing ADHD. The scales reviewed here are included primarily for illustrative purposes. They are not necessarily superior to those that do not appear, although they may be used somewhat more often. Frequently used examples of two major types of techniques are discussed. The first type is concerned mostly with ADHD (although other factors such as conduct may also be assessed). Such scales tend to be brief so that parents and teachers can repeat ratings as treatment occurs. The second type, the multidimensional scale, is longer and attempts a more in-depth evaluation of personality and behavior. Although such scales include the ADHD dimension, they are not primarily concerned with it. Five ADHD scales and two multidimensional scales are reviewed here briefly.

Conners' Rating Scales

One of the simplest and most frequently used examples of ADHD ratings is the Conners' Rating Scale, technically called the Abbreviated Teacher Rating Scale but also referred to as the Conners' Hyperactivity Index or simply as the Conners' (see Figure 5.1). The 10 items on this brief form are drawn from longer scales for parents and teachers and are believed to be most indicative of ADHD. The Conners' is often used to quickly assess ADHD characteristics and to study changes in symptoms as treatment is applied, such as when medicine is used.

Clinicians can easily convert ratings to scores. These scores have different cutoff values, depending on the age and sex of the child and on whether a parent or teacher marks the form. The differing demands of home life and school environment probably account for most of these rating inconsistencies, although parent and teacher attitudes and knowledge about ADHD can also be influential. Diagnosticians consider these factors when reviewing ratings from the Conners' or similar scales.

Lack of parent–teacher concurrence is not unique to the Conners' Rating Scale; however, the scale does have its own set of problems. For example, several of the items measure conduct disorder and oppositional defiant disorder (see Chapter 1) in addition to ADHD. If the Conners' rating were used as the sole basis for ADHD diagnosis, then children with defiance and mood control problems as well as purer ADHD symptoms would be identified. Such exclusive use of the Conners' would produce a corresponding bias against children whose symptoms are predominantly inattention and disorganization but who show no conduct problems. In addition, the short form is probably too brief to be reliable (i.e., it can be consistent). Finally, there is no method of measuring inattention as distinct from hyperactivity-impulsivity on this brief scale.

ADD–H Comprehensive Teacher Rating Scale

ADD–H Comprehensive Teacher Rating Scale (ACTeRS), featured in Figure 5.2, is a well-developed rating scale that you may encounter as part of your child's evaluation. Separate scores are available for both attention and hyperactivity

Student's name: ______________________ Gender: M F

Student's birthdate: ____ / ____ / ______ Age: ______ School grade: __________

Teacher's name: ______________________ Today's date: ____ / ____ / ____

Instructions: Below are a number of common problems that children have in school. Please rate each item according to how much of a problem it has been in the last month. For each item, ask yourself, "How much of a problem has this been in the last month?" Then circle the best answer for each one. If none, not at all, seldom, or very infrequently, you would circle "0." If very much true, or it occurs very often or frequently, you would circle 3. You would circle 1 or 2 for ratings in between. Please respond to all the items.

	NOT TRUE AT ALL (Never, Seldom)	JUST A LITTLE TRUE (Occasionally)	PRETTY MUCH TRUE (Often, Quite a Bit)	VERY MUCH TRUE (Very Often, Very Frequent)
1. Temper outbursts; explosive, unpredictable behavior	0	1	2	3
2. Excitable, impulsive	0	1	2	3
3. Restless or overactive	0	1	2	3
4. Inattentive, easily distracted	0	1	2	3
5. Fidgeting	0	1	2	3
6. Fails to finish things he/she starts	0	1	2	3

Figure 5.1. Sample items from the Conners' Global Index–Teacher. (Copyright © 1997, Multi-Health Systems, Inc. In USA: 908 Niagara Falls Boulevard, North Tonawanda, NY 14120-2060; 1-800-456-3003. In Canada: 65 Overlea Boulevard, Suite 210, Toronto, Ontario M4H 1P1; 1-800-268-6011. International: 1-416-424-1700. All rights reserved. Reproduced by permission.)

2nd Edition

Rina K. Ullmann, M.Ed.
Esther K. Sleator, M.D.
Robert L. Sprague, Ph.D.

Below are descriptions of behavior. Please read each item an pare the child's behavior with that of his or her classmates. the number that most closely corresponds with your eval Transfer the total raw score for each of the four sections to the sheet to determine normative percentile scores.

ATTENTION	Almost Never				Almost Always
1. Works well independently	1	(2)	3	4	5
2. Persists with task for reasonable amount of time	(1)	2	3	4	5
3. Completes assigned task satisfactorily with little additional assistance	1	(2)	3	4	5
4. Follows simple directions accurately	1	2	(3)	4	5
5. Follows a sequence of instructions	1	(2)	3	4	5
6. Functions well in the classroom	1	(2)	3	4	5

ADD ITEMS 1-6 AND PLACE TOTAL HERE 12

HYPERACTIVITY	Almost Never				Almost Always
7. Extremely overactive (out of seat, "on the go")	1	2	3	(4)	5
8. Overreacts	1	(2)	3	4	5
9. Fidgety (hands always busy)	1	2	(3)	4	5
10. Impulsive (acts or talks without thinking)	1	(2)	3	4	5
11. Restless (squirms in seat)	1	2	3	(4)	5

ADD ITEMS 7-11 AND PLACE TOTAL HERE 15

Figure 5.2. ADD-H Comprehensive Teacher's Rating Scale (ACTeRS), an ADHD rating form. (Copyright © 1986, 1988, 1991 by MetriTech, Inc., 4106 Fieldstone Road, Champaign, IL 61822; 217-398-4868. Reproduced by permission of the copyright holder. Permission has been granted for this publication only and does not extend to reproductions made from this publication.)

Child's Name: Chris Student

Rater: Mrs. Anderson

ID #: 71245

Date: 3/9/99

SOCIAL SKILLS	Almost Never				Almost Always
12. Behaves positively with peers/classmates	1	2	(3)	4	5
13. Verbal communication clear and "connected"	1	2	3	(4)	5
14. Nonverbal communication accurate	1	2	3	(4)	5
15. Follows group norms and social rules	1	(2)	3	4	5
16. Cites general rule when criticizing ("We aren't supposed to do that")	1	2	3	(4)	5
17. Skillful at making new friends	1	(2)	3	4	5
18. Approaches situations confidently	1	2	3	4	(5)

ADD ITEMS 12-18 AND PLACE TOTAL HERE 24

OPPOSITIONAL	Almost Never				Almost Always
19. Tries to get others into trouble	1	(2)	3	4	5
20. Starts fights over nothing	(1)	2	3	4	5
21. Makes malicious fun of people	1	(2)	3	4	5
22. Defies authority	1	(2)	3	4	5
23. Picks on others	1	(2)	3	4	5
24. Mean and cruel to other children	1	(2)	3	4	5

ADD ITEMS 19-24 AND PLACE TOTAL HERE 11

MetriTech, Inc.

symptoms (plus two other factors unrelated to ADHD). The authors of this scale, however, have emphasized inattention over hyperactivity. This emphasis may make the scale less effective in identifying children with severe hyperactivity and impulsivity. There is also no rating form for parents. Professionals must take into account both of these limitations when selecting a scale.

ADHD Rating Scale–IV

A rating form designed around the DSM-IV symptoms of ADHD has been developed by George J. DuPaul at Lehigh University. Called the ADHD Rating Scale-IV, it, in essence, lists the 18 symptoms of ADHD (encompassing both inattention and hyperactivity-impulsivity aspects) from the DSM-IV (see Chapter 1) and then asks parents or teachers to rate each on a continuum from "Never or rarely" to "Very often" present. Ratings can then be reviewed to determine whether the necessary six symptoms of either inattention or hyperactivity-impulsivity are present in order to meet the DSM-IV criteria for ADHD. To do this, clinicians may chose to treat a rating of "Often" or "Very often" to indicate the presence of that symptom. If six symptoms of inattention or six symptoms of hyperactivity-impulsivity are checked in this fashion, the child meets a key DSM-IV criterion for ADHD. Other DSM-IV criteria of duration (at least 6 months), onset (before age 7), significantly impaired functioning, and ruling out of other disorders must precede the final diagnosis.

The fact that the scale can be quantified precisely is also significant. Overall ratings for both inattention and hyperactivity-impulsivity can be calculated for the child and compared with average and cutoff scores for children of that age, sex, and rating source (i.e., parent, teacher). Empirical research has also helped clinicians decide which cutoff levels (for example, scores at the 90th percentile versus the 98th percentile) minimize the risk of falsely identifying those without the disorder and still maximize correct detection of those with the disorder. To do this, clinicians may not merely use the six-symptom cutoff level suggested by DSM-

IV. In fact, research suggests that so many boys manifest ADHD symptoms and symptoms decline so much with age that age- and gender-specific cutoff values must be used to make a proper determination of symptom severity for all children. Like other objective rating scales, the ADHD Rating Scale–IV can help show change over time while treatment is occurring.

Home and School Situations Questionnaires

Developed by Russell A. Barkley of the University of Massachusetts Medical Center, the Home and School Situations Questionnaires (see Figures 5.3 and 5.4) differ from the other scales discussed thus far. These questionnaires address where rather than which type of problems (i.e., symptoms) exist. For identification purposes, the diagnostician can count the number of situations in which problems occur (i.e., any situation checked "Yes" rather than "No") or can examine the severity of ratings for various situations (i.e., whether low- or high-number values were marked). Raters may also investigate average severity ratings across situations to determine how a child compares with others at home or in school.

The Home and School Situations Questionnaires have value beyond merely assisting in ADHD diagnosis. For instance, by examining the locations in which problems arise, professionals can determine where treatment needs to be focused. The child rated most severely in social situations may require a social skills training emphasis, whereas the child whose primary problem is school seatwork may require modification of school assignments and an incentive plan to remain on task and productive. It may come as no surprise that among the most difficult situations for children with ADHD are when parents are talking on the telephone, during visits by company, and when the child is expected to do chores. Also noteworthy is that children with ADHD have been found to exhibit fewer problems while their father is home than during most other times. These scales can also help to determine whether medication or behavioral treatments are working.

Child's name ______________________ Date ____________

Name of person completing this form ______________________

Instructions: Does your child present any problems with compliance to instructions, commands, or rules for you in any of these situations? If so, please circle the word Yes and then circle a number beside that situation that describes how severe the problem is for you. If your child is not a problem in a situation, circle No and go on to the next situation on the form.

Situtations	*Yes/No*		*If yes, how severe?* Mild								Severe
While playing alone	Yes	No	1	2	3	4	5	6	7	8	9
While playing with other children	Yes	No	1	2	3	4	5	6	7	8	9
At mealtimes	Yes	No	1	2	3	4	5	6	7	8	9
Getting dressed	Yes	No	1	2	3	4	5	6	7	8	9
Washing and bathing	Yes	No	1	2	3	4	5	6	7	8	9
While you are on the telephone	Yes	No	1	2	3	4	5	6	7	8	9
While watching television	Yes	No	1	2	3	4	5	6	7	8	9
When visitors are in your home	Yes	No	1	2	3	4	5	6	7	8	9
When you are visiting someone's home	Yes	No	1	2	3	4	5	6	7	8	9
In public places (e.g., restaurants, stores, places of worship)	Yes	No	1	2	3	4	5	6	7	8	9
When father is home	Yes	No	1	2	3	4	5	6	7	8	9
When asked to do chores	Yes	No	1	2	3	4	5	6	7	8	9
When asked to do homework	Yes	No	1	2	3	4	5	6	7	8	9
At bedtime	Yes	No	1	2	3	4	5	6	7	8	9
While in the car	Yes	No	1	2	3	4	5	6	7	8	9
When with a babysitter	Yes	No	1	2	3	4	5	6	7	8	9

------------ For office use only ------------

Total number of problem settings ____________ Mean severity score ____________

Figure 5.3. Home Situations Questionnaire, an ADHD rating form. (From Barkley, R.A. [1997]. *Defiant children: A clinician's manual for assessment and parent training* [2nd ed., p. 177]. New York: Guilford Press. Copyright © 1997 by The Guilford Press. A Division of Guilford Publications, Inc.; reprinted by permission.)

Child's name ____________________ Date ____________

Name of person completing this form ____________________

Instructions: Does this child present any problems with compliance to instructions, commands, or rules for you in any of these situations? If so, please circle the word Yes and then circle a number beside that situation that describes how severe the problem is for you. If your child is not a problem in a situation, circle No and go on to the next situation on the form.

Situtations	*Yes/No*		Mild			*If yes, how severe?*					Severe
When arriving at school	Yes	No	1	2	3	4	5	6	7	8	9
During individual desk work	Yes	No	1	2	3	4	5	6	7	8	9
During small-group activities	Yes	No	1	2	3	4	5	6	7	8	9
During free-play time in class	Yes	No	1	2	3	4	5	6	7	8	9
During lectures to the class	Yes	No	1	2	3	4	5	6	7	8	9
At recess	Yes	No	1	2	3	4	5	6	7	8	9
At lunch	Yes	No	1	2	3	4	5	6	7	8	9
In the hallways	Yes	No	1	2	3	4	5	6	7	8	9
In the bathroom	Yes	No	1	2	3	4	5	6	7	8	9
On field trips	Yes	No	1	2	3	4	5	6	7	8	9
During special assemblies	Yes	No	1	2	3	4	5	6	7	8	9
On the bus	Yes	No	1	2	3	4	5	6	7	8	9

For office use only

Total number of problem settings ____________ Mean severity score ____________

Figure 5.4. School Situations Questionnaire, an ADHD rating form. (From Barkley, R.A. [1997]. *Defiant children: A clinician's manual for assessment and parent training* [2nd ed., p. 178]. New York: Guilford Press. Copyright © 1997 by The Guilford Press. A Division of Guilford Publications, Inc.; reprinted by permission.)

Advantages and Limitations of Rating Forms for ADHD

Rating forms provide easily used, objective, and quantifiable ways to evaluate ADHD symptoms at home and in school. Because they allow ratings of symptom number and severity to be compared precisely to ratings of similar-age children, the forms represent one important element in diagnosis.

The utility of the forms is limited, however. If parents or teachers do not understand the symptoms described in the forms, they cannot produce accurate ratings. A parallel problem occurs if the rater is unfamiliar with the "Typical" range of behavior for children. Thus, unless the rater has some idea how to define a "Very much" rating of "Excitable, impulsive" (e.g., as required on the Conners' Rating Scales), then erroneous ratings may result.

Parents' and teachers' attitudes can also affect ratings and render rating tools valueless at times. The purpose of most of these scales is so transparent that markings can be tailored to the purposes of the rater, sometimes perversely so. For example, a classroom teacher who is intent on securing medication for a student has little trouble in figuring out how to mark rating scales. An instrument such as the Conners' Rating Scale simply requires ratings of "Very much" on each symptom. Conversely, those who would like to stamp out all notions of ADHD can easily mark "Not at all" for each item, regardless of their true perceptions of the student's behavior. For these reasons, the rating scales mentioned here must be regarded as only one source of data. They should never be used alone to rule in or rule out the presence of ADHD.

MULTIDIMENSIONAL RATING FORMS

As their title implies, multidimensional rating forms are concerned with several dimensions of behavior and personality, not just ADHD. Thus, anxiety, conduct problems, interpersonal difficulties, and depression may be assessed in addition to ADHD symptoms. These scales have many of the same advantages as the ADHD rating scales just discussed. It is important, however, that they also allow diagnosticians to note parents' or teachers' reports of problems in areas that may be missed by the more narrowly focused ADHD instruments. Recall that too often parents and teachers perceive the diagnostician's task as confined to determining whether ADHD is or is not present, whereas in reality the task is to determine whether one or more disorders, including ADHD, is present. Keeping this broader goal in mind, the value of these tools is self-evident. As with ADHD scales, many multidimensional measures exist, although only two commonly used examples are discussed here.

Personality Inventory for Children

In its most widely used form, the Personality Inventory for Children (PIC) consists of 280 true-or-false items suitable for use with children from 3 to 16 years of age. Each item asks parents about an aspect of behavior. The following items are adapted from the PIC multidimensional rating form:

My son/daughter is often destructive with toys. (True or False)

My son/daughter has nightmares that wake him/her up. (True or False)

My son/daughter seems anxious about leaving me. (True or False)

As an infant, my son/daughter was seldom fussy or cranky. (True or False)

My son/daughter is cruel to animals. (True or False)

Source: From Wodrich, D.L. (1997). *Children's psychological testing: A guide for nonpsychologists* (3rd ed., p. 212). Baltimore: Paul H. Brookes Publishing Co.; reprinted by permission. (*Note:* Items listed above are not actual test items.)

Items are then grouped into the following clinical scales:

Adjustment (overall index of behavior and emotional problems)

Intellectual screening (cognitive impairment)

Development (delayed or unusual development)

Somatic concern (vague physical complaints)

Depression (sadness, depression)

Family relationships (family or marital discord)

Delinquency (poor self-control, disobedience)

Withdrawal (social withdrawal and isolation)

Anxiety (fearfulness, excessive worry)

Psychosis (peculiar or odd behavior)

Hyperactivity (excesses in activity and distractibility)

Social skills (poor social skills)

In addition, there are three scales that are used to determine whether parents are responding fully and candidly. As with the previously mentioned ADHD scales, ratings can be compared with those of children of the same sex and the same general age group. Scores on each dimension can thus be noted as being above or below the minimum cutoff levels. The hyperactivity scale, for instance, contains 29 items from which the child's score is calculated. When approximately 13 or 14 of the items are marked as problematic, a score above the cutoff results. Sometimes, of course, scales other than hyperactivity are elevated. Perhaps a child who initially appeared distractible and restless is ultimately found to have symptoms more indicative of anxiety than ADHD.

Child Behavior Checklist

Another multidimensional instrument that you may encounter is the Child Behavior Checklist, which comes in several forms for parents and teachers. This checklist contains 118 items and is used with children from ages 4 to 16 years. Rather than the true-or-false items of the PIC, this scale asks for ratings from 0 for "Not true," to 1 for "Somewhat or sometimes true," to 2 for "Very true or often true." Other parts of the scale check for participation in school and social activities rather than confine the search to symptoms of negative behavior or problems.

Cutoff scores exist for such dimensions as hyperactivity, depression, obsessive-compulsive behavior, aggression, and several others. Like the PIC, the Child Behavior Checklist benefits enormously from its ability to detect a variety of problems, ADHD being but one possibility. The availability of both parent and teacher ratings also makes the Child Behavior Checklist helpful. Moreover, the ability of both the Child Behavior Checklist and Personality Inventory for Children to detect emotional, behavior, and learning problems has been validated in many research studies.

Advantages and Limitations of Multidimensional Rating Forms

The following critical questions can be answered most effectively when a multidimensional rating scale such as the PIC or the Child Behavior Checklist is used: "Do ADHD symptoms exist?" "What is their severity?" and "Are other problems also present?" Unfortunately, the length of the instruments prevents them from being readministered periodically to determine the success of treatment. In addition, the scales are generally limited to a search for problems. They fail to measure personality strengths, such as gregariousness or creativity, that may be helpful in planning for the child. Such information must come from interviews and reviews of the record, which should be part of a comprehensive assessment of the child.

CONCLUSIONS

ADHD rating scales are extremely advantageous, so much so that their use has become widespread. Especially when coupled with multidimensional rating scales, they enable the diagnostician to better understand the severity and breadth of problem behavior(s). A more effective intervention plan can thus be developed.

Chapter 6

Diagnosing ADHD from Physical, Biomedical, Laboratory, and Mental Measures

ADHD Myths

There are conclusive medical tests for ADHD.

Laboratory measures of ADHD are likely to detect most children with ADHD.

Psychological tests (e.g., IQ tests) have no primary or secondary role in ADHD assessments.

Observation, interviews, and rating forms are elements well accepted by parents in evaluating whether a child has ADHD. Many parents, however, still seem to expect something much more definitive, such as a conclusive medical test. The unfortunate truth is that there is no definitive medical test for ADHD. Some procedures, such as a physical examination, are nonetheless integral to a complete evaluation and may rule out other conditions or aid treatment planning. A review of these other assessment procedures is worthwhile and is provided in this chapter.

PHYSICAL EXAMINATION

It is generally wise to have a physical examination conducted concurrent with or as part of the interview, observation, and rating process as discussed in earlier chapters. If the diagnostician is a pediatrician, neurologist, or psychiatrist, he or she will probably conduct such an examination. If a psychologist is performing the behavioral evaluation, the physical examination is typically deferred to the child's primary care physician.

Although important, the physical examination is seldom crucial in establishing an ADHD diagnosis. For the most part, children with ADHD are indistinguishable (setting aside the obvious behavioral differences) from children without ADHD on physical examination. Nowhere does the ADHD disorder manifest itself in physical differences that may be detected even with the closest scrutiny by an expert physician. As discussed in Chapter 2, ADHD is, in most cases, an inherited disorder affecting behavior. The effects, however, are not fully understood. Although empirical research has demonstrated that children with ADHD as a group have more minor physical anomalies (e.g., two hair whorls on the head, unusual skin creases on the hands), these differences are too inconsistent to be used diagnostically.

NEUROLOGICAL EXAMINATION

Much the same is true when physicians perform a common diagnostic procedure: the neurological examination. This examination may vary from physician to physician in the degree of detail and the elements performed. Generally, it consists of evaluating reflexes, coordination, visual movement and acuity, speech and language development, and thought patterns to determine whether brain or nervous system disease or disability exists. Most children with ADHD have entirely normal examinations of this type. Some children with ADHD have minor or equivocal findings. These *soft signs,* as they may be called by diagnosticians, are believed by some to imply subtle nervous system problems even when there is no hard evidence of damage or dysfunction. Unusual or delayed motor coordination, visual or perception problems, unusual eye movements, and poor organization of activities may be among these soft signs. Because these signs are also present among children with problems other than ADHD, such as learning disabilities, their presence does little to help fix an ADHD diagnosis. Even more important, children who are free of learning problems or developmental problems sometimes exhibit these signs, too. The existence of soft signs alone doesn't prove that your child has ADHD.

The previous comments notwithstanding, there is a valid purpose for noting soft signs. Some experts have suggested that children with soft signs should be referred for more detailed testing, such as a psychoeducational or a neuropsychological evaluation (discussed later in this chapter). The logic here is that because soft signs are associated with learning problems, their presence signals a need for a closer look. In the many ADHD clinics, parent and teacher questionnaires and interview data permit detection of children who require more detailed psychological testing. The soft sign method, however, may be just as worthy. In any case, both methods allow the diagnostician to screen for potential problems. Parents should not be disappointed if the examining physician declines a detailed search for neurological soft signs. It is more important that the diagnostician have a plan for detecting children at risk for learning problems so that those who need additional psychological testing, regardless of how they are identified, are in fact referred for these services. Readers are referred to Chapter 10 for more information about learning problems among children with ADHD.

NEURODIAGNOSTIC LABORATORY TECHNIQUES

The advent of sophisticated neurodiagnostic techniques, some of which were mentioned in Chapter 2, has benefited researchers but has had little impact on the clinical diagnosis of ADHD. This fact puzzles and frustrates many parents who reason that because ADHD problems arise in the nervous system, studying the brain with the most up-to-date techniques ought to provide important information. Unfortunately, diagnostic studies such as the EEG (electroencephalography, which measures electrical activity in the brain), the CT and MRI (computed tomography and magnetic resonance imaging, respectively, both of which allow detailed study of the anatomy of the brain), and the PET (positron emission tomography, which measures the brain's use of energy as it performs tasks) do not yield significant information about ADHD for the vast majority of children with ADHD. Empirical studies involving these techniques have generally failed to detect ADHD with much precision, to measure its severity, or to determine its cause in the individual child. The techniques have also proved of little value in treatment planning, except in rare cases in which ADHD symptoms arise because of neurological disease or definable impairment.

ROLE OF BIOMEDICAL ASSESSMENT

Physical assessment and, more rarely, the use of biomedical tests do play important roles in establishing the overall diagnosis of ADHD as well as in preparing a treatment plan, despite their limited contributions in detecting ADHD itself. The purposes of the physical examination and biomedical assessment are to

1. Rule out the possibility of a rare biomedical condition as the cause of the ADHD symptoms

2. Detect additional physical problems that may require treatment
3. Establish whether there are contraindications to the use of certain medications (e.g., the psychostimulants discussed in Chapter 9)

Some biomedical problems that rarely cause ADHD symptoms, as well as physical problems that have been found to accompany ADHD at higher-than-expected rates, may be detected during a physical exam. The physical exam also enables vital signs such as blood pressure to be measured and basic physiological values such as height and weight to be collected. Problems that may be detected during examination as part of evaluation for ADHD include the following:

Potential (although rare) causes of ADHD symptoms	Biomedical problems that occur more commonly among children with ADHD
Lead poisoning	Enuresis (i.e., bedwetting)
Seizures	Encopresis (i.e., bowel problem)
Medication side effect	Motor incoordination
Brain damage (e.g., head trauma)	Somatic complaints
Stroke	Allergies
Oxygen insufficiency (e.g., severe smoke inhalation)	Middle-ear infections

This information may be an important baseline against which future comparisons can be made if medication is administered.

OTHER LABORATORY MEASURES

Psychology laboratories, usually located at large universities, have developed an impressive number of scientific techniques to measure human performance. Practitioners have hoped that some of these would have clinical value in understanding or detecting ADHD and in monitoring symptom changes. From the long list of techniques with clinical potential, however, only one, the continuous performance task (CPT), has shown much evidence of value.

The CPT consists of presenting visual, auditory, or tactile information to a subject (i.e., a child) who must attend closely and respond according to certain rules. Both subject responses (e.g., lever pressing) and the stimulus information (e.g., a series of sounds) are quite simple. The key to successful performance is to pay attention and avoid impulsive responding. Early research showing the CPT to be sensitive to concentration problems spurred further development of the CPT so that practitioners could use the technique in their offices.

Michael Gordon, a psychologist at the State University of New York Health Sciences Center at Syracuse, developed CPT hardware suitable for office use. He also devised a precise system for scoring children's performances on the CPT and conducted more than 1,000 measures on a representative group of 3- to 16-year-old children to establish norms. His research has demonstrated the effectiveness of the technique in distinguishing children with ADHD from those without it and in reflecting changes as medication is used. Gordon's procedure requires children to sit in front of a small box containing both a screen on which numbers are presented and a response button (see Figure 6.1). On one of the CPT tasks, each time the number 1 is followed by the number 9, the child is to press the response button. He or she is to refrain from pressing the button at all other times. Number sequences are presented continuously during a specified time interval. Nine minutes has proved to be sufficiently long to challenge the attention of most children. The following table lists some of the score categories and behavior measured using the continuous performance task technique:

Figure 6.1. Gordon Diagnostic System–Continuous Performance Task. (Photograph reproduced with the permission of the measure's developer, Dr. Michael Gordon, Gordon Systems, Inc., P.O. Box 746, DeWitt, NY 13214-0746.)

Score category	Definition	Behavior measured
Correct responses	Number of presses when should have	Sustained attention
Omission errors	Number of missed chances to press when should have	Sustained attention
Commission errors	Number of presses when should not have pressed	Attention impulse control

From Gordon, M. (1983). *The Gordon Diagnostic System.* DeWitt, NY: Gordon Systems, Inc.; reprinted by permission.

Many clinicians have found Gordon's modification of the CPT worthwhile because it is objective; is suitable for office use; emphasizes concentration rather than the frequently measured impulsiveness, hyperactivity, and conduct-related aspects of ADHD; and complements the ADHD rating scales (see Chapter 5). Research has shown that this technique may overlook (i.e., fail to detect because of scoring cutoffs) children who may actually have ADHD but not to overidentify (i.e., falsely diagnose children with ADHD). Several competitors of the Gordon system (e.g., the Test of Variables of Attention [TOVA]; Conners' Continuous Performance Test) exist, and clinicians may use these as well.

Unfortunately, the value of other types of laboratory procedures has yet to be empirically documented. Techniques such as the Matching for Familiar Figures and automated mazes may ultimately be clinically useful but at the time of this writing have not yet proved themselves empirically reliable.

PSYCHOLOGICAL AND MENTAL TESTS

Like laboratory psychological techniques, standardized psychological tests such as intelligence scales were at one time regarded as potentially valuable in diagnosis. This potential seemed attainable when research on one of the most popular intelligence tests, the Wechsler scales, found that some of the subtests within the scale measured traits related to attention and concentration. Clinicians and researchers noted that children with ADHD often scored lower than other children on these particular sections of the Wechsler scales. It thus became common practice to calculate this "Freedom from Distractibility" score when using the Wechsler scales and to consider the score when making an ADHD diagnosis. Subsequent research, however, found that substantial numbers of children without ADHD also score low on these sections, thus negating use of this Wechsler profile in ADHD diagnosis. Similar findings have been reported with other typically used psychological and mental tests: No pattern is sufficiently distinctive to children with ADHD to be of much practical assistance.

Nonetheless, psychological tests are important in the comprehensive assessment of children with ADHD, even if that role is ancillary in diagnosing ADHD. Intelligence tests can help establish expectations for school learning and assist in identifying strengths and weaknesses. Specialized psychological tests of memory, visual perception, and language can likewise aid in understanding the child and in creating a plan to help him or her. Individually administered tests of academic achievement allow for accurate measurement of education levels; children with unique learning problems, such as dyslexia, may reveal their problems during administration of these reading, writing, and mathematics tests. Cumulatively, these types of ability and academic tests are referred to as a *psychoeducational test battery.* Administering such a battery is one essential element in determining whether a student qualifies for special education placement (see Chapter 10).

Neuropsychological tests are sometimes employed to assess children with ADHD. These tests share many elements with those used in psychoeducational evaluation (in fact, some of the same tests may be used), but they differ in important ways. A neuropsychological evaluation is concerned with inferring brain function based on psychological test results. For example, some neuropsychological tests concern themselves with how effectively sensory or motor centers in the brain are performing. Others might be concerned with the perception of language or with how effectively the brain organizes and expresses language. As valuable as these tests are for instances in which there is known or suspected brain impairment (e.g., when an individual has sustained a head trauma), their value is less clear in most cases of ADHD. Moreover, these evaluation procedures are detailed and time consuming and thus expensive. If you have concerns about the need for either a psychoeducational or neuropsychological evaluation, you are encouraged to speak to your child's diagnostician. You should speak candidly about what you wish to accomplish by the use of such an evaluation, and you should be certain that there are valid reasons for including any particular element in the assessment.

CONCLUSIONS

As compared with diagnostic methods such as observation, interviewing, and rating-scale analysis, the measures discussed in this chapter are of secondary value in establishing an ADHD diagnosis. Yet, research continues, and the potential for better diagnoses using laboratory or biomedical techniques does indeed exist.

Chapter 7

Case Examples in Assessing Children

ADHD Myths

ADHD symptoms rarely appear during the preschool years.

Most children with ADHD remain optimistic and happy throughout their school years.

This chapter includes two case examples for parents as a means of injecting reality into the ADHD assessment process. Space limitations prevent a complete reproduction here of interview information or of ratings findings. Rather, information is presented in summary form to highlight key aspects of the process. (*Note:* The names of individuals are pseudonyms, and any similarity to actual individuals or circumstances is coincidental.)

WAYNE

Background Information

The following information was collected during the intake process, indicating that 8-year-old Wayne was having trouble with home and school behavior. The background information described the parents' perceptions of problem behavior. Wayne's parents listed the following behaviors as present to a moderate or severe degree:

- Picks on others
- Has few friends
- Fights with others
- Talks back to adults
- Disobeys parents and adults
- Has chip on his shoulder
- Can't sit still and concentrate

The parents' written comments were as follows:

> Wayne has always been all boy. He likes rough activities and is afraid of nothing. He has always played rough, but his temper has gotten worse in the last 2 years. He has had stitches three times for falls. He drank lighter fluid when he was 4, evidently just to check out the taste. Now we're afraid he might hurt his younger brother when he gets mad. He is hard to discipline. Spankings and groundings don't work. He will lie even if caught red-handed. Wayne loves football and will watch games with his dad—about the only thing he

> will do for very long at a time. We love him dearly and are worried about his future if this kind of behavior keeps up.

Parent information showed that Wayne was born following an uneventful pregnancy and delivery. He achieved developmental milestones at early ages—sitting at 5 months, ambulating independently at 10 months, using single words at 11 months, and constructing phrases at 18 months. He was easily toilet trained, both bowel and bladder, by age 24 months. His hearing and vision have been found to be normal. Wayne's parents indicated that their son was healthy and was taking no medication.

Wayne's classroom teacher listed the following behaviors as present to a moderate or severe degree:

- Does not conform to limits without external control
- Has difficulty with concentrating
- Is overactive, restless, and/or continually shifts body positions
- Disturbs other children by teasing them or provoking fights
- Argues or must have the last word in discussions
- Has tantrums
- Shows physical aggression toward objects or others
- Doesn't complete school tasks
- Is restless and fidgety

His teacher added:

> Wayne is aggressive in class and especially on the playground. He often hits for no apparent reason. He seldom is sorry. He never keeps his hands to himself in line. The other children have grown tired of his loud and rough behavior. His schoolwork is completed rapidly and carelessly or not at all. He is often disorganized. Wayne has two positives: He never stays mad for long, and he is very good in sports, especially football.

Observation of Behavior

Wayne and his family, including his 4-year-old brother, were met in the waiting room and escorted to the corridor leading to the office. Wayne's brother edged slightly ahead of him, and it was clear that the two boys were going to race to the office door. Suddenly, Wayne hit his brother with a glancing blow to the ribs and shot completely past the open office door and continued down a long corridor, only to return when he saw his parents and brother enter the office door.

Wayne's mother separated the boys as the parent interview began. Wayne sat calmly for only a few minutes and then attempted to sit by his brother, only to be redirected back to his original spot by his father. Wayne looked around the room and did not appear to follow the conversation, except to add a brief comment periodically or to disagree with his parents' statements. He seemed easily annoyed by any indication that he had done something wrong. Five minutes into the interview Wayne began to enter the conversation, in a poorly focused fashion. During the discussion of family background, Wayne spontaneously volunteered:

> Do you know what my teacher did today? She said that if Aaron got in trouble one more time he had to go to the principal's office. Aaron got his name on the board more than any other kid in our class. Aaron cannot read very well, either. He missed almost all his words in spelling, too.

The conversation was then refocused onto the background topic, and Wayne was promised a chance to tell about school later. Nonetheless, he repeatedly launched into unrelated topics and continued to do so despite redirection by his parents. Once quiet, Wayne seized large Lego-type blocks, which he repetitively popped together, separated, rotated, dropped, and flipped at his younger brother.

Wayne sat still only briefly before seeking the toys in the corner of the room—a natural tendency, although he was unconcerned with asking permission first. Several times he blocked his younger brother's access to the toys by applying shoulder blocks. Once Wayne completed a setup of the checkers game, however, his brother was welcomed, and Wayne was affectionate, encouraging, and kind to him. The game lasted approximately 3 minutes before it was clear that it was over the head of his brother, who returned to sit by his mother. Wayne investigated several other toys and games, leaving each on the floor before resuming his original seat.

Later Wayne and his father were taken to the observation room, where Wayne was presented with several pages of simple addition and subtraction problems. During the 10-minute observation period, Wayne turned and looked at his father (who was seated beside and slightly behind him) on three occasions, only to receive, in each instance, a harsh look from his father. He quickly returned to his work. Objectively, his percentage of on-task behavior was 92.5%. Subjectively, Wayne appeared only mildly restless in this situation.

Parent Interview

Wayne's parents reconfirmed some of the health and developmental information of the intake form. They described their son as a wonderful baby who adapted well to their home and its routines, developed normal rhythms, bonded well, and was a joy to them. As a toddler, Wayne was "busy and curious"; he frequently attempted to climb or to get into places where parents assumed no baby could go. When he learned to walk, his curiosity and activity levels intensified. His parents recall that when Wayne finished playing, "the room looked like a tornado had hit it." They remembered their son's first contact with other toddlers vividly because he attempted to dominate others even at an early age. Competition for a toy often resulted in Wayne pushing the other child down and grabbing the desired plaything. By age 2 years, they noted that he was "intense." If frustrated, he was quick to display a tantrum, even though he was generally pleasant and affectionate if not frustrated. He was likewise recalled as being easily excitable, laughing loudly during cartoons and talking nonstop if taken by his father to a football game.

By age 3 or 4 years, Wayne's parents found Wayne more difficult to manage and more strong-willed. According to his mother, "If he made up his mind on something, then it was very difficult to change." Both parents were surprised that spankings were of almost no value by this time. If spanked by his mother, he refused to cry; if spanked by his father, he cried only briefly. In either case, he was apt to return undeterred to the same behavior that initially prompted the punishment. By this age, Wayne preferred to play outside. Here his behavior was generally acceptable, except that he liked to climb so much that there was constant worry that he would fall and hurt himself, which he did several times.

His mother recalled a frightening incident that occurred at age 5 years when the family was in their front yard. A neighbor was walking two leashed Doberman pinschers down the sidewalk. Wayne abruptly raced toward them, apparently startled one of the dogs, and was knocked down as the dog snarled. Although Wayne was momentarily frightened, both parents were shocked that he showed so little apprehension about approaching these formidable-looking animals to begin with.

Wayne loved sports and was good at them. He had more trouble with indoor activities, however, in which he seemed to become quickly bored. Although others played board games or watched television, Wayne generally had little interest in these activities. Indoors, his play was sufficiently loud and rough to alienate most potential playmates. By age 6 or 7 years, Wayne was reported by his parents as having few friends. Older children would allow him to play sports with them, but few same-age peers ever telephoned him or were willing to play if he telephoned them.

Wayne's parents had been married for 2 years when he was born. It was the first marriage for each parent, and each described their relationship as good except for the strains of raising their older son. In contrast to Wayne, his 4-year-old brother was characterized by his parents as easy to discipline, although slightly overactive as well. Although neither parent had learning or ADHD-related problems, Wayne's father indicated that as a child he always preferred outdoor and physically active pursuits. He recalled his own school days as "long and boring." A paternal first cousin had a history of severe behavior problems before dropping out of school but was never diagnosed as having ADHD.

Teacher Interview

A telephone interview was conducted with Wayne's classroom teacher. She stated that Wayne could not keep up with his third-grade classmates. Closer questioning, however, revealed that Wayne was capable of reading, spelling, computing mathematics problems, and writing adequately; but he was failing to do so. He was described as so frequently in trouble for his behavior or so careless and inattentive with his work that "his productiveness [was] not up to the standards of a third-grade student in [his] school district." Although concerned about work completion, his teacher was even more concerned about what she called "his behavior and his attitude."

The classroom discipline system, which consisted of a series of warnings and escalating consequences, was ineffective in controlling Wayne. For example, he had been warned to keep his hands to himself but violated that rule so many times that he had to miss recess. Although Wayne disliked missing recess, he continued to "pick at and provoke" classmates. On the playground, his behavior was even worse. Here several pushing matches had progressed into full-blown fights when Wayne lost his temper. He had been sent home from school on three occasions for these fights.

His teacher indicated that Wayne had passed many of the criterion-referenced achievement tests covering topics that had just been taught in class. In contrast, his day-to-day classwork was poor. His spelling and arithmetic assignments were frequently incomplete or woefully inaccurate. Wayne often started activities too quickly and did not listen to his teacher's directions even if his attention appeared to be fully focused beforehand. Neither the school psychologist nor the school counselor had had any involvement with Wayne to date.

Rating Forms and Questionnaires

Wayne's parents completed the Personality Inventory for Children (PIC), the Home Situations Questionnaire, and the ADHD Rating Scale (see Chapter 5). Figure 7.1 summarizes Wayne's PIC scores. Note that both the hyperactivity (HPR) and delinquency (DLQ) scales were elevated.

Figure 7.2 summarizes all of these scores concerning ADHD. Wayne's parents rated him above the cutoff levels on each of the brief ADHD measures. (Note that PIC hyperactivity scale scores are listed here also on the extreme right of the figure.) The situations in which Wayne's behavior was rated as most problematic by his parents were in public places, at bedtime, occasions when he plays with other children, occasions when he is asked to do chores, and occasions when asked to do homework. These ratings were consistent with his parents' comments during the parent interview.

Wayne's teacher assisted by completing the Teacher Report Form from the Child Behavior Checklist, the School Situations Questionnaire, and the ADHD Rating Scale (see Chapter 5). Wayne's score exceeded the cutoff value on the scales that measure inattention and aggression on the Teacher Rating Form, which is hardly surprising, given this teacher's prior reports. Wayne's score on the ADHD Rating Scale also exceeded the clinical cutoff.

Child Interview

After the parent interview, Wayne was interviewed alone. At the outset, he was asked his understanding of the purpose of his visit. "I think they are mad at me for not getting my work done and fighting at school" was his response. Wayne went on to attribute most of his school problems to classmates who "start fights." He indicated that his teacher was "nice and fair." Wayne was friendly, extremely comfortable talking to an adult, and only slightly restless when provided

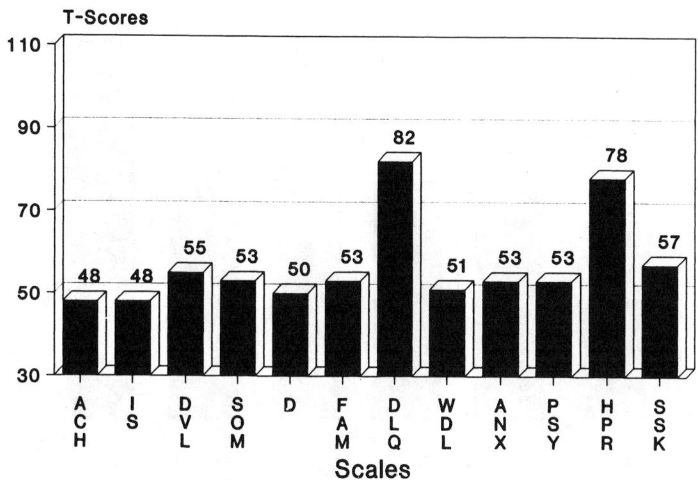

Figure 7.1. Summary of Wayne's scores on the Personality Inventory for Children. (ACH = achievement, IS = intellectual screening, DVL = development, SOM = somatic concerns, D = depression, FAM = family relationships, DLQ = delinquency, WDL = withdrawal, ANX = anxiety, PSY = psychosis, HPR = hyperactivity, SSK = social skills.)

the individual attention of the interview. Inattention to social cues and impulsivity were evident, however. Wayne frequently digressed from the topic at hand to launch into discussions about camping trips and football. He had difficulty ignoring the games and toys he had earlier placed on the floor in front of him, even though he was told that games could be played only during a subsequent office visit.

Wayne did admit to occasional difficulty with controlling his temper. He also added that some schoolwork was "boring." He denied, however, problems with concentration, sitting still, or thinking before acting. As one might expect, Wayne appeared a bit more sad as he discussed loss of recesses and weekends that typically involved little peer contact. Nonetheless, he denied any feelings of sadness and discouragement.

Both the content and the manner of his responses to two questions were telling. Asked what he would like to be when he grew up, Wayne responded that he would like to be a professional football player, at which time he jumped

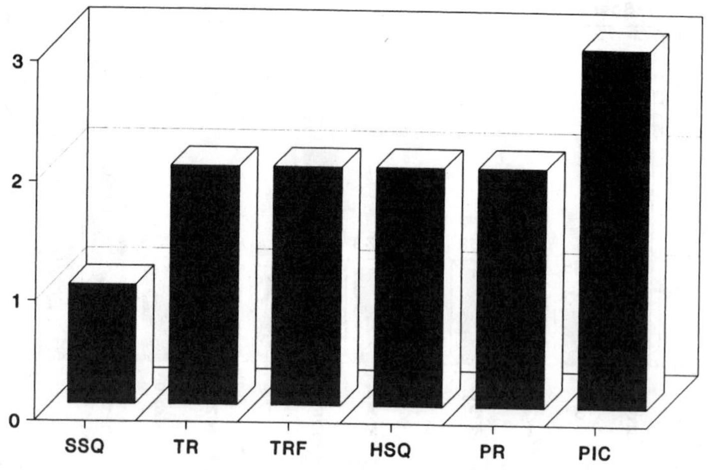

Figure 7.2. Summary of Wayne's scores on ADHD rating forms. (SSQ = School Situations Questionnaire, TR = teacher rating [ADHD rating scale], TRF = teacher's rating form [attention problems scale], HSQ = Home Situations Questionnaire, PR = parent rating [ADHD rating scale], PIC = Personality Inventory for Children [hyperactivity scale], 0 = normal, 1 = mild, 2 = moderate, 3 = severe.)

from the couch and screamed loudly, "Hut one, hut two, hut three," took an imaginary snap from the center, and faked a downfield pass. He did this so quickly and spontaneously that there appeared to be little forethought or recognition that he was in an office, not at a playground. When asked his three fondest wishes, Wayne responded quickly, "A million bucks, a million wishes, and no school."

Physical Examination

Wayne had been seen by his pediatrician recently. After conducting a physical examination and ordering laboratory tests, she concluded that he was healthy and that there was no biomedical problem or disease that could account for his ADHD symptoms.

Conclusions

Parent and teacher reports, coupled with the confirmatory information that they provided on rating scales, allowed the ADHD diagnosis to be made confidently. The following symptoms (see Table 1.1) from the DSM-IV criteria related to inattention were concluded to be present:

- Often has difficulty sustaining attention in task or play activities
- Often does not seem to listen when spoken to directly
- Often does not follow through on instructions and fails to finish schoolwork, chores, or duties in the workplace
- Often has difficulty organizing tasks and activities
- Often avoids, dislikes, or is reluctant to engage in tasks that require sustained mental effort
- Often loses things necessary for tasks or activities

In addition, the following symptoms from the DSM-IV criteria (see Table 1.1) related to hyperactivity-impulsivity were concluded to be present:

- Often fidgets with hands or feet or squirms in seat
- Often leaves seat in classroom or in other situations in which remaining seated is expected
- Often runs about or climbs excessively in situations in which it is inappropriate
- Is often "on the go" or often acts as if "driven by a motor"
- Often talks excessively
- Often interrupts or intrudes on others

DSM-IV criteria stipulate that symptoms must have at least a 6-month duration, must have been evident before age 7 years, and must cause impairment in two or more settings. In Wayne's case, symptoms had been present continuously since age 3 or 4 years and were causing him significant impairment in his school and home functioning. Wayne thus meets all necessary criteria for a DSM-IV diagnosis of ADHD–Combined Type.

ADHD is only one element of Wayne's problem. Careful review of parent and teacher reports and interview data suggests that impulse and mood control elements plus resistance to authority and a tendency to blame others also exist. Despite repeated warnings, Wayne's conduct is seriously undercontrolled, especially in school. Wayne meets the diagnostic criteria (see Table 1.3 for oppositional defiant disorder as well, by virtue of the following symptoms:

- Often loses temper
- Often argues with adults
- Often actively defies or refuses to comply with adults' requests or rules
- Often is touchy or easily annoyed by others
- Often is angry and resentful

It is likely that Wayne's problems with judgment, foresight, and impulse control underlie some of his conduct problems and resistance to authority. As discussed previously, for many children with ADHD, the rewards and punishments that typically are sufficient to influence behavior are ineffective. For Wayne, even repeated loss of recess or at-home spankings have failed to deter him. His comment that school is boring, coupled with his obvious inability to stick with monotonous classwork, suggests that he experiences deficient amounts of inherent reward for performing these tasks. Other children without ADHD problems may experience enough inherent reward in performing these tasks to keep them attending and motivated. Wayne does not.

Wayne's future is at special risk. Without changes, Wayne is likely to develop an increasingly poor attitude toward school and to further solidify his defiance and resistance to rules. Although he denies it, signs of discouragement are beginning to surface, as evidenced by his sad facial expression at times and his comments about wishing there were no more school.

Recommendations

Although the focus of this chapter is on the assessment of ADHD, it is worthwhile to conclude this case example with an outline of the types of recommendations that would be made for a child such as Wayne. (Subsequent chapters offer more detailed dimensions of interventions to help children with ADHD.) Recommendations for Wayne include the following:

1. Provide Wayne's parents with basic information about ADHD and about oppositional defiant disorder.
2. Assist Wayne's parents in developing a discipline system at home.
3. Enroll Wayne in a social skills training group.
4. Discuss Wayne's diagnosis, the need to modify school procedures, and the necessity of providing him services under Section 504 of the Rehabilitation Act of 1973 (see Chapter 10) with his classroom teacher, building principal, and school psychologist.
5. Forgo a comprehensive psychological evaluation at this time, but consider one if the preceding recommendations fail to alleviate school problems.
6. Refer Wayne to an ADHD clinic for possible trial on medication.

JESSICA

Background Information

Jessica's mother was obviously ambivalent about seeing psychologists and psychiatrists about her 10-year-old daughter's "problem." Her intake information was as follows:

> I am not certain that my daughter really has a problem, but something must be done because Jessica is starting to feel bad about herself. At home, she is fine most of the time, except that she doesn't pay attention to what she is doing. It takes her forever to clean her room or to help out with the

> dishes. If I ask her to do something, she is apt to forget what I said and to be back a few moments later asking me to repeat myself. She must be able to read the frustration in my voice. As frustrating as home is, we could tolerate it if school were not a problem. Jessica's teachers love her, but she is almost failing. The school psychologist tested her for learning disabilities but concluded that she doesn't have that problem. He felt like she might have an attention-deficit or hyperactivity-type problem. Her pediatrician was unsure because Jessica didn't seem "hyper" in the office. He suggested that we obtain a more detailed evaluation.

Jessica's pediatrician confirmed in a written evaluation that Jessica was a healthy girl and had no physical problems that were causing the behavior her mother outlined. Jessica's parents listed the following problems:

- Spends most of her time alone (mild problem)
- Is sad much of the time (moderate problem)
- Acts younger than her actual age (moderate problem)
- Daydreams a lot (moderate problem)
- Often appears to be in a daze (moderate problem)
- Doesn't finish tasks and/or has a short attention span (mild problem)

The intake information indicated that Jessica's mother had experienced an uncomplicated pregnancy. Labor was protracted; after nearly 18 hours, a cesarean birth was accomplished. The baby required oxygen because of a breathing problem, but she ultimately did well and left the hospital at age 4 days, when her mother was able. She sat, crawled, walked, spoke her first word and first sentence, and was toilet trained on time. She was recalled to be a "busy baby who was extremely happy." Her mother indicated that Jessica had mild allergies that occasionally required treatment with over-the-counter medication. She was listed as free of hearing or vision problems.

Jessica's fourth-grade teacher checked the following problems:

- Is overly critical of herself
- Does not complete tasks
- Is easily distracted by ordinary classroom stimuli (e.g., movements of others, noises)
- Doesn't pay attention
- Exhibits poor work skills
- Has difficulty with understanding directions
- Is restless and fidgety

In addition, Jessica's teacher estimated Jessica's handwriting, mathematics, and reading comprehension to be 1–2 years below her grade level. Jessica's teacher commented:

> Jessica is a sweet girl who unfortunately is falling further and further behind in class. She has difficulty in keeping up with her classmates, at least partially because she is inattentive and disorganized. She doesn't listen well, yet she becomes upset (usually self-directed) when she cannot understand what to do. Sometimes she asks to stay in at recess to complete what the other students have completed during class. If I provide her with easier work, she usually gets it done. Otherwise, it is always a struggle for her. The other children like her, except for the times when she can more or less drive people crazy by talking too much. Jessica seems spacey and distractible rather than hyperactive.

Observation of Behavior

Jessica appeared confident and outgoing as she and her mother entered the office. Jessica assumed the lead in answering questions, often preempting her mother's comments. Jessica not only answered but went on to provide spontaneous comments about her school and home life. Nonetheless, she showed sufficient self-control to quiet down quickly when her mother signaled her to do so. Jessica scanned the room; looked out the window; and, at times, lost track of the conversation so that questions to her required repeating. The only sign of restlessness observed was that she repetitively slid her foot back and forth on the carpet as her mother answered questions.

In the observation room, Jessica worked at mathematics problems while her mother completed rating forms. Jessica refrained from speaking to her mother there, but she was extremely restless. She rocked in her seat and stretched her arms after every few problems. More significant, she repeatedly drifted from her arithmetic problems to look around the room. She was off-task during 6 of the 40 ten-second observation intervals (i.e., 15% of the time). Her proportion of on-task behavior was 85%.

Parent Interview

Jessica and her mother live alone. Her parents were divorced 6 years ago, and she rarely sees her father, who resides in another state. Jessica's mother said, "Perhaps as a result, Jessica and I have always been close. I know I'm reluctant to punish her because of the potential impact on our relationship. Sometimes now the closeness is too much. I feel like I have no private life." Because of Jessica's disorganization and forgetfulness, her mother has resorted to virtually constant supervision and direction. Even when Jessica was 5 or 6, she contributed little to her own dressing. At present, Jessica has to be followed around the house to ensure that she brushes her teeth, combs her hair, collects her books, and picks up her lunch money before leaving for school.

Jessica's baby sitters had likewise identified her as disorganized. She might pull out one set of toys, only to leave them and start with another. Her attention span was poor as a preschooler. When naptime stories were read, Jessica showed no interest. By contrast, she has always been able to flourish with undivided adult attention, often sitting and talking for extended intervals.

Jessica's mother described her as "pretty cautious physically but pretty unafraid socially." When taken to Disneyland, she avoided some of the more adventuresome rides but started conversations with adults, teenagers, children, or even staff while waiting in line. Jessica's mother continued, "Even though Jessica seems so grown up when she talks with me, something goes wrong when she is with other children. She either talks too much or won't play what they want, at least for very long. Can a child be both immature and overmature at the same time?"

Homework was identified as a particularly difficult task. Despite attempts to provide structure, Jessica "invariably insists on sharpening her pencil, getting drinks, going to the bathroom, and calling me for help at the first sign of frustration. It seems as though Jessica takes twice as long as necessary to complete everything, especially homework." Only with detailed questioning was Jessica's mother able to recall a great deal of "rocking and fidgeting when she works, even when she's getting things done." Jessica's mother asked, obviously perplexed, "But still, if she were hyperactive, how could she watch television for hours on end with no problems?"

Jessica's mother stated that her daughter had recently shown more signs of "being down on herself." After reprimands or during weekends without playmates, Jessica often complains of being unhappy. She has told her mother, "I know you're my best friend, but I feel like sometimes it isn't enough."

Jessica's mother concluded the interview by indicating that she doubted her daughter had ADHD. She stated that an after-school tutor with whom Jessica had worked insisted that she was not hyperactive. Jessica's mother pleaded that Jessica "isn't that much of a problem at home." Jessica's mother was clearly puzzled that Jessica could have an obvious problem in all situations except when Jessica was with her.

Teacher Interview

In a telephone interview, Jessica's teacher expanded on the statements contained in the previously completed teacher intake form. She expressed the greatest concern about Jessica's falling behind academically: "Without better work habits, Jessica may not be ready to go on to the fifth grade." With closer questioning, her teacher was unsure about Jessica's exact level of skill development in reading, spelling, or mathematics. What was clear was that Jessica was not completing work. When questioned directly about ADHD symptoms, her teacher identified restlessness, especially in-seat movement, poor sustained attention, frequent out-of-seat behavior (e.g., pencil sharpening), talkativeness, and a lack of planning and organization. Jessica's behavior presented absolutely no problem. On the contrary, she had obviously become one of her teacher's favorites. Recently, as her relationship with her peers waned, Jessica had come to spend her lunch recesses in the classroom visiting with her teacher. Her teacher added, "In some ways, Jessica seems more mature than her age; she can talk about adult topics almost like a friend of mine rather than a child."

Prior Psychological Testing

Because it was stored in the school's confidential file, an evaluation completed by the school psychologist 1 year earlier had not been seen by Jessica's mother. That evaluation had found Jessica to have a verbal IQ score of 113, a performance IQ (i.e., nonverbal) score of 108, and a full-scale IQ (i.e., composite) score of 111. The school psychologist found her to have no problems with language, memory, visual perception, or fine motor control. Equally important, Jessica's scores on individually administered tests of reading, spelling, and mathematics were average. The diagnostician noted distractibility, occasional impulsivity, and mild restlessness. A classroom observation, conducted as part of the evaluation, noted Jessica's frequent attempts to talk with classmates rather than complete her seatwork.

Rating Forms

Jessica's teacher and parent ADHD ratings were not in complete agreement. Her teacher identified eight of nine ADHD symptoms related to inattention from the DSM-IV list, with her scores on the "inattention-overactivity" dimension of the ADHD Rating Scale–IV exceeding the cutoff level. Similarly, scores on the School Situations Questionnaire exceeded cutoff values for both the number of situations and the mean severity of those situations that were rated. Consistent with other teacher ratings were scores on the Child Behavior Checklist–Teacher Rating Form (see Figure 7.3). Here, Jessica's teacher's responses identified not only attentional problems and difficulty in getting along with others but also hinted at discouragement or depression.

Jessica's mother rated her daughter as much less symptomatic on the brief ADHD-related scales. The scores on the ADHD Rating Scale–IV and the Home Situations Questionnaire scores did not exceed cutoff values. But Jessica's score on the hyperactivity scale of the PIC was elevated above the clinical cutoff. No other PIC scales were so elevated, although Jessica's score on the depression scale approached significance. Her mother seemed to be noticing some signs of both inattention/hyperactivity-impulsivity and discouragement/depression, although less assuredly so than her teacher.

Child Interview

Jessica was fun to talk with—highly verbal, expressive, and more than capable of carrying on an adultlike conversation. Yet her conversation, both in style and in content, was too adult. Rather than tell about her school, current styles, or children's television shows, Jessica recounted R-rated movies that she had seen at home, asked about the personal life of the diagnostician ("How much do you get paid at this job? Are you married?"), and wanted to know whether she was "hyper." She did all of this in a fairly controlled way, with good eye contact and appropriate voice inflection. For the first 10 minutes or so of the conversation, Jessica was well focused; thereafter, however, her attention wandered. At this point, she interjected the previously mentioned off-topic questions and provided comments unrelated to the discussion.

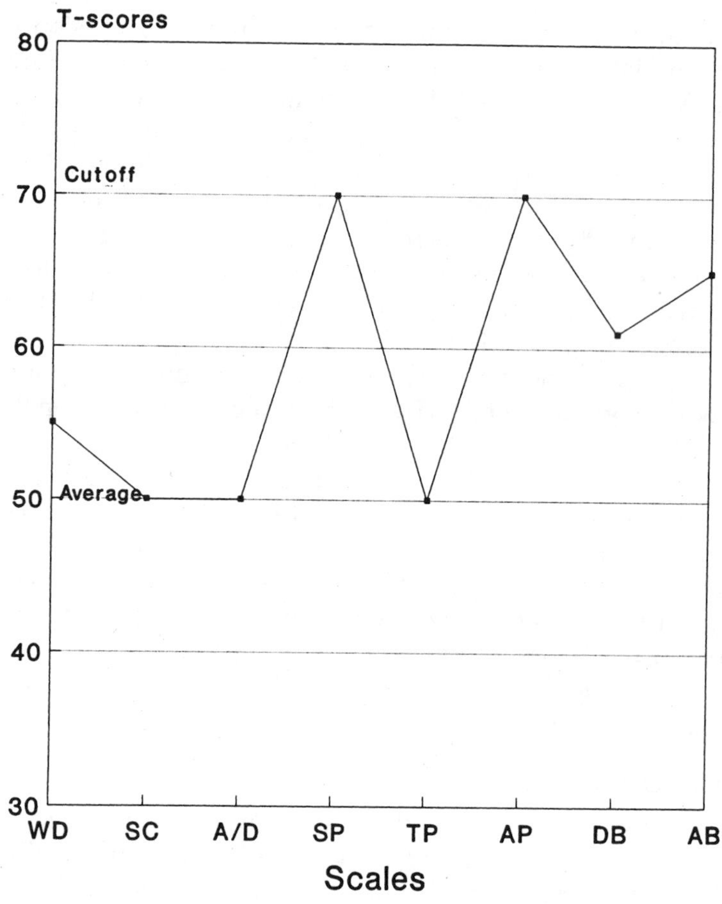

Figure 7.3. Jessica's scores on Child Behavior Checklist–Teacher Rating Form. (WD = withdrawn, SC = somatic complaints, A/D = anxious/depressed, SP = social problems, TP = thought problems, AP = attention problems, DB = delinquent behavior, AB = aggressive behavior.)

Jessica was aware that she was failing to complete her schoolwork. She was less sure about the presence of attentional problems but ultimately commented, "It must be a problem because I'm obviously not getting my work done." She denied feeling hyperactive or having trouble slowing down and thinking before reacting. She stated that her clearest emotion was one of boredom, especially at school. In her words, "I really can't stand to do those worksheets they want you to do. My teacher is the greatest, so don't tell her; but the stuff is awfully boring." When directly questioned, Jessica confirmed feelings of poor self-esteem, including unhappiness with her appearance, lack of confidence about her school ability, and concern about her capability of winning friends. She also admitted to occasionally feeling "sad," only to later relabel this feeling as "boredom." She stated that she had never wished she were dead but had "wished I had never been born when I get too bored and bummed out." Jessica's fondest wishes were to be 18, to get all A's without doing the work, and to have a new house for her and her mother.

Conclusions

Arriving at an accurate assessment was more difficult for Jessica than for Wayne. A diagnosis of ADHD, predominately inattentive type, for Jessica was clear only after several different data sources were collected and carefully interpreted. In Jessica's case, the following ADHD symptoms (see Table 1.1) of inattention from DSM-IV were noted:

- Often fails to pay close attention to details or makes careless mistakes in schoolwork, work, or other activities
- Often has difficulty with sustaining attention in tasks or play activities
- Often does not follow through on instructions and fails to finish schoolwork, chores, or duties in the workplace
- Often has difficulty with organizing tasks and activities
- Often avoids, dislikes, or is reluctant to engage in tasks that require sustained mental effort
- Often loses things that are necessary for tasks or activities
- Often is forgetful in daily activities

Only two symptoms of ADHD related to hyperactivity-impulsivity could be confirmed:

- Often fidgets with hands or feet or squirms in seat
- Often talks excessively

Inattention-related symptoms had adequate duration (greater than 6 months), had early enough onset (before age 7 years), and were causing sufficiently impaired performance at home and in school to allow a formal ADHD diagnosis, predominately inattentive type, to be made.

Several key points for parents should be kept in mind. First, even though Jessica's mother had been told by the tutor that her daughter did not have ADHD, Jessica nonetheless was affected by this disorder to the degree that it was having a significant negative impact on her life, despite her mother's not being particularly distressed about her home behavior. Jessica's mother had clearly developed a high tolerance for her behavior, and, because Jessica was an only child, there was no sibling in the home with whom to compare her behavior daily. Jessica's example thus demonstrates that a diagnosis of ADHD should be made only after objective and careful evaluation by professionals specifically trained to identify the disorder. Sometimes a parent's own assessment is inaccurate, as was the tutor's, who saw Jessica within a limited time frame and a narrow setting.

Second, in this example, it is not surprising that scores from home and school rating forms did not completely agree. The demands to pay attention, control impulses, and follow school rules were, in Jessica's case, far more stringent at school than at home, where her mother's undivided attention, encouragement, and direction were virtually constant. Moreover, Jessica's outgoing social style as well as her excessive pretenses of maturity appeared to match well with her mother's desires for her daughter. Thus, Jessica was less symptomatic at home, and her mother failed to recognize some of the symptoms that were present.

Third, it is significant that only on the multidimensional questionnaire (i.e., the PIC) did Jessica's mother rate her daughter as symptomatic for ADHD. The brief ADHD Rating Scales are obvious in their content and purpose. Because Jessica's mother doubted that her daughter had ADHD, she simply checked her as having few problems on those scales. Jessica's mother was probably more open-minded as she completed the 280 items on the PIC, of which only 29 deal with ADHD. Given a more objective response set, Jessica's problems were better detected.

Fourth, a comprehensive assessment ensured that a treatment plan could also be comprehensive. Jessica was becoming discouraged about repeated failure. Thus, there were problems not just with ADHD but with self-esteem as well. Similarly, Jessica's pseudo-mature approach to interpersonal relationships and her relationship with her mother should be addressed in treatment. Assisting Jessica to act in a more age-appropriate fashion and helping her and her mother to sort out their respective roles in the family will probably benefit Jessica's long-term social adjustment.

The following recommendations would have been made for Jessica:

1. Arrange for family therapy.
2. Enroll Jessica in a social skills training group.
3. Institute a revised school program emphasizing clear expectations and limits and providing a token economy (i.e., a point system for acceptable behavior with points being traded in for rewards).
4. Refer Jessica to an ADHD clinic for consideration of a trial on medication.

Because both ADHD and mood elements are present, an antidepressant or a stimulant medication would probably be considered by the attending physician. Treatment issues are discussed in later chapters.

CLOSING COMMENTS

No two children with ADHD are identical. Although they share a core group of symptoms of either inattention or hyperactivity-impulsivity, they differ in the manifestation of those symptoms; in symptom severity; and, most important, in other characteristics such as co-existing emotional, interpersonal, and school learning problems. Each child and his or her family also possess unique strengths and talents. A thorough evaluation that includes interviews, observation, and often objective rating techniques represents the best method of assessing children suspected of attentional and overactivity problems. Such an assessment permits not just the establishment of a simple diagnosis such as ADHD but, more important, the development of an intervention plan. Child clinicians who understand not only the syndrome of ADHD but also child development, the treatment of emotional problems, and the process of education can help give your child the optimum chance to grow and develop.

Section III

How Is ADHD Treated?

Chapter 8

Behavior Management to Help the Child with ADHD

ADHD Myths

Because ADHD is primarily inherited, behavior modification techniques are of little value.

Parents can figure out most behavior modification plans on their own.

Behavior modification plans require a great deal of extra parental effort.

Behavior modification plans depend on purchased rewards such as stickers or candy.

"How should I treat my child when she does something wrong?"

"Was I wrong to ground my son for hitting?"

"Should I back off from correcting my child so much, since I know that he has ADHD?"

Questions about discipline are among the most-pressing concerns of parents whose children have ADHD. This chapter addresses many of these questions. The remaining chapters in this section focus on other issues of great urgency for parents—how medication may help and where and how to secure a proper education—in addition to examining interventions such as counseling and social skills training and issues in financing. For suggestions on improving your and your child's home and school situations, these chapters are crucial. I begin with the topic of parenting.

BEHAVIOR MANAGEMENT: SEEKING PROFESSIONAL ASSISTANCE

Fortunately, a well-developed body of knowledge exists about parenting difficult children, including those with ADHD. Parents can be taught skills and techniques, called *behavior modification* or *behavior management,* that are designed to improve children's behavior. Besides offering a coherent method for approaching the toughest aspects of parenting, these techniques are empirically proved to be effective. For example, children whose parents have been taught behavioral strategies to manage noncompliance and defiance have shown significant improvement over similar children whose parents received no such training. Equally important, gains were often maintained for several years and sometimes were even extended to behaviors not directly treated, such as aggression.

One point is crucial when using behavioral techniques with children with ADHD: Techniques must be suited to the difficult nature of the child. Research shows that children with ADHD, because they require so much discipline, often tax parenting skills severely and sometimes force parents into heavy-handed discipline. Although many "how-to" parenting books exist, the strategies described in such books are aimed at temperamentally easy children—those who exhibit flexibility, an even temper, and a desire to please. Few such books are adapted for parents of truly difficult children. As discussed in Chapter 1, many children with ADHD are strong-willed and noncompliant and have explosive tempers. Thus, most basic behavior management guidebooks may leave parents of children with ADHD frustrated because the straightforward techniques that they espouse backfire when applied to children with ADHD.

Parents of children with ADHD often find that they need face-to-face meetings with a professional to help decide how to discipline. Indeed, rather than rely on general and necessarily superficial outlines of behavioral techniques, many parents find success only when a trained behavioral therapist, such as a psychologist or counselor trained to work with ADHD children, assists them. Sometimes a professionally led parent-training group is sufficient. At other times, individual sessions are required to ensure that basic principles are understood, that implementation fits the family's circumstances, and that the disciplinary plan is working.

The material following is designed to provide you, as parents, with some basic behavior modification ideas and techniques. If your child's problems are relatively mild, these techniques may be attempted after you read the material. If your child has more severe problems, it is suggested that the material be read prior to working with a professional who can tailor a program to your unique circumstances. These ideas may seem simple, but implementing them can be extremely difficult without professional assistance.

BASIC IDEAS IN BEHAVIOR MANAGEMENT

Behavior management's most basic idea is that children, like all other humans and animals, learn many of their behaviors from their environment. Children with ADHD, although compromised by problems with impulse control and attending, nonetheless learn many behaviors from the world around them. Just as some unacceptable behaviors are learned from the environment, these behaviors can also be unlearned and more-acceptable behaviors can be learned to take their place.

Why are some behaviors learned and others not? A partial answer to that question is simply that learned behavior works. Behaviors that result in consequences that the individual deems desirable are likely to be retained or strengthened and may ultimately become habitual. Behaviors that result in undesirable consequences are likely to be discarded or weakened. What each individual experiences as a consequence of his or her actions determines, at least to some extent, whether the individual attempts that behavior again. For the most part, all humans, including children with ADHD, are pragmatic.

The following simple example can explain why children sometimes behave as they do. Jeremy is the class clown. Each time he makes a burping noise, several classmates laugh. Jeremy's behavior (i.e., burping) is followed by desirable consequences (i.e., attention from peers, laughter), which strengthens this behavior and heightens its probability of recurring. From the teacher's viewpoint, the behavior is unacceptable; but from Jeremy's viewpoint, it works because he receives a positive consequence. Despite adults' wishes to the contrary, this behavior is likely to continue unless changes are made in the consequences that Jeremy receives for burping.

It is easy to see how a behavior change program for Jeremy may be instituted. If he is burping to make classmates laugh, he can be induced to stop burping if classmates ignore this behavior. A simple plan to encourage inattention to Jeremy at these times could be implemented. Although Jeremy may not like this new arrangement, and even though he has not changed his mind about inappropriate attention seeking, he nevertheless may cease this bad

come to favor the target behavior rather than the problem behavior. There are many ways to accomplish this. Juán's example is again used here to briefly explain this process; various types of positive and negative consequences are then discussed more fully in subsequent sections. In this example, reducing positive consequences for Juán's problem behavior may be a first step. As such, parents may be encouraged to avoid rushing into conflicts or at least to minimize discussion once they are involved in conflicts between the brothers. Likewise, arranging for less screaming by the brother may help. Both of these measures are designed to reduce the chance of positive consequences following the problem behavior.

Additional simple approaches may include adding positive consequences when target behaviors occur—for example, "I like the way you are sitting with your hands to yourself"—or, perhaps, the use of privileges—"Juán, since you did a good job keeping your hands to yourself, you can ride in the front when we go pick up your sister" (assuming that riding in the front seat is desirable for Juán and that he is large enough to sit in the front seat safely). Simple approaches such as these may tip the scale so that there are more positives for the target behavior than for the problem behavior. Over time, these arrangements ought to help discourage problem behaviors and encourage target behaviors.

Unfortunately, this plan would fail miserably for many children unless negative consequences were used. Many children with ADHD respond only briefly and undramatically to praise or to other positives. Likewise, negative consequences work only briefly and less dramatically for children with ADHD than they do for other children. The very bases of reward and punishment may operate slightly differently for these children. An immediate negative consequence for continuing the hitting, such as isolation in time-out (discussed in the next section) would probably be required to deter this behavior. This rearrangement of consequences for Juán's behavior could be written as follows:

BEHAVIOR		CONSEQUENCES
Problem		
Hitting	⟶	Time-out (–)
Target		
Keeping his hands to himself	⟶	Attention (+)
		Freedom of movement (+)

Hence, time-out is listed as a negative (–) following hitting. Note that with this rearrangement of consequences, the target behavior suddenly becomes more advantageous to the child, whereas the problem behavior becomes less advantageous. Although it is not the entire solution to misbehavior, such rearrangement often helps to improve behavior substantially, especially when used repetitively and systematically. More is said later in this chapter about using behavioral techniques as an overall approach to discipline. We next turn to positive and negative consequences that typically work to provide you with some initial ideas.

POSITIVE CONSEQUENCES

Parents often mistakenly assume that the use of positives must involve purchasing candy and using it as a bribe to get their child to do as they are told. This is not advocated here. Instead, the general notion is to use already available privileges—consequences perceived as pleasurable by the child—as a way to encourage good behavior. Many of these positives are social in nature; they are not tangible. Attention from parents, siblings, or peers is often the most powerful and easily utilized positive consequence.

Unfortunately, there are not universally positive consequences. It all depends on how your child reacts to them. For example, most children love to be praised; but some hate it. Furthermore, even children who typically respond well to praise may prefer to forgo it under certain circumstances. They may not want praise from someone with whom they are unhappy (e.g., a parent immediately after a fight) or to be told "Good job" by someone with low popularity when peers are present. Most children would also prefer that their parents not be too angry with them, although at times they may desire so ardently to annoy parents that they will withstand parental anger. Thus, at times, an upset parent may actually be a positive consequence, even though most of the time it is a negative one. These warnings about overgeneralization notwithstanding, some general ideas for positives follow.

Attention as a Positive Consequence

Wendy talks rudely—that is the problem behavior. Her mother wants her to talk more politely—that is the target behavior. At present, the consequences for both polite and rude talk are a topic of continuing discussion with her mother, as shown in the following table:

BEHAVIOR		CONSEQUENCE
Problem		
Rude talk	⟶	Attention (+)
Target		
Polite talk	⟶	Attention (+)

No matter how rudely Wendy talks, her mother continues to talk with her. Like most parents, however, Wendy's mother has told Wendy that she shouldn't talk rudely and has provided her daughter with a detailed rationale for why speaking rudely is not desirable. Wendy's mother makes a common error: She attempts to discipline primarily with words rather than with action. Her wordy discussions inadvertently provide Wendy attention; thus, a change is required.

We might suggest a simple plan whereby positive consequences are used to promote the target behavior—polite talk. Wendy's mother might be encouraged to say something such as "I'm sorry, but I find rude talk unacceptable. If you continue to talk rudely, I will no longer talk with you. If you talk politely, I will be happy to talk with you." She may then either leave the area or direct her attention away (i.e., cease to make eye contact, cease to talk) if Wendy persists with rude talk. Because the goal is to encourage polite talk by Wendy, as soon as Wendy switches to polite talk, her mother would immediately return her full attention to her daughter. Obviously, in this situation, there is one very powerful positive consequence—her mother's attention. In this arrangement, problem behavior is no longer followed by a positive consequence; only acceptable (i.e., target) behavior is followed by these consequences, as shown in the following table:

BEHAVIOR		CONSEQUENCES
Problem		
Rude talk	→	Inattention (–)
Target		
Polite talk	→	Attention (+)

This strategy has a good chance of working for several reasons. First, Wendy probably knows how to engage in the target behavior—she merely has neglected to do so at this point or has purposely chosen to do otherwise. Second, there are immediate powerful consequences for engaging in the target behavior.

There are practical problems, too, however. First, Wendy's behavior is likely to become worse (i.e., more intense, more dramatic, more threatening) before it improves. This is a well-known occurrence when old ways of behaving are disrupted. If parents are unable to withstand the child's temporarily worsening behavior, then this particular strategy is not recommended. Second, some parents would find the worsened behavior almost impossible to ignore. Still other parents would disagree with using this technique, considering it rude or unkind. In these cases, alternative techniques would be sought out. Again, behavior management provides methods for understanding why behaviors occur and for finding simple ways to change them. Although the behavior change plans are not always usable, a logical approach to discipline problems often helps parents understand why behavior occurs and how it might be changed.

Preferred or Habitual Activities as Positive Consequences

Most parents fail to recognize an array of powerful consequences capable of motivating desired behavior. These are activities that the child is already doing, is anticipating doing soon, or would do if given a chance.

Ross and his brother Rick always fight in the car. Their parents described the problem as yelling, hitting, and getting out of their seatbelts. Target behaviors were identified as using their inside voice, keeping their hands to themselves, and remaining in their seatbelts. The parents realized that the boys may enjoy annoying them, but they did not recognize other potential positive and negative consequences. In fact, they could not think of immediate consequences capable of improving their children's behavior, as indicated by the following table:

BEHAVIOR		CONSEQUENCES
Problem		
Yell, hit, get out of seatbelts	⟶	Annoy parents (–) (+) ?
Target		
Use inside voice, keep hands to themselves, keep their seatbelts on	⟶	(0)

It was then suggested that the boys might prefer being in a moving car as opposed to a stationary one. A moving vehicle is often pleasurable compared to a stopped one. If so, this preference could possibly be used to motivate behavior change.

Ross and Rick's parents instructed the boys as they entered the car, "Rules for riding are that everyone must have a fastened seatbelt, use their inside voice, and keep their hands to themselves. As long as everyone follows the rules, the car will keep moving. If the rules are not followed, we may have to stop and wait until everyone is following the rules." Now there is a significant inducement to follow the rules because positive consequences follow immediately (in fact, simultaneously) upon good behavior, and problem behavior receives an immediate negative consequence, as shown in the following table:

BEHAVIOR		CONSEQUENCES
Problem		
Yell, hit, get out of seat	——→	Stopped car (–)
Target		
Use inside voice, keep hands to themselves, keep seatbelts on	——→	Moving car (+)

Again, parents may complain that this arrangement is unfair to the child who was not at fault or to themselves as innocent bystanders. Alternatively, perhaps, it will be suggested that children will not find stopping in the car unpleasant. Typically, however, they do, provided that parents carefully avoid attending to them while stopped. The point remains, however, that thinking of consequences in a systematic way helps generate solutions that can be tested to determine their effectiveness.

A similar and even more common example is evident when children are in transition from one activity to another, when there is often a strong desire to get on with the next activity. For example, children preparing to go to recess may push or crowd in line. Wise teachers often say, "As soon as everyone is lined up straight, is looking at me, and is quiet, we will be able to go outside." Children generally shape up quickly when such a strong, immediate positive consequence awaits their compliance.

Privileges and Rewards in a Formal Positive Consequence System

Sometimes positive consequences can be used to help develop good habits rather than merely coping with pressing discipline problems as they arise. If a clear list of wished-for target behaviors exists (e.g., learn to make bed and clean room, complete homework on time) and if strongly motivating privileges or rewards are identifiable, developing a formal system may be worthwhile. Sometimes a briefly written list of behaviors and privileges is sufficient. If the child completes all homework each night by 7:00 P.M., then he or she earns an extra hour of free time. This arrangement should ideally remain in place for at least several weeks or months as a way to help develop the habit of prompt homework completion.

More formal and complicated systems also work well for some children. Sometimes these are referred to as *token economies.* Figure 8.1 outlines an agreement between Janet, a teenager with ADHD, and her parents. Target behaviors include clothes and books laid out for school each evening and room clean each day (i.e., bed made, floor picked up, dirty clothes in hamper). For each behavior that is completed in an acceptable fashion, points are earned. These are then traded for privileges and rewards listed on the reward menu. Prepared forms are used easily to list target behaviors, points awarded, and reward menu (see Figure 8.1). Older children work well with points. In lieu of points, younger children may require actual tokens, which can be traded for privileges.

Although these programs have been shown to improve behavior, they are not without some practical drawbacks. First, if considering using a system such as this, you must decide what you hope to accomplish. For many families, long-term change is sought, and a long-term commitment to the system may be necessary. Many families find adhering to this type of arrangement difficult in the long run. In addition, many parents fail to provide a rich enough array of

Home Reward Program

Name: Janet Date: 12-13 to 12-19

Target Behaviors	#1 Room clean = 1 pt. each	#2 Ready in evening = 1 pt. each
Monday	1	1
Tuesday	0	0
Wednesday	1	0
Thursday	1	1
Friday	0	
Saturday	1	
Sunday	1	1
POINTS:	5	3

MENU:

Movie	=	5	Points	Late night	=	5	Points
Extra allowance	=	2	Points	Special snack	=	1	Points

Figure 8.1. An example of a token economy reward system. (Zero [0], no points.)

privileges, or their trade-ins are too remote or too infrequent, or they place too many behaviors on the target list. Formal systems thus are generally best used in collaboration with a counselor or psychologist who is familiar with your child and family, at least in the beginning.

Prompt, Positive Consequences

Even our best efforts at using positive consequences may fail. Parents then naturally question whether behavior management really works. In most instances, it is the way in which behavioral techniques are applied rather than the principles themselves that is faulty. When failure occurs, two possible remedies are suggested: The first is to use more immediate consequences, and the second is to use a behavioral principle called *shaping* (discussed in the next subsection).

Regarding prompt consequences, adults should try to remember that we are accustomed to looking at the world in one way and children probably in another. For us, the end of this week seems quite immediate. If told by a supervisor that increased work hours on Monday would result in a cash bonus on Friday afternoon, we would probably think about this impending consequence, and we might well extend our workday. Many children, in contrast, would respond less dramatically. If told on Monday morning, for example, that they would receive a positive consequence on Friday if they increased their school productiveness that week, many children would not do so. Friday seems too remote to have much impact on Monday's or Tuesday's behavior.

Prompt consequences are generally even more important for children with ADHD. Recall that a cardinal feature of ADHD is impulsivity, or an inability to plan carefully before acting. Impulsivity also means that immediate actions that the child finds fun or interesting influence behavior more than remote consequences. Thus, poking at a classmate who walks by is more inviting than adhering to class rules by keeping one's hands to oneself. The prospect of punishment for poking fails to offset the immediate fun of doing it. Children with ADHD seem even less able to anticipate delayed consequences. In recognition of that fact, parents do well to follow good behavior with positive consequences as quickly as possible. At times, these consequences must be truly immediate. The following scenario illustrates how an extremely strong positive consequence can lose its effectiveness when it is too long in coming.

Dale loved to watch *Sesame Street* on television. His mother ardently desired that he place his dirty dishes in the sink and return the milk to the refrigerator after finishing breakfast. Recognizing the value of positive consequences, Dale's mother told him that if he put his dishes in the sink and the milk in the refrigerator (i.e., the target behavior), then he could watch *Sesame Street* (i.e., the positive consequence). Failure to do these things (i.e., the problem behavior) would result in no television (i.e., the negative consequence). Unfortunately, Dale consistently failed to do these two things, appearing totally unconcerned about television until a few minutes before his beloved program began, at which time he invariably would have a tantrum when told he had not earned the privilege of watching *Sesame Street.* Dale wished to earn this privilege, and he certainly knew how to engage in the desired behavior. He simply failed to anticipate upcoming consequences, even with his mother's reminders. For Dale, as for many young children, long intervals between a target behavior and a positive consequence may not be sufficiently motivating, as illustrated in the following table:

BEHAVIOR		CONSEQUENCES
Problem		
Fails to clear away dishes	1 or more hours elapse →	No television (–)
Target		
Clears away dishes	1 or more hours elapse →	Television (+)

An alternative plan emphasizing immediate consequences was used. Dale's mother recorded Monday's edition of *Sesame Street* on the videocassette recorder while she and Dale were on an outing. On Tuesday, he was offered Monday's program immediately upon performing the desired behaviors: "Dale, as soon as you put your dishes and milk away, you can watch your program." This deal quickly induced Dale to execute his chores, whereupon he raced for the television set. Contrast the promptness of consequences in the first program with those of the second program listed in the following table:

BEHAVIOR		CONSEQUENCES
Problem		
Fails to clear away dishes	1 minute →	No television (–)
Target		
Clears away dishes	1 minute →	Television (+)

Shaping New Behavior through Positive Consequences

Shortening the interval between the target behavior and the positive consequences may not suffice, however. When children do not yet possess the desired actions in their array of available behaviors, then a behavioral plan that teaches as well as motivates them may be required. Consider the example of Kim, a 4-year-old with ADHD.

Kim's parents had read about behavior modification and hoped to improve her conduct in the grocery store—an area long plagued by problem behaviors for Kim—by devising a behavioral plan. Kim's parents began correctly by explicitly identifying problem behaviors, which consisted of Kim running away from them and grabbing items from the shelves. After considering all potential positive consequences, the parents devised a plan whereby, rather than put candy in the cart first as had been their custom, they would make buying candy contingent on Kim's exhibiting appropriate target behaviors: "Kim, if you hold onto the cart all the way through the store, then Mommy and Daddy will get candy before we leave." It didn't work, however. Kim had never learned to hold onto the cart for more than 10–15 seconds, yet her parents started with a plan that required her to do it for more than 30 minutes!

Shaping, or teaching new behavior by successive approximations, can help. Instead of shooting for the difficult, final target behavior, the shaping technique begins with small successes that approximate the target and then slowly builds on them in the hope of eventually reaching the final goal. Positive consequences are used to provide motivation and to signal to the child that he or she is on the correct path of learning.

Using this strategy, Kim's parents developed a plan aimed at extremely small amounts of target behavior, each of which was to be followed immediately by a positive consequence. After receiving directions, Kim was awarded a small piece of candy if she walked with her hand on the cart for the distance of one-half of one grocery store aisle. She was also encouraged with praise, such as "Good job of holding on like a big girl, Kim!" But she could earn no more candy until she had traversed another half aisle with her hand on the cart. This procedure was employed in half-aisle increments throughout the grocery shopping trip. One step at a time, Kim proceeded through the entire store holding onto the cart. This was her small initial goal, and she was successful in meeting it.

The demand for success was then slowly increased. A standard of holding onto the cart down one entire aisle was established. Once this was mastered, a new standard of several aisles without interruption, to be traded for several pieces of candy, was established and ultimately mastered within a few grocery store visits. Unfortunately, Kim's age and the severity of her overactivity prevented her from walking all the way through the store prior to earning a reward. Because this is an extremely difficult task for this child, expectations may need to be reduced. Nonetheless, the approach of slowly building the child's skills one step at a time by using available consequences offers much help to parents, as the following table illustrates:

FIRST TARGET		
Hold on for short distance	→	Candy (+) Praise (+)
SECOND TARGET		
Hold on for very short distance	→	"
THIRD TARGET		
Hold on for longer distance	→	"
FOURTH TARGET		
Hold on for entire distance	→	"

NEGATIVE CONSEQUENCES

Without negative consequences to help curtail their unacceptable behavior, many children with ADHD would be unmanageable. Unfortunately, when it comes to using negative consequences, many parents have trouble. Parents are apt to select the wrong negative consequence or to implement it incorrectly or at the wrong times. Part of the problem stems from our unavoidable emotional involvement with our children. After all, as parents, we are only human. A portion, however, stems from mistaken ideas about how and why negative consequences work.

Spanking as a Negative Consequence

To spank or not to spank? That is the question parents often ask. Rather than search for a right or wrong answer, it is often more important, I believe, to investigate the rationale behind spanking. If there is a rationale for spanking, it ought to be that spanking is a viable negative consequence. According to that line of thinking, parents are attempting to convey a point to the child, such as "If you play too roughly, then you will be spanked." Hypothetically, the repeated use of this negative consequence offers the hope of discouraging unacceptable behavior such as rough play.

Once the rationale is understood, the practical question of implementing spanking must be examined. Parents might ask themselves how many times per day they are willing to spank their child. Few parents answer that they are willing to do so more than one or two times per day. They next might ask themselves how many times per day might their child misbehave—that is, how many times a negative consequence might be required. Few parents would answer one to two times; most indicate 15, 20, or 30. An inequity is thus evident between those behaviors that potentially merit negative consequences and the family's ability to use spanking as a consequence. If, for example, a child engages in 10 potentially punishable behaviors per day but knows parents will spank only once, then only a 10% chance of a negative consequence exists. Why not misbehave and live with the 90% chance that a negative consequence is not forthcoming? Setting aside the potential disadvantages of parents' modeling unacceptable behavior and the potential damage to a child's self-esteem, spanking simply fails to work as a consistent deterrent for most children with significant behavior problems. Most children with ADHD simply misbehave too much to make spanking a viable option.

Time-Out as a Negative Consequence

For many families, time-out proves to be a more usable consequence and thus a more credible deterrent. Many parents mistakenly assume that time-out is a place, such as a time-out chair. In reality, time-out is a principle the particulars of which need to be suited individually to each child and each circumstance. The time-out principle rests on the idea that if a child is where the action is, where it is stimulating, and where he or she prefers to be, then a temporary loss of the privilege can be used as a mild punishment or a negative consequence. Usually, a corner, an isolated area marked by tape on the floor, or a sparsely filled spare room works best. Because the idea is to reduce stimulation and make the consequence uninteresting, parents must take care not to pay too much attention when using this consequence. Thus, lecturing on misbehavior as the child is sent to time-out or responding to the child's comments while he or she is in time-out should be avoided to the extent possible. This is often difficult, as children dislike the boredom of time-out and seek to lessen it by engaging parents, often in clever ways: "Why am I the only one ever to get punished? I have to go pee really bad!" Parents are encouraged to ignore these attempts at baiting during the brief time-out interval. Most preschoolers require no more than 2 or 3 minutes, and school-age children need 5 minutes for time-out to work.

Jack, a 10-year-old with ADHD, likes to annoy his two younger sisters. A typical day after school finds the three of them watching television while their mother prepares dinner in the adjacent kitchen, only to be interrupted frequently by complaints about Jack's changing the television channel in midprogram or grabbing his sisters' possessions. Relying on behavioral procedures, Jack's mother is quite directive: "Jack, you need to stay in your chair and keep your hands to yourself. No channel changes without asking me first. If you do this, you can stay to watch television. If you touch your sisters or their things or change the channel, you will have a time-out."

Assuming that Jack meets these expectations, he stays. If he violates them, he serves the time-out penalty, as illustrated in the following table:

BEHAVIOR		CONSEQUENCES
Problem		
Bothers his siblings	⟶	Time-out (–)
Target		
In his seat, hands to himself, channel unchanged	⟶	Freedom to watch television (+)

Clearly, this arrangement has some prospect of working because the problem and target behaviors are both made clear, and there are positive consequences for engaging in the target behavior (i.e., allowed to watch television and interact with his sisters) and negative consequences for problem behavior (i.e., time-out and loss of privileges). If Jack were to require a time-out, his mother could merely signal the consequence. Although difficult to do, parents should strive to remain calm and in control. Signs of anger, as reflected in facial expression or voice tone, may inadvertently signal to the child that they have upset the parent. In some instances, making parents angry is a desired consequence for the child. If so, a reaction from Mom or Dad may only encourage the very behavior that the parents are seeking to discourage.

Parents should also avoid much discussion after the time-out. Jack may feel quite unhappy about serving his 5 minutes in time-out, but this distress may be reduced if his mother goes into a lengthy discussion with him. Jack may see this as a good trade-off. Even though he had to endure a 5-minute time-out, the enjoyment of his individual time with his mother offsets the negative effects of the time-out. Time-out, then, ceases to be much of a negative consequence. By the same token, attempting to squeeze apologies or promises for future improvement out of the child often backfires. If the child has served the time, you have made your point. Drop it there.

Of course, many children refuse to go willingly to time-out or refuse to stay once there. This leaves parents with difficult choices. Young children or those who can easily be handled physically may do best if their parents escort them to time-out and hold them there if necessary. Tantrums may result, and parents should be certain that they are prepared to withstand the tantrums prior to taking physical action. Especially in the beginning, these tantrums can be long and violent. After it is clear that parents will insist on a time-out no matter how severe the tantrum, then most children become increasingly willing to comply with time-out. Being held from behind while both parent and child are seated may be the best procedure. Besides controlling the child and avoiding injury to both parties, this arrangement prevents eye contact with the child. Of course, conversation should generally be withheld during this time.

One special word of warning is in order when considering time-out as a disciplinary procedure. There are exceptional children, most of them preschoolers with a history of moodiness, whose tantrums are so long and loud that they are virtually unable to quiet themselves. Assigning them to time-out may precipitate one of these unwanted tantrums. If your child has this degree of moodiness, then working with a professional to devise behavioral strategies, which may or may not include time-out, is essential.

Older and larger noncompliant children or teenagers present another challenge. This is especially true if the youngster has an explosive temper or is belligerent. Many parents state that they are unwilling or unable to coerce their children physically into time-out. After time-out is assigned and rejected, parents confront two unpleasant choices. One choice is simply to capitulate—that is, to drop the time-out demand and let life return to normal. For many, this is the poorer of the two choices. Another choice is for parents to drop the subject in the short run but bide their time until the child can be induced to take the previously assigned time-out.

The scenario may be as follows. Lee, age 13 years, is told to take a time-out for swearing at his mother. He declines, and his mother is aware that she cannot force the issue physically. Rather than hound Lee to comply, she immediately removes her attention, ceases eye contact, and suspends any verbal exchanges. Lee's initial reaction is a smile, perhaps assuming that he can do as he wishes without consequences. After a few minutes, however, he approaches his mother with a question. Instead of answering, she forgoes eye contact and in a soft tone states, "After you have done your time-out, I will talk with you." Lee scoffs and walks away. Later he again tries to initiate conversation but meets the same reaction from his mother. This time he angrily swears under his breath. His mother continues to ignore him, even though this taxes her self-control to the maximum. As the family's typical lunchtime approaches, he inquires about the offerings, only to be calmly reminded of the time-out that is due before lunch will be prepared for him. He swears loudly now. Again, his mother marshals her power of self-control to ignore him. Finally, 2 hours after the first encounter, he requests a ride to a friend's house. When told the requirement is to serve time-out first, he grudgingly sits for 5 minutes in the square. After he does so, he is immediately taken to his friends' house without another word from his mother. Compliance with the time-out request is the target behavior at this point. His mother provided him with a positive consequence promptly after he complied. For some extremely difficult children, getting them to take a time-out, even using difficult and lengthy steps such as these, may be worth the effort. After the child complies with a time-out request once, subsequent compliance with time-out requests often becomes easier. This scenario may not always eventuate, but it represents a rational attempt to use consequences to work through a difficult disciplinary situation. Again, individual plans are best worked out with the help of a professional.

A final word about time-out is in order. Parents are encouraged to remember why time-out works—it is a consequence of boredom. Often time-out fails to work because it lacks the element of boredom that makes it so effective. For example, sometimes a parent inadvertently poses time-out as a negative consequence for an even less desirable alternative: "Ed, I want you to go take a bath now. If you don't get up and do it right away, then I will put you in time-out." Ed may well prefer time-out to the bathtub. If so, the intended negative consequence (i.e., isolation) turns out to be a positive consequence (i.e., a chance to be away from the bathtub). Parents must seek other strategies at that point. Perhaps telling Ed that he can continue to work on his model ship as soon as his bath is complete would work. Time-out can be an effective technique, but it has limitations. Trying to solve all behavior problems by applying time-out will fail.

Physical Prompt as a Negative Consequence

At times, parents are unwilling to wait for time-out to work, and there may be an easier and more direct negative consequence. A physical prompt involves moving the child through the requested behavior by physical force if necessary. For many children who enjoy resisting, this is an unpleasant prospect that either induces them to do what they were told or discourages future resistance.

Six-year-old Olivia becomes so wrapped up in her play that she often ignores her parents' directions to stop. Sometimes she defiantly responds "No" or "In a minute" to directions. Her parents have tried to explain why they need prompt cooperation, but to no avail. When in an irritable mood, Olivia seems to enjoy dragging her feet and annoying her parents. Her mother, in particular, finds Olivia's resistance infuriating. Time-out works sometimes, but it is not always viable. A mental health counselor encouraged Olivia's parents to try a physical prompt.

When Olivia, who was putting together a puzzle, ignored her mother's request to pick up her shoes and socks and join the family for dinner, a chance for a physical prompt arose as indicated in the following table:

BEHAVIOR		CONSEQUENCES
Problem		
Ignores request	→	Physical prompt (–)
Target		
Complies with request promptly	→	Allowed to do activity on her own (+)

Olivia's mother told Olivia calmly, "Either pick up your shoes and socks and come to dinner now, or I will help you. If you do it on your own, I'll leave you alone." Olivia refused, so her mother placed her hand on top of Olivia's and "helped" her to pick up her shoes and socks. She then nudged Olivia to her room to deposit these items. Halfway to her room, Olivia pleaded, "I'll do it myself, just leave me alone," at which point her mother acquiesced by silently following behind her until she was seated at the table.

A physical prompt, even more than time-out, requires finesse. If parents become angry on the one hand or are too accommodating in their help on the other, then the child may feel that his or her resistance is worth it. Of course, parents must never physically hurt the child or be abusive in any way. The parent who learns to move the resisting child through the assigned activity rather assertively while conveying an attitude of "this is no inconvenience to me" often finds this technique invaluable. In contrast to time-out, this technique is generally of value only if used with younger children (8 years old or younger) and only if used rarely—no more than once or twice per day.

UNDERSTANDING ANTECEDENTS AND SITUATIONS IN ORDER TO INFLUENCE BEHAVIOR

Behavior management techniques emphasize changing behavior through controlling consequences. Sometimes, however, parents are happy simply to make their lives run more smoothly; changing habits is not always their goal. The same careful observation techniques that permit behavior–consequence links to be detected can be applied more broadly. Rather than look at what happens after behavior occurs, sometimes it is advisable to look at what happens beforehand. By determining in which situations or at which times acceptable and unacceptable behaviors are likely, parents may be able to set the occasion for their child to behave well.

Consider the example of a boy who is apt to become frustrated and blow up while attempting homework. Using the process discussed previously, parents decided that what they desired (i.e., the target behavior) was quiet, on-task effort at work completion, and what they wished to decrease (i.e., the problem behaviors) was shouting, cursing, and throwing objects. When parents examined their son's behavior patterns closely, they noticed that blow-ups tended to occur when their son was working on math problems but rarely when he attempted other subjects, such as social studies or spelling, and never at school. Furthermore, they discovered that these outbursts almost never occurred when his teacher provided him with a calculator. Thus, the antecedent for his problem behavior was concluded to be to work on math problems at home without the use of a calculator. Because acceptable behavior generally occurred when other subjects were studied or when a calculator was available, parents opted to follow a simple path for improving the boy's homework-related behavior. They arranged for math to routinely be completed at school (where no blow-ups had occurred) and to complete only other subjects at home. If, on occasion, math work was not completed at school, the student's teacher was to lend him a calculator for use at home. When parents implemented this plan, outbursts were reduced to about 10% of their previous level.

At home and school, it can prove quite beneficial to examine antecedents of problem (and acceptable) behavior. Problem antecedents may include task demands (e.g., whether what is being requested is simple or difficult), social factors (e.g., whether peers are present or absent and who they are), caregiver factors (e.g., whether mother, father, or teacher are present), and times of day (e.g., mornings, bedtime). Parents are encouraged to consider these factors and to incorporate opportunities to set up good behavior routinely as part of an overall management strategy for their child.

BEHAVIOR MANAGEMENT AS A WAY OF LIFE

Many parents' reaction to a suggested behavior management program is that it sounds like a great deal of effort as well as a great deal to remember. Is behavior management really practical, then? The answer is an emphatic *yes*!

Consider how much time you spend daily, as it is, disciplining your child. How much more work could it be to use behavioral principles? The biggest switch for parents who adopt behavioral techniques occurs with regard to *when,* not how much, effort is expended. As parents, we are apt to cope with problems after they arise. We scold or lecture in the hope of inducing change, or we simply vent frustration that things are going so badly. In contrast, a behavioral approach emphasizes creating a plan before the problem behavior has begun.

Recall the four questions that led parents through the steps of behavior change (Which problem behavior would I like to eliminate? Which behavior would be more acceptable? What are the consequences of the problem behavior and the target behavior? How can I rearrange consequences to discourage the problem behavior and encourage the target behavior?). If parents learn to ask themselves these questions when they anticipate problems, then many problems can be avoided. When a situation that is likely to result in a problem arises, the behaviorally astute parent creates a preventive plan. The children's watching television in the next room, the family's going for a car trip, or the family's mealtime may signal to parents that it is time to make explicit expectations for positive behavior and to spell out positive and negative consequences. This structure maximizes chances for good behavior. For the child who anticipates consequences poorly (i.e., is impulsive), this outline is essential.

This type of arrangement has the enormous additional advantage of allowing parents to focus on success. By specifying target behavior, everyone is aware of what is expected and can notice when it has occurred. Rather than chide their child for misbehavior, parents can praise their child for good behavior. Success can beget further success.

Many parents comment that they, too, learn new behaviors. Their use of behavioral techniques, especially those outlining expectations and consequences, becomes second nature. These habits reach such an ingrained level that their use is no longer an effort. Only when new or difficult situations present themselves must parents revert to careful, step-by-step development of a behavioral plan. If well versed in behavioral strategies, most parents are quite capable of doing this. By working with a behavioral professional, of course, detailed plans and guidance can also be provided.

Remember, however, that the suggestions in this chapter are only the bare bones of behavior management. Professionals who work with children are familiar with behavioral techniques that are effective for a variety of unique problems ranging from aggression to lack of play skills. Such professionals can modify these techniques to fit your child and your family's circumstances as well as provide you with a framework and a general rationale for discipline. Recalling the warning that behavioral techniques do not alleviate attentional or hyperactivity problems, you may take heart that their judicious use can help maximize your child's development while making home life more pleasant.

CONCLUSIONS

Because many children with ADHD have accompanying behavior problems, parents are encouraged to learn techniques for behavior management. By learning to identify both problem behaviors and desired alternative behaviors and by using consequences (and sometimes antecedents) that promote behavior change, parents can do much to help their children. The principles that are presented in this chapter thus compose a foundation of knowledge on which individual plans specific to your child can be developed with the help of a counselor or a psychologist.

Chapter 9

Medication Treatment of ADHD

Eric Benjamin

ADHD Myths

Ritalin is the only medication used to treat ADHD.

Several days or weeks are required before Ritalin begins to help children with ADHD.

Ritalin use increases the likelihood that your child will become addicted to drugs.

Herbal and natural treatments have been shown to be far safer than prescription medications.

Children often develop tolerance to ADHD medications so that, after a while, the medications no longer work.

Because ADHD is the result of alterations, distortions, or abnormalities in the physiological functioning of the central nervous system (i.e., the brain), physicians have been called on to treat the disorder with medication. What, in fact, is the brain abnormality that medical professionals are treating? In diabetes, medical professionals know about the failure to produce insulin in specific cells in the pancreas. What is the specific malfunction that causes ADHD? Answering this question has been a problem because it is very difficult to study the function of living brain tissue directly. EEGs (i.e., electroencephalograms) help assess for seizures, and tests such as CT (i.e., computed tomography) scans and MRI (i.e., magnetic resonance imaging) look at brain structure; but these tests do not offer any help in diagnosing ADHD, because neither seizure activity nor structural abnormalities are the cause of ADHD.

Methods have been developed, however, to monitor brain function (e.g., PET [positron emission tomography] scans, functional MRIs). Researchers can observe which regions of the brain are quiet or active under certain controlled conditions. The most recent findings derived by using these methods were the result of work by Ernst and colleagues in 1998, and they indicated that abnormal dopamine (one of the chemicals involved in the disordered process associated with ADHD) production occurs in the specific sites in the frontal cortex of adults with ADHD. Parents may find it encouraging that there is evidence that there are areas of the brain that function differently in those with ADHD. Because these tests are very expensive, are still in the research phase, and have not yet been applied to children across all age groups, they are not yet part of the ADHD assessment process. That is, they are presently of no clinical use; but they are nonetheless helpful in revealing differences in how the brain of an individual with ADHD functions.

ADHD AND BRAIN CHEMICALS

What is the brain chemical involved in ADHD? The medications that are effective for ADHD change the concentration of dopamine and sometimes of norepinephrine, two chemicals or neurotransmitters in the brain. Nerve cells (i.e., neurons), when they activate, cause the desired response in the part of the brain in which they are located. If a neuron activates in the part of the brain controlling right-finger movement, for example, then the right finger will move. Likewise, neurons that are active in the regions of the brain that allow us to focus result in attention to task. These neurons have microscopic gaps between them. The neurotransmitter fills these gaps and controls the neuronal activity. Even using this simplified account, one can see how it is important to have the correct amount of neurotransmitter in the gaps to stay focused.

Just as a lack of insulin in the pancreas is the disordered process in diabetes, an imbalance of dopamine and possibly norepinephrine in specific brain regions (i.e., the brain stem, the prefrontal cortex, and surrounding areas) appears to be the disordered process in ADHD. Not surprisingly, medications that are prescribed to treat ADHD alter the concentration of dopamine and norepinephrine, thus correcting many behavioral abnormalities in children with ADHD.

PARENTS' FEAR OF MEDICAL TREATMENT FOR ADHD

Despite our increased understanding of human behavior and its relationship to brain chemistry, it is understandable that parents continue to be anxious and fearful about using medicine to treat their child with ADHD. They express a myriad of concerns, some of which are legitimate but many of which are based on misinformation. In order to treat your child successfully, it is important to be as informed as possible. In this section, I attempt to address some of the unfounded fears that parents frequently have concerning medical treatment of their child with ADHD.

Fear of Overdiagnosis

The apparent increase in diagnosis of ADHD is a parental worry that I hear expressed a great deal. Some parents say,

"It seems that all the kids in school are on medication," leading to a belief that ADHD is overdiagnosed and therefore that medication for ADHD is being overprescribed. A report summarized the findings of the American Medical Association's Council on Scientific Affairs, published in *JAMA: The Journal of the American Medical Association* in April 1998. Based on a review of scientific studies from 1975 to 1997, the report concluded that 3%–6% of school-age children may have ADHD but that only 2%–3% are actually receiving treatment. It was concluded that there was no evidence of overdiagnosis or overprescription of medication. Indeed, ADHD is still underdiagnosed.

It is important to note that National Institute of Mental Health studies have shown that 13%–16% of the child population (about 1 in 7) have psychiatric problems (including mood and anxiety disorders) during childhood and that half of these are quite serious. In a classroom of 35 children, up to 5 children could therefore have a psychiatric problem that would benefit from treatment, including medication. Because all of these findings and treatments are fairly recent (having developed in the 1980s or 1990s), it can appear to the uninformed observer that there is an epidemic of childhood psychiatric disorders. In reality, greater public awareness, increased access to services, and expanded media coverage explain this perception of a growing problem.

Fear of Influencing Brain Chemistry

Many parents express fear of administering medicine that targets the brain. They say, "I can see fixing an arm or a leg; but working with the brain, well, I don't want to mess around with the brain. My child's behavior is not a physical problem that you can see."

Much of this kind of fear is the result of beliefs about personality development proposed by Sigmund Freud in the early part of the 20th century. Freud's doctrine, which suggests that early life events largely determine the personality that one develops during childhood and carries forward into adulthood, deeply affects parents' expectations with regard to their child's behavior and treatment. The idea of an internal conflict leading to willful, poor behavior is a Freudian concept. Consistent with this perspective, parents often think that if they can just get to the core of what's bothering their child, then their child will stop being inattentive, hyperactive, and impulsive. This line of thinking supports the false notion that the child "is just lazy and can do it but isn't trying on purpose." Parents, therefore, sometimes believe that their child "just needs to talk about what's bothering" him or her and then his or her behavior will improve. As a result, parents do not seek medical treatment for their child.

In the same way that parents hold their child responsible for behavior over which he or she may have limited control, they can also hold themselves overly responsible for their child's misbehavior. Given this perspective, they may view medicine as an "easy fix"—"what people who can't parent well or who don't spend enough time with their children do"—which again keeps them from seeking medical help.

Fear of Medication Leading to Drug Abuse

A story told to me by a parent of a child with ADHD during an initial assessment summarizes how easily the understanding of medical treatment for ADHD can be distorted. The parent had seen a mother of a child with ADHD on a popular television talk show claiming that Ritalin had caused her son to become a drug addict. The mother described how she had been a substance abuser as a child, had eventually overcome that problem, had had a son who was extremely active, and then had reluctantly started him on Ritalin at age 5 years. It seems that her son did well; but at puberty, she stopped giving him the medicine, thinking it would affect his maturation. One week later, he was abusing drugs. She then blamed his taking Ritalin as the cause of his unfortunate substance abuse. The parent seeking help was worried that Ritalin would cause drug abuse in her child.

After reviewing the facts, this parent was able to see the true relationship in this case. The parent on television had (untreated) ADHD, which led to her drug abuse, for which there exists a high risk. Her son likely inherited some of her ADHD characteristics and thus had a heightened risk for drug abuse. Although Ritalin has no proved effect on puberty or on any maturational process, this parent mistakenly stopped giving Ritalin to her son, which allowed the child's underlying risk to express itself.

An analogy would be that if an adolescent with insulin-dependent diabetes stopped taking his insulin, his diabetes would cause him to go into a coma. It would make no sense to attribute the coma to the fact that he took insulin in prior years. It would seem silly to blame the diabetic coma on prior successful use of insulin. Similarly, it was this boy's characteristics of impulsivity, poor judgment, and thrill seeking, now untreated, that caused him to take street drugs.

Furthermore, in a study in which a large group of boys with nonmedicated ADHD were followed for 15 years, workers found that 50% of them exhibited antisocial behavior, were incarcerated, or abused drugs and/or alcohol by the end of their teenage years. Parents of children with ADHD may have themselves struggled to overcome drug and alcohol problems, perhaps because their own ADHD was not medicated properly. As noted previously, children of parents whose ADHD was not medicated properly are at high risk to repeat these behaviors. It is understandable that the last thing these parents want to do is to give their child medication, because they fear that this will further increase their child's risk of substance abuse. However, children who are prescribed medication to control their inattention, hyperactivity, impulsivity, and low frustration tolerance are much less likely to follow these same family patterns of substance abuse. Ironically, it is not taking medication for ADHD that increases their risk for drug or alcohol abuse.

On a final note, in my many years of experience in treating individuals with ADHD, I have never seen any person addicted to the kinds of drugs used to treat the disorder. Stimulants are the most commonly prescribed medication for ADHD, and, even at the highest therapeutic levels used in treatment, they do not cause euphoria and are not addictive. A hard-core ex–drug addict and parent of a patient with ADHD once told me that taking methylphenidate (i.e., Ritalin)—the most commonly prescribed medicine for ADHD—in huge doses intravenously was his last, desperate choice when no other street drug was available. He said a junkie will shoot anything, but Ritalin was at the bottom of the list.

Fear of Medicines Perceived to Be Unnatural

Another influence on parents' treatment expectations is the food and nutrition supplement industry. Because this industry purports to support the principle that natural is good and artificial is bad, many parents may try supplements and herbal remedies before seeking medical care. Parents say they would prefer to use natural remedies instead of medications; however, they may not know that carbons, hydrogens, and nitrogens (the basic elements of life), which are synthesized in a laboratory to treat a medical condition, would be no different from a substance found in nature that is isolated and concentrated for the same purpose. Indeed, there is no difference—both, when used to heal our body, are being used as medicines.

Which drugs are safest? Until the alternative treatments for ADHD are more extensively researched, common sense tells us that the compounds that are rigorously tested and approved by the U.S. Food and Drug Administration (FDA) and that deliver the same dose in each pill would be safer. Yet parents may buy supplements and give them to their child because a friend of a friend said her son did better with them. Ironically, parents may be jeopardizing their child's health in an attempt to avoid using prescribed medication. Supplements can be riskier because purity, dose, and efficacy are not FDA-monitored. Many people died in the 1990s from a tainted batch of tryptophan, a nonprescription supplement used to help ameliorate sleep problems. Those who readily embrace alternative substances may wish to consider whether safety is more apparent than real.

Other General Fears

In practice since 1984, I still routinely learn of new fictions about ADHD and its medical treatment. Some parents, especially fathers, believe that boys with these behaviors are just being boys. This is often because ADHD runs in families and fathers may identify these behaviors as similar to their own when they were children. In addition, many parents are influenced by reports from the World Wide Web, which is loaded with medical and other information and opinion, much of which is erroneous. Parents often come to my office having been exposed to a great deal but do not know what is fact or fiction. It is critical for parents to discuss with their child's physician their fears regarding using medication. If they do not, misattribution of behaviors to medication rather than to ADHD itself can lead to difficulty in treatment. Once the myths have been dispelled, it is easier to discuss parents' legitimate concerns regarding the medical treatment of ADHD. These concerns, primarily regarding tics and decreased growth, are examined with regard to specific medicines discussed a little later in this chapter.

In summary, parental concerns about the medical treatment of ADHD with medication are influenced by outdated beliefs about human behavior, by the inherent fear of using medication that influences brain chemistry, by recommendations from the multibillion-dollar nutrition supplement industry, and by an abundance of data available on the World Wide Web (some facts, some fiction). Thus, it is often a reluctant, anxious parent who comes to my office saying, "We've tried everything, nothing works, and we are ready to consider medicine as a last resort."

MEDICINES USED TO TREAT ADHD

The stimulant class of medications are the most commonly prescribed for ADHD and affect dopamine concentrations in the involved brain regions. They improve the child's ability to tolerate frustration, to think before acting impulsively, to concentrate and attend, and to process auditory and visual information. When the medication is dosed appropriately and given consistently, report cards will probably show better academic grades and behavior ratings, the child's self-esteem will improve, conflict at home may diminish markedly, and the risk of substance abuse and criminal behavior may diminish. The therapeutic effects are generally noted within 20–30 minutes after taking the first dose.

The word *stimulant* is often confusing because people tend to explain their function in a literal context. Parents may try to understand how something that is a stimulant, like an "upper," can calm children. In pharmacology textbooks (e.g., *Remington's Pharmaceutical Sciences*), a central nervous system stimulant is a drug that increases the activity of some portion of the brain or the spinal cord. Drugs that act on the cerebral cortex—in the brain regions described previously—increase mental alertness, the ability to focus, and the ability to think before acting. Therefore, they are not sedatives.

Commonly Prescribed Stimulants

The stimulant class of medications includes methylphenidate (i.e., Ritalin), dextroamphetamine (i.e., Dexedrine, Dextrostat), and Adderall (a combination of dextroamphetamine sulfate, dextroamphetamine saccharate, and amphetamine sulfate and amphetamine aspartate). Until 1999, methylphenidate was the most prescribed stimulant for ADHD, although Adderall is increasingly being prescribed.

In selecting a medicine for your child, the stimulants are the first choice for many reasons. One of the most important reasons is that they have been used for many years, so the long-term side effects, a serious concern for parents, are better known. Parents are often amazed to hear that the stimulant dextroamphetamine was first noted to ameliorate hyperactivity in children in a 1937 study. Consequently, one can look at the long-term side effects of stimulants over three generations of treated children, a rare luxury in an era of new medicines. Choosing among the stimulants is based on some subtle differences, many of which are indicated in the following table:

Generic	Brand	Duration of effect	Dosages available (in milligrams)
Methylphenidate	Ritalin	2–4 hours	5, 10, 20
	Ritalin SR	4–8 hours	20
Dextroamphetamine	Dexedrine Tab	4–6 hours	5, 10 (Dextrostat)
	Dexedrine Spansule	6–8 hours	5, 10, 15
Dextroamphetamine Sulfate and Saccharate Amphetamine Sulfate and Aspartate	Adderall	5–7 hours	5, 10, 20, 30

Ritalin, Dexedrine, and Adderall differ in their duration of effect. Ritalin lasts up to 2–4 hours per dose; Dexedrine, 4–6 hours; and Adderall, 5–7 hours. Ritalin is available in 5-, 10-, and 20-milligram tabs, and Dexedrine is available in 5-milligram tabs. A 10-milligram tab of Ritalin is equivalent to 5 milligrams of Dexedrine. Slow-release Ritalin (i.e., Ritalin SR) lasts 4–8 hours, and slow-release Dexedrine (i.e., Dexedrine Spansule) lasts 6–8 hours. Ritalin SR is available only in 20-milligram doses, and Dexedrine Spansule is available in 5-, 10-, and 15-milligram doses. The 20-milligram Ritalin SR is equivalent to 10 milligrams of Ritalin over the time frame of its effect. The same principle holds for Dexedrine Spansule (i.e., a 10-milligram Dexedrine Spansule tab equals a 5-milligram Dexedrine tab, but over a longer time frame). Adderall doses are generally twice as potent as Ritalin doses (i.e., 10 milligrams of Adderall equal 20 milligrams of Ritalin); but these conversions are just guidelines, are not always predictable, and vary among children.

I have found that smaller, more frequent doses are better tolerated in children younger than age 6 years. Small doses of Ritalin every 3 hours seem to work best most often in young children. In the ADHD clinic at Phoenix Children's Hospital, the general rule is that as the child gets older, the doses and the dosing interval (i.e., the time between doses) increase. A 5-year-old may take 5 milligrams of Ritalin at 7:00 A.M., 10:00 A.M., 1:00 P.M., and 4:00 P.M., whereas a 10-year-old might take 10–15 milligrams of Ritalin at 7:00 A.M., 11:00 A.M., and 3:00 P.M.

When children reach middle school, just as they are approaching adolescence, they often become reluctant to go to the school nurse. Prior to this time, parents can dictate to their children when they take their medication. It has been my experience that only when parents are ambivalent about medication have compliance problems been common in children younger than 12 years of age. As children become preteens and teens, however, they typically begin to assert more autonomy and may then challenge the medication regimen. A positive parental attitude toward medication, along with a doctor who is sensitive to these developmental issues, help to maintain a successful treatment plan for the child with ADHD.

With this in mind, as a child approaches middle school, longer-acting medications can be tried in order to avoid dosing in school or minimizing visits to the school nurse. I have found Dexedrine Spansule to be more reliable than current Ritalin SR preparations; however, new formulations of Ritalin SR are being developed that may be more reliable and longer acting. Adderall has been effective in twice-a-day dosing as well. Each child may do better on one or the other, so it is important to experiment to find the medication and dosing regimen best suited for your child. The choice of Ritalin versus Dexedrine versus Adderall, after total dose and dose intervals are accounted for, is dependent on the side effects of these medications (discussed in another section of this chapter) in each child. Clearly, the regimen should be individualized to the child to maximize positive response and to minimize or eliminate side effects. The duration of treatment can vary based on their personal life agendas as children become adults (e.g., jobs, relationships). Increasing numbers of people with ADHD are finding Ritalin helpful into their adult years.

Toxicity Research has examined the toxicity of methylphenidate (i.e., Ritalin) in laboratory animals since the late 1950s. The literature reports remarkably few adverse reactions or serious toxicity in humans. Even reports of adverse effects from intentional overdose are rare. Data have indicated that there is a very large margin of safety, approaching 100 to 1, between a single dose, which represents the approximate human clinical dose, and one that is lethal. Therefore, there is a huge margin of error for toxicity.

Rebound In about 10% of children, a phenomenon called *rebound* occurs. Parents may witness an exaggeration of the child's symptoms of low frustration tolerance, irritability, and hyperactivity that occur when the medicine is wearing off. This rebound effect usually lasts about 20–45 minutes and results from a rapid decrease in stimulant blood level from high to low; therefore, parents should constantly note the time of their child's behaviors—both improvements and problems—to understand just how long each dose lasts, when it wears off, and whether there is a rebound period. A child may do well for 3 hours, have a rebound, then do well again, followed by another rebound, and so forth. A composite school report may be poor because of the rebound periods, but the child's behavior may be excellent when the medicine is working.

Rebound is treated by making sure that each dose lasts long enough for the next dose to start working. It generally takes only 20–30 minutes for a dose to become effective. At the end of the day, smaller incremental doses can be given 30 minutes before the rebound period to decrease the rate of change in blood levels. For example, if a child is doing well on 15-milligram doses of Ritalin at 7:00 A.M., 11:00 A.M., and 3:00 P.M. but becomes very irritable at 6:30 P.M., then a 5-

milligram dose of Ritalin at 6:00 P.M. can be helpful. Monitoring of stimulant blood levels by drawing the child's blood and sending it out for laboratory analysis, however, is not necessary or helpful and is rarely used in the clinic.

Headache and Stomachache The most common short-term side effects of stimulants include headache (5%) and stomachache (5%). These usually occur at the onset of treatment and often result from not eating enough, particularly at breakfast. Since some children don't like to eat breakfast, this can be a problem. This, however, can be an opportunity to work on developing good nutritional habits for breakfast. The *Physicians' Desk Reference* states that stimulants should be taken 30–45 minutes before a meal. In the clinic, however, it does not appear that the stimulants lose effectiveness when taken with food. Your physician therefore may recommend that you give the morning dose with breakfast if stomachaches or headaches occur. These two symptoms usually remit after 1 week on the medication. If they don't, then switching to an alternate stimulant is often recommended. Some children have headaches or stomachaches on Ritalin but not on Dexedrine or Adderall, and vice versa.

Because headaches and stomachaches are early-onset side effects, these problems can persist if medications are stopped on weekends. On Monday morning, it is as if treatment is starting again, and the adjustment to these side effects begins anew. Many physicians cite other reasons for not stopping medication on weekends. One of these is that children must focus in social situations to develop appropriate social skills, and thus the weekend may be a critical time for them. Another is that weekends may be less structured than school days and thus put impulsive children at greater risk for conduct problems, defiant behavior, and other at-risk behaviors.

Decreased Appetite Decreased appetite occurs 30%–50% of the time. In general, the higher the dose of stimulant, the greater the appetite-suppressant effect. At lower doses, some very active small children actually eat more because they are able to sit still long enough to consume their meals. Maintaining weight or minimizing weight loss, however, is a key aspect of tolerating stimulants. Children who take stimulants should eat big breakfasts and are likely to be very hungry in the evenings. It is important to learn when the last dose wears off in order to offer dinner at that time. Additional high-calorie snacks—for example, instant breakfasts, nutritious snacks, and ice cream (if there is no cholesterol or triglyceride elevation)—are often given before bedtime. Experience in the clinic indicates that most children who take stimulants are thinner than they would be if they did not take stimulants; but with careful timing of meals and appropriate use of high-calorie snacks, it is rare for a child not to be able to continue on medication.

Some parents hesitate to provide sweet snacks for children with ADHD. The myth that sugar causes hyperactivity remains the most entrenched fallacy of all. There has never been a well-controlled study that has proved this correlation scientifically. Indeed, parents' expectation that sugar causes hyperactivity has been shown to bias their assessment of their child's behavior: Parents rated their child's behavior as more active when they were told that the child had received sugar, regardless of whether the child actually had.

This concept is important because calorie consumption is the goal, and children in general like sweet foods. With the exception of children who have diabetes, children with other illnesses requiring special diets, or children with poor dentition, parents of children who have problems with maintaining weight on stimulants can generally be encouraged to find snacks to help maintain their child's weight.

Difficulty with Falling Asleep About 10%–20% of children with ADHD have trouble with settling down at night. Sometimes, when stimulants are started, children settle down more easily. Stimulants can cause insomnia, however, particularly difficulty with falling asleep. In these cases, the last dose is often decreased. When this is not possible because the dose becomes ineffective, then the addition of another medicine (e.g., clonidine, imipramine) before bedtime can help sleep induction. I discuss these medicines in more detail in another section of this chapter.

Tics Can stimulants produce tics? In the clinic, I occasionally see that stimulants exaggerate tics (i.e., involuntary motor movements or vocalizations). A child who develops eye-blinking tics while on stimulants and who has never had tics before and has a negative family history for tics (i.e., nobody in his or her biological family has had tics) is likely getting too high a stimulant dose. The tics remit once the medicine is stopped. Such episodes are infrequent; most often, a child who develops motor or vocal tics while on Ritalin either has had milder, previously unnoticed tics that are exaggerated or has a family history of tics. The latter case suggests that the child has a biological vulnerability to tics and eventually would have had them even without stimulants. There is a group of children with significant tics who warrant a diagnosis of Tourette syndrome (TS) or other tic disorder. Research shows that about 50%–60% of these children also have ADHD.

Because of the overlap in diagnoses (TS and ADHD) and the ability of stimulants to exacerbate tics, it is obviously very important to ascertain whether a child or a family member has had tics prior to starting the child on stimulants. This is not, however, an absolute contraindication of the use of stimulants. Clinicians treating these children have reported that treating children with both TS and ADHD with stimulants results in increased tics 50% of the time and significant overall benefit 50% of the time.

Decreased Growth Between 1972, when the question of decreased growth was first addressed, and 1988, there were more than 16 studies that examined the effects of stimulants on height. Seven researchers found an effect on height during a 1- to 2-year period. Only one group reported a decrease in height after 4 years. Longer-term studies (i.e., 5–10 years) reported no effect on height. Recent studies noted no difference in growth patterns of medicated versus nonmedicated children with ADHD. The children with ADHD appeared ultimately to reach their predicted height, regardless of whether they took medication; but their growth spurts occurred later as compared with children without ADHD. Thus, it appears that stimulants have no permanent, significant effect on growth. Further research is needed to see whether these most recent findings—that the developmental aspects of ADHD itself may alter growth patterns but not final height—are supported.

Additional Medications for ADHD

Some children, even after trying all three commonly prescribed stimulant medications, may not tolerate them. Other medication options are available in these circumstances. The following table lists, and the following subsections discuss, some of the other medications that are prescribed:

Generic	Brand	Benefits	Side effects
Methamphetamine	Desoxyn	Elevates mood Long-acting potential	Possible abuse
Pemoline	Cylert	Long-acting	Liver toxicity (1:2,000)
Tricyclic antidepressants			
Imipramine Desipramine Nortriptyline	Tofranil Norpramin Pamelor, Aventyl	Improve concentration Decrease anxiety Elevate mood	Intracardiac conduction delay (greater than a 2-milligram/kilogram dose)
Central α-2 agonists			
Clonidine	Catapres	Calming	Sedation
Guanfacine	Tenex	Decrease impulsivity Decrease tics	Lowers blood pressure May depress mood
Bupropion	Wellbutrin	Decreases impulsivity, irritability	Seizures possible at greater than 450 milligrams per day Elevates mood

Methamphetamine Methamphetamine (i.e., Desoxyn) is another stimulant, and it is often well tolerated. It is not as often prescribed as the stimulants mentioned previously, because in sad, depressed children with ADHD, it has some mild mood-enhancing effects that, clinicians caution, creates a potential for abuse unlike the other stimulants. I have found it helpful for a carefully selected small group of children and have noted good outcomes and no abuse problems.

Pemoline Pemoline (i.e., Cylert) is a stimulant-like compound that is often categorized as a stimulant but has slightly different pharmacological properties. Its side-effect profile is very similar to that of the stimulants. The primary advantage of pemoline is that it is the longest-acting medication of all those discussed in this chapter (except possibly Desoxyn). This is important for adolescents who "hate" going to the school nurse and then come home to a latchkey situation. A morning dose may allow for sufficient coverage until dinnertime. Sometimes a second dose in the early afternoon is necessary.

The primary disadvantage of pemoline is that there is a 1-in-2,000 chance that liver enzymes (i.e., transaminases) can become elevated; therefore, liver function tests should be done every 6 months by ordering a specific blood test. A very small percentage of the 1 in 2,000 patients who have liver function test abnormalities can later experience liver ailments. In such a case, the child might experience pain under the right diaphragm (where the liver is located) accompanied by nausea, vomiting, or jaundice. These symptoms require immediate medical evaluation.

It is ironic that pemoline is classified as a Type IV drug by the FDA but that the stimulants are in a more restricted Type II class. As I have described previously, the stimulants are quite safe, nonaddictive, extremely difficult to overdose on, and have no significant organ toxicity or long-term side effects. Pemoline, although generally quite safe, does have a risk, albeit very low, for inducing serious liver problems. Type II drugs require special precautions. In some states, these include triplicate copies of prescriptions; in all states, prescriptions cannot be issued with additional refills. This means that stimulant medications require a new prescription each month, an often bothersome issue for patients, whereas pemoline can be prescribed with refills. The difficulty in refilling stimulants contrasted with the easier access to potentially less safe medication seems contrary to the intent of the FDA's typing of medications and often is confusing to parents.

Tricyclic Antidepressants The tricyclic antidepressants have been used with children since the 1960s. Since tricyclics improve mood, they are often used when anxiety or depressed mood coexist with ADHD. Imipramine (i.e., Tofranil) and its chemical end product desipramine (i.e., Norpramin) have both been shown to improve concentration and decrease impulsivity in children with ADHD. These medicines are often effective initially in doses that are lower than what is needed to treat depression. In many children, the benefits are lost after 3–6 months on lower doses, at which point higher doses may be needed.

Prior to starting imipramine or desipramine, a cardiac history should be obtained. Five cases of unexplained sudden death during desipramine but not imipramine treatment have been reported. A causal relationship between desipramine and these deaths has not been established, however. I do not recommend using desipramine, because the medications otherwise available and discussed in this section are so relatively safe and effective.

Nortriptyline (i.e., Pamelor, Aventyl) is a demethylated metabolite (i.e., chemical end product) of amitriptyline (i.e., Elavil). It can be very helpful in preschool children who are impulsive, hyperactive, defiant, and negativistic. It is available as a syrup and is easy to dispense to young children. Its side effects and monitoring are the same as those described for imipramine.

A few words of caution are in order regarding the use of tricyclics in general. Although tricyclics do not make tics worse and are otherwise well tolerated, a child with abnormal heart rhythms should not take them; a benign heart murmur, however, is not a contraindication. Unlike stimulants, these medications can be dangerous in overdoses of 10–20 times the prescribed dose, so parents must prevent their children's inadvertent access to them. Side effects include sedation; dry mouth; constipation; and, very rarely, hand tremor. Tricyclics should be tapered when discontinued because 10% of children experience stomachaches or vomiting if doses above a certain value are suddenly stopped.

Thus, with careful monitoring, the tricyclics, particularly imipramine and nortriptyline, are often helpful in children with ADHD who can't tolerate stimulants or who have tics or concomitant anxiety and depression.

Central α-2 Agonists The central α-2 agonists, clonidine (i.e., Catapres) and guanfacine (i.e., Tenex), are noted to decrease impulsivity, improve frustration tolerance, and decrease tics. They affect the neurotransmitter chemical norepinephrine and regulate the firing of brain neurons using this neurotransmitter. Children who have ADHD and tics therefore benefit from these medications. It is helpful to quiet the tics and impulsivity first. If inattention and poor concentration continue, then the addition of the stimulants is often well tolerated, and tics are unlikely to get worse with the use of this two-drug combination.

Central α-2 agonists are sedating and were formulated to treat hypertension. In 1975, workers at Yale University discovered their benefits for tics and ADHD. Sleepiness can prohibit their tolerability in some children. Gradually increasing the dose minimizes both sedation and hypotensive effects. If a child complains of lightheadedness, then the dose should be tapered as tolerated. Because these medications affect norepinephrine concentrations, they can alter mood states. A few children with a predisposition to depression or who present with sad mood may become depressed as a result of using one of these medications. Antidepressants may be more helpful adjunctive medications for these children.

Clonidine is available in 0.1-, 0.2-, and 0.3-milligram tabs, and guanfacine is available in 1- and 2-milligram tabs. Fractions of these doses (i.e., one-quarter to one-half tabs) are used two to four times daily initially and increased until tics and ADHD symptoms improve. Guanfacine maintains a little longer clinical effect, but the duration of both medications varies by patient and by dose given.

Some clinicians also use these medications to facilitate sleep in children with ADHD. They are very effective in inducing sleep and then allowing the child's natural sleep pattern to keep him or her asleep, and they produce no "hangover" effect in the morning. Along with trouble falling asleep, some children with ADHD cannot stay asleep and may be up during the night. This can be dangerous because they may impulsively set fires or get into other mischief. To keep these children asleep, the tricyclics imipramine and nortriptyline may be required.

Bupropion (i.e., Wellbutrin, Zyban) is an antidepressant with some stimulant-like pharmacologic properties that is used not only as an antidepressant (i.e., Wellbutrin) but also to help people stop smoking (i.e., Zyban). It is also helpful in patients with ADHD, irritability, anger, and depressed mood. (If there is more anxiety than irritability and anger, then tricyclics may be used first.)

Bupropion is formulated as a slow release (i.e., Wellbutrin SR) in 100- and 150-milligram tabs. It was originally formulated in shorter-acting tabs, but these preparations are less effective in distributing the dose. Doses range from 50–450 milligrams daily. In the clinic, I rarely issue a prescription above 300 milligrams daily. A typical dose would be 100–150 milligrams of Wellbutrin SR before and after school. It is generally well tolerated, and there is no need to administer it at school. Adolescents in particular may benefit and be more compliant because of its dosing schedule, its ability to decrease irritability and anger, its low incidence of side effects, and its significant effect on concentration. The one drawback is that bupropion lowers seizure threshold in doses of more than 450 milligrams daily. Careful monitoring of daily intake is thus necessary.

Newer Medications What about new medications as the 21st century turns? The atypical antipsychotics have offered new hope for people with psychosis because, unlike their predecessors, they have no long-term risk of inducing tardive dyskinesia (a permanent movement disorder).

Risperidone (i.e., Risperdal) is one of these new agents and the only one to date that has been shown to help control some ADHD symptoms (as first revealed by workers in Scandinavia). I sometimes use small doses of this medicine in concert with the stimulants in patients who have difficult-to-control conduct problems, aggression, and severe temper tantrums along with ADHD. It can be remarkably effective in controlling these behaviors. Side effects include sedation, which is usually less than that of the α-2 agonists (discussed previously) and increased appetite, which is often balanced by the depressed appetite caused by the stimulants. Tremors and muscle cramps (i.e., dystonias) can occur, often at higher doses, and are reversible and treatable with certain anticholinergic agents (i.e., benztropine mesylate).

Workers have noted that the antidepressant venlafaxine (i.e., Effexor) and the noradrenergic compound tomoxetine have been clinically effective in adults with ADHD. Further clinical trials in children are forthcoming.

Selective Serotonin Reuptake Inhibitors The 1990s were significant for the introduction of the selective serotonin reuptake inhibitors (SSRIs) (e.g., Celexa, Luvox, Paxil, Prozac, Zoloft). Although these medications treat a whole spectrum of mood and anxiety disorders, they are *not* effective in treating ADHD. Indeed, because they can be activating, they tend to induce impulsivity or disinhibition rather than diminish such behaviors. When a child with complex problems requires treatment with multiple medications, a physician may decide that they can be used with stimulants when anxiety is severe enough that the tricyclics are ineffective or when tricyclics are contraindicated. In these instances, picking among the SSRIs often results in selection of one that is less activating and less well tolerated with the stimulants. A study of Prozac and Ritalin has found them to be safe when given together and often helpful for co-existing depression and ADHD.

ADHD and Bipolar Affective Disorder

As discussed at recent national conferences, as many as 10%–20% of children with ADHD seen in clinics may develop bipolar affective disorder (i.e., manic depression). It does appear to be a group of children who often do well on stimulants early on but need gradually increasing doses. Eventually, irritability, severe mood swings, grandiose and aggressive behaviors, sleep and appetite disruption, pressured speech, racing thoughts, and psychotic symptoms may evolve. This, of course, represents a much more significant disorder than ADHD. These children have positive family histories (i.e., parents, siblings) for bipolar affective disorder.

The addition of mood stabilizers (e.g., carbamazepine, gabapentin, lithium, valproic acid) is then needed. Sometimes the symptoms remit, but at other times concomitant use of both a stimulant and a mood stabilizer is necessary. In the clinic, I have found this combination to be safe and effective in such children who have both ADHD and bipolar affective disorder. Adderall and Pemoline tend to induce psychosis occasionally in these vulnerable individuals, so I usually choose methylphenidate (i.e., Ritalin), which is less likely to do so. Because stimulants increase dopamine, however, and increased dopamine in certain regions of the brain causes psychosis, these combinations should be monitored closely. Obviously, for these rare and complex cases, a close working relationship with an expert physician is an essential element of a child's treatment.

CONCLUSIONS

Understanding of the medicines used to treat ADHD has blossomed. Physicians with expertise in their use are finding these treatments to be safe and, generally, extremely effective. When used as part of a multimodal approach to treatment, the results can be remarkable. Since 1990, I have seen young, impulsive, inattentive, disruptive elementary school children who are labeled the "bad child" grow up to become focused, proud, engageable, and productive adolescents and adults.

The challenge continues to be parents' education about ADHD. Physicians must maintain a constant awareness that treating these behavior problems with medication requires a sensitivity to parents' concerns, misunderstandings, and anxieties. It is hoped that this chapter has helped to diminish these factors and will enable parents who previously would not use medication for their child to consider doing so.

Chapter 10

ADHD and Eligibility for Special School Services

ADHD Myths

All children with ADHD qualify for special education services.

No children with ADHD qualify for special education services.

Only services provided under special education laws are mandatory in U.S. schools.

Many children with ADHD experience their greatest problems at school. It is common for parents to feel frustrated that school personnel fail to recognize the presence of ADHD or to assign their child's poor achievement or disruptive behavior to non-ADHD causes. Often parents complain that even when the presence of ADHD is confirmed, teachers are too busy to provide individualization for their son or daughter and instead request that parents themselves fix the problem through some change in discipline techniques or by taking the child to a physician for medication. Fortunately, beginning in the early 1990s, these kinds of situations began to change as the federal government provided clarification about the responsibility and obligation of public schools to meet the needs of students with ADHD. Unfortunately, there are still instances in which this important information remains unknown or is disregarded.

Because ADHD has broad implications for classroom learning, federal agencies (i.e., the Office of Special Education Programs and Rehabilitative Services, the U.S. Office of Civil Rights, the U.S. Department of Education) have clarified state and local responsibilities under federal law for addressing the school needs of children with ADHD. As the parent of a student who is either diagnosed with ADHD or is suspected of having ADHD, you are encouraged to learn as much as possible about the rights of students with disabilities and particularly about the rights of children with ADHD. This chapter summarizes the position of the Department of Education on educating students with ADHD. Federal law represents a minimum guarantee of student rights, although state laws and regulations may offer greater rights to students and parents.

ELIGIBILITY FOR SPECIAL EDUCATION AND RELATED SERVICES

The Individuals with Disabilities Education Act (IDEA) of 1990 (PL 101-476) and its amendments in 1991 (PL 102-119) and 1997 (PL 105-17), the latest update of the Education for

All Handicapped Children Act of 1975 (PL 94-142), authorizes and funds special education services. In 1990, while debating the IDEA legislation, the U.S. Congress seriously considered including ADHD in the definition of *children with disabilities.* Had they done so, ADHD would have become a separate disability category within special education. This change would have made students with ADHD eligible for services under IDEA by virtue of their having this disorder, just as children with other disabilities (e.g., learning disabilities, hearing impairments) are eligible if they are determined to be in need of special education and related services. Because many students with ADHD are readily able to qualify for special education services under the IDEA without creation of a separate category (as discussed later in this chapter), however, the Department of Education took the position that there was no need to create a new, separate special education category for students with ADHD. Thus, although no change was made to the categories of children eligible for special education services, it was recognized that confusion exists, and subsequently the federal government attempted to make clear their position, as described later in this chapter.

Services Afforded under the Individuals with Disabilities Education Act

For children with disabilities who are found eligible for special education and related services under IDEA, the law stipulates that a *free appropriate public education* be provided. That is, special education instruction and related services such as counseling are provided at no cost to parents if their children are eligible for special education. The services that are provided must be delineated in an individualized education program (IEP) for each child. This is a plan that details which special education and related services will be provided, by which instruction personnel, and how progress toward each student's educational goals will be measured. The law also provides that various rights and protections, such as the right to an independent evaluation, the right for parent input into the student's education program, and the right to review all records, must be extended to children with disabilities and their parents.

To be eligible for the special education services outlined by IDEA, a student must undergo an evaluation and be found to have one or more of the thirteen disabilities specified in IDEA. The student must also actually need or require such special education and related services. Because ADHD was not made a special education category under IDEA, some but not all children with ADHD are eligible for services. It is the responsibility of local school districts to provide special education and related services to children with ADHD who are determined to have one of the disabilities listed as qualifying a student for special education services (discussed in the sections following) and to be in actual need of special education and related services. Following is a list of key terms in qualifying children with ADHD for school services:

IDEA (the Individuals with Disabilities Education Act): Formerly called the Education for All Handicapped Children Act of 1975, this federal law governs special education services.

Learning disabilities: One of the thirteen categories of disability in which students may qualify for special education services under IDEA. In many states, students are identified by a severe discrepancy between their IQ scores and their academic achievement. Accompanying problems, such as with memory or perception, are required in some states.

Seriously emotionally disturbed: One of the thirteen categories of disability in which students may qualify for special services under the IDEA. Students are usually identified by longstanding problems of mood, interpersonal relationships, anxiety, thinking, or behavior that hinder their school progress.

Other health impaired: One of the thirteen categories of disability in which students may qualify for special education services under the IDEA. Students with ADHD may qualify for services if their problem is deemed an ongoing or acute health problem that "results in limited alertness adversely affecting educational performance."

Section 504 of the Rehabilitation Act of 1973: This is a non–special education provision that can be invoked to offer services to students with disabilities. Some students receive services if ADHD is viewed as a "physical or mental impairment which substantially limits a major life activity."

Special education services must meet each child's unique educational needs, including those arising from the ADHD condition. The IDEA stipulates that a full continuum of alternative placements must be available, including instruction in general classes, special classes, and special schools; home instruction; and instruction in hospitals and institutions. Significantly, IDEA requires that students must be educated in the least restrictive environment (LRE), such as a general classroom, that meets their needs. The following are a few of the special education disability categories into which children with ADHD often fall in order to receive special services:

- Learning disabilities
- Serious emotional disturbance
- Other health impairment

Each of these categories is discussed in the subsections that follow. It is important to recognize that only those students who are found eligible in one of these categories qualify for special education services.

Eligibility for Special Education by Virtue of Learning Disabilities

One of the categories of disabilities under which students with ADHD may be found eligible for special education services is *learning disabilities.* Children with ADHD have a substantially higher rate of learning disabilities than children without ADHD. Just like children without ADHD, those with ADHD must satisfy the criteria for learning disabilities if they are to receive this designation and are to be afforded special education and related services. The federal definition of a *specific learning disability* follows:

> [A] disorder in one or more of the basic psychological processes involved in understanding or in using language, spoken or written, that may manifest itself in an imperfect ability to listen, think, read, write, spell, or do mathematical calculations. The term [*learning disabilities*] includes such conditions as perceptual disabilities, brain injury, minimal brain dysfunction, dyslexia, and developmental aphasia. The term does not apply to children who have learning problems that are primarily the result of visual, hearing, or motor disabilities, of mental retardation, of emotional disturbance, or of environmental, cultural, or economic disadvantage. (PL 102-119, 20 U.S.C. § 1401[a][1])

This definition was clarified by accompanying federal regulations. These federal regulations specify that children qualify as having learning disabilities only if certain conditions are met. Practically speaking, a learning disability designation is possible only if 1) the child does not achieve commensurate with his or her peers (thus requiring special education or related services) in one or more of the following areas, and 2) a significant discrepancy exists between a student's ability and his or her achievement in at least one of the following areas:

- Oral expression
- Listening comprehension
- Written expression
- Basic reading skills
- Reading comprehension
- Mathematics calculation
- Mathematics reasoning

Testing and evaluation of the child suspected of having a learning disability are often performed by a school psychologist and are termed a *psychoeducational evaluation.* Some states, however, require or encourage other forms of testing and evaluation that assist both in determining whether that child has a learning disability and in developing a program to meet the child's needs. Findings from the child's evaluation are among the sources of information that a multidisciplinary team uses to decide whether any child, including one with ADHD, is eligible for services under IDEA.

Eligibility for Special Education by Virtue of Serious Emotional Disturbance

Another category under which students with ADHD may qualify for special education services is serious emotional disturbance. Here, too, students with ADHD must meet the established criteria. They neither automatically qualified nor automatically disqualified for services because they have ADHD. The federal definition of *serious emotional disturbance* is as follows: a condition exhibiting one or more of the following characteristics over a long period of time and to a marked degree that adversely affects a child's educational performance:

1. An inability to learn which cannot be explained by intellectual, sensory, or health factors
2. An inability to build or maintain satisfactory interpersonal relationships with peers and teachers
3. Inappropriate types of behavior or feelings under normal circumstances
4. A general pervasive mood of unhappiness or depression
5. A tendency to develop physical symptoms or fears associated with personal or school problems (PL 102-119, 20 U.S.C. § 1401[a][1])

Serious emotional disturbance includes schizophrenia. The term does not apply to children who are socially maladjusted, unless it is determined that they have a serious emotional disturbance.

To be identified as having a disability in this category, students must exhibit one of the five previous characteristics to a marked degree, the problem must have been evident for a substantial time period, and the problem must affect the student's educational performance. Some but not all children with ADHD meet these criteria.

Eligibility for Special Education by Virtue of "Other Health Impaired" Category

Other health impaired is another one of the thirteen disability categories under which students with ADHD may qualify for special education services. Many health problems can potentially create eligibility for special services under this category. There is no exhaustive list, but among its provisions, the category "Other health impaired" includes all chronic and acute impairments that result in limited alertness that adversely affects educational performance. If a student with ADHD has a chronic (i.e., longstanding) or acute (i.e., recent onset) health problem (ADHD itself may be considered to be a health problem) that results in limited alertness (e.g., poor attention to classroom instruction), then he or she may be considered as having a disability and thus be eligible for special education services solely on the basis of the ADHD impairment. That is, a child with ADHD may be eligible under the "Other health impaired" category without having learning disabilities or serious emotional disturbance. Again, the mere diagnosis of ADHD is insufficient to create special education eligibility. The student must still meet the criteria to be eligible for services subsequent to a review of all available data and determination that such services are required by the school's multidisciplinary team and the student's parents.

EVALUATIONS FOR SPECIAL EDUCATION SERVICES

Local school districts as well as state agencies have an affirmative obligation to evaluate children suspected of having any of the disabilities discussed thus far. IDEA requires state agencies and local school districts to have procedures for locating, identifying, and evaluating all children who are suspected of having a disability and who are in need of special education and related services. This responsibility is known as the Child Find program. It is applicable to all children from birth to 21 years of age, regardless of the severity of their disabilities.

The obligation to identify students with disabilities includes the requirement that evaluations of children suspected of needing special education and related services be conducted without undue delay. There are other requirements as well. Local school districts may not refuse to evaluate a child for special services who has a prior medical diagnosis of ADHD solely because of that diagnosis, as sometimes occurred before the federal position on ADHD was clarified. Another point that is equally important is one that has been mentioned previously but is worth repeating: *A medical diagnosis of ADHD alone is insufficient to render a child eligible for special education services.* Thus, a physician's statement that a child has ADHD does not create automatic eligibility. The student still must be found eligible by meeting the criteria for one or more of the special education categories and have a demonstrated need for specially designed instruction.

During the early 1990s, students such as an overactive and severely underachieving child named Jeremy, for example, may not have received needed special education services. Jeremy's parents may have been reluctant to share information about his ADHD diagnosis. Parents were often concerned that such a diagnosis, particularly if established by a physician, would suggest to school personnel that the problem was a medical rather than an education-related one. In some instances, children like Jeremy were overlooked (in fact, not even considered) for special education services, even though they may have had a strong need for services and met the definition of having a condition or disability, such as learning disabilities or serious emotional disturbance, that made them eligible for special education and related services.

By the late 1990s, the federal government's position that ADHD is *not* a contraindication for special services was widely recognized, and the situation for students seemed to have changed. It is not uncommon for physicians or other nonschool diagnosticians to establish an ADHD diagnosis that is openly transmitted to the student's school. For example, a child named Barry has undergone a detailed evaluation at an ADHD clinic and has been found to meet DSM-IV criteria for ADHD, combined type. Barry's parents recognize that he is making average grades but believe that he could do better with supplemental services. Accordingly, they present a report of the clinic's finding to Barry's local school and request that he be enrolled immediately in special education services to enhance his school performance. In both Jeremy's and Barry's cases, the local school district must review outside information and, in consultation with parents, determine whether each child qualifies for services.

IDEA spells out the required sequence of events for a child to receive special education and related services once he or she is considered eligible. To begin, a full, individualized evaluation of the child's educational needs must be conducted prior to placement in a special education program or related services. This evaluation must be conducted by a multidisciplinary team (i.e., professionals from various disciplines such as education, psychology, medicine, or nursing). The evaluation team must include at least one teacher or other specialist with knowledge of the suspected disability.

Because disagreements sometimes arise with regard to evaluations (as may occur in the case of Jeremy or Barry), IDEA addresses these potential concerns. If a parent disagrees with the local school district's refusal to evaluate a student or with the school district's determination that a student does not have a disability (i.e., is not eligible for special education services), then remedies are available. These remedies include an important parental right: the right to request a due process hearing. The due process hearing offers a chance for parents to present their concerns, for the local school district to make its position clear, and for a binding opinion to be rendered by an independent hearing officer.

SECTION 504 OF THE REHABILITATION ACT OF 1973

The previous discussion indicates that some students with ADHD do not qualify for special education under IDEA. Important alternatives may nonetheless exist for these students. Section 504 of the Rehabilitation Act of 1973 and its implementing regulations may afford your child a means of gaining the services that he or she needs. The fact that some children may not qualify for special education services under IDEA but may still be recognized under Section 504 is of great importance. It also appears to be the source of the most confusion among school personnel who still believe that services are available only to those children identified as eligible under IDEA.

Section 504 prohibits discrimination on the basis of disability by recipients of federal funds. Most public schools in the United States receive some federal funds. Because Section 504 is a civil rights law rather than a funding law, its requirements are framed in different terms from those of IDEA. Although the Section 504 regulation was written with an eye toward consistency with IDEA, it is more general, and there are some important differences. One crucial difference is that some children who are determined to have a disability under Section 504 may be afforded protection under Section 504 but may not be eligible for special education under one of the disability categories under IDEA.

Definition of *Disability* in Section 504

Section 504 requires every recipient of federal funding operating a public elementary or secondary education program to address the needs of children with disabilities. Under Section 504, students with disabilities must have their needs met as adequately as the needs of students without disabilities.

The definition of *person with a disability* is thus crucial. As defined in the Section 504 regulation, a *person with a disability* is any person who has a physical or mental impairment substantially limiting a major life activity such as learning, has a record of such an impairment, or is regarded as having such an impairment. Thus, depending on the severity of their conditions, children with ADHD may fit within that definition.

Programs and Services under Section 504

Under Section 504, a local school district must provide a free appropriate public education to each qualified child with a disability. In this sense, children identified under Section 504 and IDEA are offered similar basic guarantees. A free appropriate public education, under Section 504, consists of general or special education and related aids and services. These must match individual students' needs. Under Section 504, if there is reason to believe that a child has ADHD and is in need of special education and related services, the local school district must evaluate the child to determine whether he or she has a disability according to Section 504. Generally, this evaluation consists of a child study team or an individualized education planning committee (composed of teachers, special educators, an administrator, a nurse, and a school psychologist) convening to review previously collected information about the child. Often the same team has reviewed the child's information and has determined that the child is not eligible for special education under the IDEA. If the district determines that the child does not have a disability under Section 504, the parent has the right to contest that determination. If the child is found to have a disability under Section 504, however, steps are taken to aid the student. The local school district then determines the child's educational needs. General or special education services might be offered, or related aids or services alone might be found sufficient. An IEP developed in accordance with IDEA is one means of meeting the free appropriate public education requirement of Section 504, but a formal IEP document is not mandated by Section 504.

As is true under IDEA, a child's education must be provided in a general education environment to the maximum extent appropriate. For example, students eligible under Section 504 are to be educated in the general classroom, with modifications, unless it is demonstrated that education in this environment would not be appropriate even with the use of supplementary aids and services. If a student needs only modifications in the general education learning environment, then it is impermissible to remove the child from the general classroom. General classroom teachers are important in identifying appropriate education adaptations and interventions for many students with ADHD. Chapter 12 discusses a number of interventions that can occur within the child's classroom without extensive support or elaborate aids.

State education agencies and local school districts have been encouraged by the federal government to take steps to coordinate their services under IDEA and Section 504. Similarly, they have been encouraged to train general education teachers and other school personnel. The goal is first to enhance awareness among school personnel about ADHD and its manifestations and second to provide for the adaptations that can be implemented in general education programs to address the instruction needs of students with ADHD.

Examples of the types of interventions that are expected to be implemented under Section 504 were made clear in a memorandum authored by the U.S. Department of Education in the early 1990s:

> Providing a structured learning environment; repeating and simplifying instructions about in-class and homework assignments; supplementing verbal instructions with visual instructions; using behavioral management techniques; adjusting class schedules; modifying test delivery; using tape recorders, computer-aided instruction, and other audiovisual equipment; selecting modified textbooks or workbooks; and tailoring homework assignments.

The federal government has identified other ways to meet the special needs of students with disabilities. These range from consultation services to special resources and may include reducing class size; using one-to-one tutorials; employing classroom aides and notetakers; involving a service coordinator to oversee implementation of special programs and services; and modifying nonacademic times such as lunchtime, recess, and physical education. It is believed that through adaptations and interventions in general classroom, many of which may be required by Section 504, local school districts are able to provide effective instruction for many students with ADHD.

Procedural Safeguards of Students' Rights under Section 504

Procedures to protect the rights of students and parents are included under Section 504; they are less specific, however, than those under IDEA. The Section 504 regulations require local school districts to make available a system of procedural safeguards. These safeguards permit parents to challenge actions regarding identification, evaluation, or educational placement of their child with a disability who they believe needs special education or related services. Safeguards under Section 504 include notification of programs and placement decisions, an opportunity for parents to examine records, an impartial hearing with the opportunity for parents' participation and representation by counsel, and a review procedure. School districts and state education agencies may use the same due process procedures for resolving disputes under both IDEA and Section 504, but a separate procedure can also be used under Section 504.

Other protections may be afforded children with ADHD as a result of court cases. For example, it may be inappropriate to use expulsion or suspension procedures as a way to discipline behavior that results from the student's disabling condition (i.e., ADHD). Also, corporal punishment—in schools that permit it—may be inappropriate unless its use has been carefully considered and made part of the student's formal, written IEP.

CONCLUSIONS

It is important for parents and school personnel to understand the laws and regulations regarding the education of children with ADHD. Often parents must serve as advocates for their children. Becoming informed about the rights of children with ADHD and being willing to share information with school personnel can be of considerable value. Parents should study the material in this chapter and in Chapters 11 and 12 to develop an overall appreciation of their child's rights and the ways that these can be met, when necessary, by classroom adjustments and specialized teaching techniques.

Chapter 11

Finding the Best School Placement

ADHD Myths

Private school placements are almost always better than public school placements for students with ADHD.

Local school districts must pay for all private school placements if parents of students with ADHD insist.

Military schools are almost always helpful for rebellious boys, including those with ADHD.

Among the foremost concerns expressed by parents is where to educate their child with ADHD. This concern is justified, based on findings that an estimated 23%–30% of children with ADHD have problems with achieving at the level predicted by their IQ scores and that 30%–70% of children with ADHD fail at least 1 year of school. Without an appropriate education program, many such children drop out of school. Finding the right education environment for them is thus crucial.

GENERAL PUBLIC SCHOOL CLASS PLACEMENT: NO SPECIAL DESIGNATION

As Chapter 10 suggests, services for many children with ADHD can be provided in public schools, many times in your child's general classroom and often with no labels involved. You are encouraged to consider this option first because with no labels there is no stigma, and, provided that your child's needs can be met adequately, the child experiences little or no negative impact. This option, however, requires teachers to do what is necessary, even though no formal label of ADHD is involved, no special funding occurs, and administrative support may not be offered. If a viable plan is feasible under these conditions, that is fine: Labeling in itself has no special value as long as the child's condition is understood and his or her needs are fulfilled. Many experienced teachers can individualize their instruction so that the child with ADHD succeeds, especially if other aspects of the child's life are successful. Other teachers find that by working with a school psychologist or a school counselor—or, alternatively, with an out-of-school professional—a fairly straightforward plan can be devised and implemented. The plan is not sufficiently unique that special education designations are called for; both parents and teachers are satisfied to leave things on an informal basis.

ASSISTANCE IN THE GENERAL CLASSROOM UNDER SECTION 504

Chapter 12 discusses some of the many techniques that can be used to help children with ADHD in a general classroom.

Implementing these techniques may require special support or assistance, however. Often the local school district must concur with the ADHD diagnosis and sanction an individualized program if the child's needs are to be met. By invoking Section 504 of the Rehabilitation Act of 1973, the school is required to provide necessary support personnel or modifications; but the child is not identified as a special education student, and no special education labels are entered into his or her school records. Recall that, under Section 504, programming changes may be made but only the ADHD label is used. A program authorized by Section 504 may be an excellent compromise because the child receives a minimum of stigmatizing labels but may receive substantial services.

RESOURCE SPECIAL EDUCATION ASSISTANCE

Another variant of leaving the child in his or her general classroom is to use resource special education services if the child qualifies for them. Many students with ADHD qualify for special education services in the categories of learning disabilities, serious emotional disturbance, or "Other health impaired," as discussed in Chapter 10. For those who do qualify, a resource special education placement may be the best choice. With this arrangement, as with the non–special education option just mentioned, the student remains primarily in the general education classroom; but a special education teacher provides direct tutoring or instruction services and assists the general education teacher by securing distinctive materials or arranging novel teaching methods, or both. Gaining access to trained special education personnel, receiving a formal designation as a student with special needs, and yet having the chance to receive services in the context of the general classroom make this the preferable option for many students. As emphasized in Chapters 10 and 12, extensive services can be delivered in such an arrangement; no preexisting limit on the amount or the character of resource services exists.

Unfortunately, many students who could potentially benefit from resource special education services are denied them because they lack eligibility. Teachers and parents are thus left to work out acceptable programs under Section 504 provisions or by relying solely on the good will of the school.

SELF-CONTAINED SPECIAL EDUCATION PLACEMENT

Some students who are eligible for special education placement require more than resource assistance. If this is the case, the next option to be considered is a self-contained classroom. This is an ungraded class, usually consisting of no more than 12 students and a special education teacher. Often one or more aides are also available. The advantages here are obvious. Individualized instruction is possible; the teacher-to-student ratio is maximized; and exotic programming, such as using a classwide token economy assigning points for acceptable behavior and trading those points for rewards, is feasible. Students benefit from an uninterrupted day's instruction by the same teacher(s), thus maximizing detection and implementation of the best and most individualized teaching methods.

This is a costly option for the school district, and it has the disadvantage of segregating children with problems from their peers. The latter can be stigmatizing. It may also preclude the chance for children with ADHD to learn more acceptable behavior by depriving them of exposure to suitable peer models. For these reasons, relatively few children are placed in self-contained special education classes. Those that are typically have failed in the generally classroom, even with considerable resource assistance.

SPECIAL EDUCATION SCHOOL AND RESIDENTIAL SCHOOL PLACEMENT

A very few children with ADHD cannot be educated successfully in a self-contained classroom located on the campus of a public school. Of this group, some attend classes in quite specialized, off-campus special schools. Large districts might manage their own schools of this type—a 30-student school for children with serious emotional disturbance is an example. Contracting with a private special education school is another option. Some students' problems are so formidable that residence on the campus of a special school, where class is attended during the day, is mandatory. This residential option is the most restrictive and extreme of those discussed here. Some districts have never planned or implemented such a placement and do not anticipate doing so in the future.

Children who require such a stringent placement usually have several severe problems (i.e., ADHD and severe conduct disorder). The severity of ADHD alone is almost never sufficient to prompt such a placement. As a parent, you would generally be advised to seek this option only if all else had failed. The advantages of extreme control, individualization of treatment, and staff expertise are generally negated by the disruption in the child's typical education and social life. Of course, for the child who would be incapable of receiving an education elsewhere, this option is acceptable.

VALUE AND LIMITATIONS OF SPECIAL EDUCATION SERVICES

Special education services (whether resource, self-contained, or special school environment) are of immense value. For many children, these services make the difference between school failure and success, happiness and satisfaction, and sadness and despair. Without special education services, many children would learn little; many would drop out of school at the earliest opportunity.

The fact that services are provided without expense to parents is an obvious and important advantage. The cost to the public school of providing services and accommodations for one child easily can amount to several thousand dollars per year. Participation in special education also means that certified, professionally qualified teachers are providing services. Moreover, there are obvious legal safeguards for your child. For example, each child must be placed in the LRE, a provision requiring that schools consider an array of services for each child, from the simple and nonintrusive to the complex and potentially intrusive.

PRIVATE GENERAL SCHOOL PLACEMENT

A common reaction of parents on learning of their child's ADHD diagnosis is to seek a private school so that their child can be educated better. The desire for more individualized, or what is perceived as more compassionate, instruction is often the motivation for a private school placement. Although some private schools' favorable teacher-to-student ratios and their commitment to children make for good placements, often such placements are a poor idea for several reasons.

Many private schools have neither the resources nor the desire to educate children with ADHD. Teachers in private schools may know less about learning difficulties and behavior and attentional problems than public school teachers do. Private schools, by definition, do not serve all students as public schools do. Accordingly, they may lack techniques for individualizing instruction and the know-how to encourage acceptable behavior. Even when individual accommodations are possible, private schools may balk at the requisite staffing demands and the diversion of teaching time away from their other students. Thus, some private schools exclude students with ADHD. Special education services may be provided by local school districts to children with disabilities who attend private schools as spelled out in federal law. Logistical problems associated with the use of part-time or itinerant special education teachers often plague this practice, however.

A candid discussion of your child's needs and a dispassionate appraisal of the school's ability to meet them is advised before agreeing to a private school placement. You may want to 1) ask pointed questions about other students with ADHD who have enrolled or 2) request to view examples of programs worked out for them. At any rate, a healthy skepticism backed by an insistence on facts is suggested.

PRIVATE SPECIAL SCHOOL PLACEMENT

The rare private school that is organized specifically for children with learning, behavior, or attentional problems may offer the same advantages as the special education schools discussed previously. In some exceptional instances, such a school may offer unique advantages, too. For instance, a special school located at a university or a medical school might link treatment with the latest research findings or have experts on hand to contribute to the program.

Private special schools that lack these valuable but uncommon advantages may not, unfortunately, compare favorably with their public education special school counterparts, mostly because of lack of finances. It is difficult for programs supported solely by tuition from parents and perhaps endowments to compete for professional staff with publicly supported schools. Thus, a private school often cannot attract or retain quality teachers or garner the necessary funds for building improvement, materials, and supplies. This is so because any program devoted to special students must have an extremely rich teacher-to-student ratio, which costs more. Although local factors vary, generally speaking, public education's access to federal and state money makes it more favorable than private programs. Often parents are better served by working with the public school by explaining their child's unique needs rather than exercising the private education option. At times, of course, considerable lobbying is called for, and outside professionals may need to be called on to explain the rationale for more services.

A word of caution is in order about unilateral placements in specialized schools. Some parents may place their child in private, specialized environments and later claim that the provision of a free appropriate public education sanctions such a move. Parents then expect the local school district to pick up the cost of such placements. Retroactive authorization for placements like this are rare and generally are not supported by the 1997 IDEA Amendments. Parents should proceed cautiously because they may incur personal financial obligations if they place their youngster in this manner.

MILITARY AND STRUCTURED BOARDING SCHOOLS

Structure, consisting of clear expectations and consequences to back up those expectations, has already been said to benefit many children with ADHD, as does a predictable daily routine. Some live-in programs devoted exclusively to caring for children and teenagers can provide a degree of structure that is unattainable at home. Military schools and boarding schools with carefully planned patterns of daily activities are examples of placements that sometimes help children or teenagers with ADHD.

Military schools have a reputation for imposing discipline and structure on their student bodies. Military schools promote an obvious code of conduct, they typically impose group and individual consequences for not adhering to that code, and their students' days are usually filled with organized activities so that there is little free time. Moreover, an organizational plan that places individuals into prearranged groups or units may, for some, provide a chance for acceptance that is difficult to obtain otherwise. Some children may develop a sense of pride and competence here that eluded them elsewhere.

The risk in this type of arrangement, however, is inflexibility. Rules that are too rigid to accommodate individual differences (e.g., the student unable to sustain attention during long tasks) may cause some to fail unnecessarily. Children with co-existing conduct or oppositional problems (see Chapter 1) may also experience recurrent conflict with authority. Some children, however, seem better able to control their antisocial tendencies when tight external controls are present. Obviously, the specifics of each program's approach and its prior success with various types of youngsters need to be explored before enrollment.

Many of the same issues exist with other private boarding schools, except that these programs seem to vary greatly in their degree of structure and in how they cope with individual differences. Programs that welcome individual differences exist, as do programs that exclude students with special problems. Sourcebooks describing boarding and military schools are available in most bookstores. Parents should research several facilities before making a final decision.

HOME SCHOOLING

Rarely, parents give up all hope of finding an acceptable placement for their child. Often, in desperation, these parents turn to home schooling. Many states have laws that allow parents to keep their child at home, purchase texts and school materials, and follow a prescribed curriculum. Local associations of parents frequently exist to offer support and guidance.

For parents who feel that they understand and manage their child as no one else can, this seems like a plausible option. Certainly, the child can receive a high degree of individual attention, and the potential parent–school friction can be eliminated in cases in which behavior or learning problems accompany ADHD.

The downside to home schooling, however, warrants careful consideration. Parents who take on the demanding job of teaching in addition to the demanding job of parenting may find that they end up doing neither job well. This is especially true if your child is extremely symptomatic for ADHD, has accompanying conduct or oppositional problems, or has difficulty with learning. To teach a difficult child all day and then slip into the after-school role of a parent who must both discipline and nurture that child is extremely demanding.

There are other considerations, too. The child with learning problems may require the most experienced and skilled of teachers. In some instances, parents may simply lack the skills to teach their child. Peer relationships are another issue. Already at risk for social skills deficiencies, the child with ADHD who is home-schooled is further deprived of a chance to develop social skills. He or she may become quite isolated from peers and may risk developing long-term social interaction problems. A child who is taught at home may find him- or herself increasingly unaware of the rules for social exchange or of the topics and interests that are common to peers and may lack acquaintances with whom to interact. Special effort must be made, therefore, to ensure that the home-schooled child is provided with opportunities for meaningful social interaction.

CONCLUSIONS

Although potentially bewildering to parents, the diversity of education programs available in many communities across the United States is quite advantageous for the child with ADHD. This is so because children with ADHD themselves are so varied. Selecting the best option requires a careful evaluation of the child as well as knowledge regarding educational resources and eligibility for special programs. You are encouraged to seek out the most knowledgeable and qualified professionals to assist you in this task. Of course, the better informed you are about available options and resources, the more effective advocacy you can provide for your child.

Chapter 12

Classroom Techniques

ADHD Myths

Reprimands and negative feedback have no role in teaching students with ADHD.

There are few, if any, classroom techniques that truly motivate students with ADHD.

Chapters 10 and 11 address how to qualify your child with ADHD for special services and where to educate your child. This chapter explores techniques that can be used in the classroom to best educate a child with ADHD.

Before discussing specifics of instruction, it is important to gain a little perspective. No parent can expect to call the shots within his or her child's classroom. That prerogative is the teacher's. Parents who attempt to tell a classroom teacher how to do his or her job will probably alienate their child's classroom teacher, who is their most important ally. Yet, we have seen that outside input, sometimes directly from a parent, may be required. This chapter contains ideas to assist you in your role as your child's advocate. It is cautioned, however, that development of a cooperative, open relationship with your child's teacher, as well as a certain amount of diplomacy, may be required before these ideas can be conveyed to him or her. I also caution that no amount of advocacy by parents can substitute for the expert instruction of a quality teacher. No plan yet devised is half as valuable as a good teacher.

GOAL OF EDUCATION

At its core, education's goal is to teach academic skills—that is, initially, to teach basic skills in reading, spelling, and mathematics, and, later, to teach more-advanced subjects such as science and social studies. Consumed with attempting to meet this daunting task, teachers cannot be expected to "cure" ADHD simultaneously. Even if that is their intent, no educational method for doing so exists. Thus, more modest education goals must be selected.

Just as the goal at home is to lessen the impact of ADHD and to encourage development of good habits, much the same is true at school. An ideal program for a student with ADHD is one that prevents his or her attentional or self-control problems from hindering his or her learning. That is, as is true for students in general, the student with ADHD should be viewed as benefiting most from school when he or she is able to acquire academic competencies. By understanding the nature of ADHD, educators can make modifications to help ensure that learning does occur and that academic competencies do develop.

EDUCATION TECHNIQUES

Securing the Child's Attention Before Giving Directions

The first step in learning is following directions, and the first step in following directions is attending to them. Students with ADHD, however, are apt to miss verbal directions because physically they are occupied with something else or their minds are wandering. The child who is absorbed in rolling a pencil repetitively off the desk or is daydreaming about after-school baseball games will miss directions. Thus, the child's work productivity will suffer, and the child's skill development will lag.

Thus, good teachers have learned the crucial first step of securing students' attention when working with students with ADHD. Many teachers request the class' attention, then pause until all eyes are on them. More than other students, of course, the child with ADHD may require special treatment. He or she may then require direct eye contact with the teacher before instructions are provided. For some children with ADHD, eye contact with the teacher may be required virtually continuously throughout the presentation of directions. Generally, teachers have found that eye contact is the best guarantee of focused attention.

Checking to Ensure Understanding

Students are even more likely to attend to verbal directions if the instructions are followed by an immediate check for understanding. A teacher's individual verification that the message was understood furnishes the student with a motive for paying attention (to look good and avoid embarrassment). The quick check also guarantees that key points are understood or that directions can be followed. Some teachers require students with ADHD to repeat directions, write the essential points out on paper, or highlight essential elements with a pen or pencil if directions are provided in writing.

Assigning Preferential Seating

Students seated close to the teacher have a better chance of making eye contact during the vital directions phase. This helps them attend and follow directions. They also work better under close teacher scrutiny. Off-task behavior is noticed and redirected most easily if the teacher is close at hand and has a direct line of vision to the student. Likewise, it is often easier for the teacher to notice and encourage on-task, productive behavior when the child is close by.

Reducing Classroom Distractions

Placement of a child with ADHD close to distractions such as a pencil sharpener, a window, or noisy classmates is unwise. The common-sense notion that novel stimuli or excessive noise distracts children with ADHD seems to be true. If your child's teacher has not already considered reducing classroom distractions, it may be a good idea to make such a recommendation. The best location, however, must be left to the teacher's discretion.

More radical attempts to control stimulation are generally not suggested. For instance, it was once advocated that classrooms be stripped of all potential distracting stimuli (e.g., colorful bulletin boards, windows, noisy tile flooring). It was hoped that by lowering the general distraction level, this stimulus reduction technique would aid children with ADHD. It was also suggested that some children be placed in three-sided study carrels or facing barren walls. These procedures have failed to be supported by empirical research, however.

Shortening Assignments and Providing Breaks

Children with ADHD can often complete short assignments but not long ones. Shortening assignments can help them.

As an example, the child who tires, drifts off-task, or quits a 20-minute spelling assignment may do adequately on a 10-minute assignment. Such a reduction is particularly wise if the child can actually master the skill with a briefer assignment.

In addition, repetitious work such as arithmetic computations or copying from a dictionary requires careful scrutiny. Because the impairments underlying ADHD may include lack of sustained effort when reward levels are low, presenting low-interest, low-stimulation tasks to a child with ADHD risks exaggerating his or her impairments. Tasks of this type not only reduce attention to task but also invite behavior problems and contribute to long-term discouragement. For many children, repeated practice is not necessary to master a skill. For students with ADHD, it makes sense to determine whether the assigned exercises are really necessary. Reducing assignment lengths or inserting breaks may be especially important when tedious and uninteresting work must be completed.

Making Assignments More Interesting and Stimulating

Like children without ADHD, many children with ADHD benefit from novel presentations and more stimulating subject matter instead of repetitive or tedious drills. For example, inserting colored type into the midst of a lengthy passage may help recapture a child's flagging attention. Switching type fonts, altering the shapes of objects to be counted, providing texture (e.g., sandpaper letters) or allowing the use of new or different writing tools midway through long assignments may help. These considerations seem to matter most on simple rote tasks.

Of course, identifying the child's unique interests and skills so that they can be capitalized on may help, especially on more complex tasks. For instance, a seventh-grade boy who quickly tires of percentage problems may work far longer if computing batting averages of a favorite baseball player (also a percentage problem). Alternatively, the child who shows minimal interest in a generic writing assignment may light up at the prospect of writing about a favorite subject such as space travel. High-interest reading material matched with the child's independent reading level may also encourage attention and foster the desire to learn.

Providing Reasonable Choices

Modifying the task somewhat by providing the student reasonable choices has been shown to work in some situations. For example, offering the student a menu of required tasks (e.g., spelling, worksheets, arithmetic problems) and allowing him or her to select or prioritize them may encourage a sense of control and independence. Research suggests that simple modifications such as these may encourage more time on task and greater effort; they may also diminish disruptive behavior. Some teachers not surprisingly find this suggestion objectionable because it transfers control to the student (which may be seen as reducing the teacher's authority). Also, it may be seen as offering special privileges to some students, thus raising the prospect of favoritism. Nonetheless, because it is easy to accomplish and takes little teacher effort, this approach may be worth considering.

Providing Computer-Assisted Instruction

Classroom computers are widely available and have been touted loudly as aides to instruction. Indeed, they are commonly cited as having advantages that may be especially well suited to teaching children with ADHD because they allow individualization of instructional content, pacing of presentations, high levels of visual and auditory stimulation, and prompt feedback about success or failure. Surprisingly, few studies have investigated their effectiveness for students with ADHD. Those that have have reported significant spurts in work completion in the short run. Their longer-term impact does not appear to have been studied yet. Depending on their availability, the teacher may wish to attempt to use them as instruction tools for children with ADHD. As with other techniques presented in this chapter, each technique should be attempted on a trial basis until it is clear that its use is effective.

Capitalizing on Strengths and Avoiding Weaknesses

Identifying and using a child's strengths to help him or her succeed while avoiding the child's weaknesses may aid motivation and attention. For instance, a child with ADHD who is plagued by fine motor problems but blessed with language strengths may require teaching modifications that take these facts into account. Failure to reduce written assignments for this child guarantees problems. Allowing the child to report his or her understanding of class material orally as opposed to in writing, however, can help enormously. These modifications are likely not only to make this child successful but also to enhance his or her self-image. As pointed out in Chapter 6, a psychoeducational evaluation may help pinpoint individual strengths and weaknesses, thus permitting intelligent education planning.

Providing Peer Tutoring

This notion involves one student assisting, instructing, or guiding and encouraging (e.g., through feedback) another student with his or her academic work. Activities might include joint reading involving turn taking, explanation or guidance during the completion of arithmetic problems, immediate feedback and reassurance about work accuracy and completion, and on-the-spot explanations when errors occur during learning. Some studies have suggested that these techniques have helped promote engagement with academic materials, better academic performance, and better social interaction. Sometimes entire classrooms work as teams; in other instances, only two students are involved. The former may require such drastic changes in classroom procedures that few teachers would be willing to attempt it. Teachers are much more apt to permit two students (one with ADHD) to work together, at least on a trial basis. To maximize the chances of this procedure working, teachers are encouraged to provide an overall plan, make expectations clear at the outset of each instruction period, and arrange guidance and encouragement for participating students. Merely assigning two students to work together without affording guidance and structure is unlikely to result in success.

CLASSROOM PROGRAMS FOR IMPROVING BEHAVIOR AND INCREASING PRODUCTIVITY

Positive Attention and Rewards

For the child who finds too few rewards inherent in completing work (e.g., the bored, disinterested student), external rewards can be added. The simplest and potentially most plentiful rewards are teacher praise and attention. When appropriate behavior (e.g., sitting with attention focused and working) is followed by attention and praise, this behavior may be strengthened. Teachers, owing mostly to their heavy work demands, often fail to notice and praise appropriate behavior promptly and frequently enough to produce much positive impact. To counteract this shortcoming, programs that encourage monitoring of a particular student's behavior and praising him or her, if warranted, are often suggested for children with ADHD. Some of the suggested plans are simple yet clever. For example, Russell A. Barkley and his colleagues suggested placing a large, smiling face adjacent to the classroom clock so that each time the teacher glances at the clock, he or she is reminded to check on the identified student. If on task, the child is praised; if off task, the child is ignored or reprimanded. The smiling face reminder may help ensure 15–20 daily chances for praise. Of course, timers with chimes or other devices can work just as well as visual reminders.

Incentive Programs and Token Economies

As valuable as attention and praise are, they often lack sufficient potency to promote ongoing motivation. Added incentives are frequently required. It is known that the addition of rewards can increase work productivity and improve behavior. These incentives might be special privileges, such as gaining more recess time or serving as line leader, or tangible rewards, such as baseball cards or stickers. The tangible rewards are often referred to as *backup reinforcers.*

In their simplest form, incentives may be dispensed for successful performance without a detailed, prearranged, or formal plan. A teacher might merely state, "If you complete all your worksheets this morning, then you can be line leader for recess." The teacher should build flexibility into these plans by considering work demands, the student's current behavior, and available rewards.

A token economy—a prearranged system of assigning points for acceptable behavior and trading those points for rewards—expands and formalizes this idea of positive consequences for successful behavior. Either academic performance or conduct can be targeted. Consider the program for a student who fails to complete work, as outlined in Figure 12.1. Points may be awarded simply for work completed or for work completed accurately. Thus, one point might be credited for each 10 mathematical problems finished, one point for a spelling worksheet, and two points for answering reading questions. The child's teacher would monitor work production closely and assign points promptly. Points could be exchanged at prescribed times, perhaps at 10:00 A.M., noon, and 2:30 P.M. A unique menu of rewards could be created for each child, or a common menu could be used for several students or even for an entire classroom.

Behavior problems may be treated, too. Consider the child who, impulsively and unsolicited, answers classroom questions. This child might be awarded points if he or she remains quiet for specified time intervals. One point might be awarded for each half-hour of control. Alternatively, the child might be awarded points for engaging in a behavior incompatible with shouting out answers. Under this plan, the child would be awarded three points each time the child raised his or her hand, waited, and was finally selected by the teacher to answer. Other procedures are discussed

Name: Sam
Date: 7-17-99

	Math	Spelling	Reading
1 pt. =	10 problems	1 worksheet	1 reading question
Points earned	~~1~~ ~~2~~ ~~3~~ 4 (3)	~~1~~ 2 3 4 (1)	~~1~~ ~~2~~ 3 4 (2)

This sheet is for the time interval between 8:00 and 10:00. Record points in bank, file this sheet, and begin new sheet at second time listed.

Figure 12.1. Token economy program, used as an incentive to the child to complete work. One point is earned for each 10 math problems, each spelling work sheet, and each reading question completed.

later in this chapter for reducing this type of unacceptable behavior.

Chapter 8 in this book emphasizes the need for structure when planning interventions for a child with ADHD. Simply put, *structure* in this case means that clearly stated expectations exist and that positive and negative consequences can be dispensed quickly based on the child's behavior. By their very nature, token economies guarantee structure. As an example, a basic set of classroom rules may be posted. These might include the following:

- Keep hands and feet to self
- Use inside voice
- Remain in seat
- Work on assigned material
- Raise hand to speak

For each interval (perhaps 15 minutes) during which these rules are followed, students are awarded points. Failure in any category, such as leaving one's seat, would result in withholding of points during that interval. Because expectations are outlined clearly, the teacher can supplement points. For example, verbal rewards can be used, such as, "Dan, I liked the way you raised your hand. Why don't you tell the class what your answer is." Little attention is required to correct inappropriate behaviors, and reprimands and redirections can occur clearly and easily: "Betsy, remember to follow rule number 2." This direction can be used to tell a student to modulate voice tone without dwelling on the specifics of the student's misbehavior or giving the student undue teacher attention.

Although token economies may appear simple, they can be complex. Among the demands of an effective program are selecting an appropriate reward menu, revising it periodically as interest for some items or privileges wanes, properly calibrating the price of menu items, providing sufficiently prompt and numerous trade-in times, and selecting reasonable target behaviors with fair point values. When an incentive or token program fails, or when initial success ceases (both of which are common), a careful revision of the plan can often put things back on track. Expert advice, such as from a special education teacher trained in behavior modification, a counselor, or a psychologist, may be required.

To review, token economies offer several advantages in working with the child with ADHD:

1. They can be targeted to either academic performance or classroom behavior.
2. By their nature, they guarantee structure.
3. They can be modified and revised to fit the changing needs, interests, or circumstances of the student.

Reprimands and Redirection

Most teachers and parents would prefer to rely on positive consequences. In an ideal world, praise and love would overcome all problems. Empirical research, however, has shown that reprimands and redirection (verbally instructing the child back to a task or indicating acceptable behavior to them) promote on-task behavior, productivity, and suitable classroom behavior. For many children, reprimands may actually be essential for school success. Thus, it would be wrong to expect your child's teacher to forgo reprimands or to use a program consisting only of positive attention and praise. Of course, some reprimands are better than others. Repeated or severe reprimands can demoralize students and damage their self-esteem. "Prudent" reprimands—those that are delivered in a calm, firm, consistent, and immediate manner—are advocated rather than those that are overly emotional, vague, or delayed. Besides having greater effectiveness in promoting desired behaviors, reprimands of this type are less likely to damage the child's self-esteem and hamper the child's motivation to succeed.

Response Cost

Response cost is a penalty technique involving loss of privileges, rewards, or tokens based on the occurrence of unacceptable behavior. Response cost can be used as an aspect of a token economy program (previously discussed) or as a separate procedure, such as when an expected privilege is revoked because of misbehavior. Often children with ADHD require immediate negative consequences to deter inappropriate behavior or to help stop it once it has occurred. Thus, penalty techniques such as response cost and time-out (discussed next) may be vital. These techniques can help the student with ADHD inhibit inappropriate responding, such as shouting out or hitting.

It is easy to incorporate response cost into a token economy. Points may be accumulated for work productivity and acceptable behavior but lost whenever unacceptable behavior occurs, such as hitting a peer or leaving one's seat. To promote fairness and avoid arbitrary penalties, unacceptable behavior and its penalty value are often spelled out in advance.

Michael Gordon, a psychologist at the State University of New York at Syracuse, devised a variant of the traditional response cost technique incorporating electronic sophistication. Called the *Attention Trainer,* Gordon's device is a small plastic apparatus that sits on the student's desk and credits a point each minute, presuming that the student is on task, working, and following class rules. The student can glance at the device's face easily to determine his or her point total. The teacher, however, is equipped with a portable transmitter capable of subtracting from the child's total from a distance. Points are subtracted for rule violations, just as they would be when other response costs procedures are used. The Attention Trainer's precision, its portability, and its convenient system of point tabulation have made it popular in trials with teachers. Research studies also have shown it to be effective.

Response costs can also be used without a formal token economy. This is especially helpful for the child with ADHD who remains in a general classroom. For example, a particularly loud and disruptive student might be given a deck of coupons at the start of each school day. Each coupon might signify a privilege, such as recess, free time to interact with a classmate, access to a preferred location in the classroom, and so forth. The student would retain each coupon and would exchange it for the indicated privilege unless a rule violation occurred. Each violation would result in the teacher confiscating one coupon. The fact that penalties follow immediately upon the occurrence of misbehavior and the conspicuousness of the loss (i.e., the student sees the confiscation) often makes the response cost technique effective for students with ADHD.

Time-Out

Chapter 8 discusses time-out as a control strategy for home use. As discussed, time-out can be an especially successful strategy for children with ADHD, but only under certain circumstances. Unfortunately, those circumstances, which include a pleasing environment from which the child can be excluded so that a negative consequence is experienced, are rarer at school than at home. At home, most children find it unpleasant to be sent out of the family room or away from the family's center of action. Being isolated from the interactions and activities of the family is unpleasant. Many students, however, enjoy being sent from their classroom to an isolation area. Rather than being a negative consequence, isolation may thus actually be experienced as a reward! Practical problems exist as well. An isolation area may not be available, and many children with ADHD refuse to go willingly. In addition, the classroom may be disrupted if time-out is used under the wrong circumstances, because some children may struggle or have a tantrum, especially when the procedure is first used.

Still, there are times when traditional time-out can be used. A special classroom setting may include its own isolation room to be used for time-out. An isolated area, however, which is a less-restrictive option than an isolation room, can often be adapted to a special class setting as well. If the teacher makes class instruction interesting enough, and particularly if attention is plentiful or rewards are possible (e.g., a token economy), traditional time-out can work well.

Variations on traditional time-out may be easier to implement. For example, a teacher may set up a classroom so that students can be awarded points on an ongoing basis, perhaps every 10 minutes. With frequent rewards possible, the teacher can handle misbehavior by imposing a nonexclusionary time-out. A misbehaving student may have his point card turned down, denoting that he or she is briefly ineligible to receive rewards. After a short interval during which rewards are withheld, the card can be turned up, indicating renewed eligibility for rewards. Another alternative to exclusionary time-out involves a clock whose accumulated time is exchangeable for points and rewards. The clock is simply stopped for brief intervals when a specified misbehavior occurs. Besides ease of implementation, these nonexclusionary time-out procedures may be less damaging to the child's self-esteem and less demoralizing than the exclusionary options. Teachers who understand the time-out principle can devise similar programs.

Home–School Incentive Programs

Sometimes parents must assist classroom teachers with a home–school incentive program to help their children become productive and learn to control their behavior. Although the interval between behavior at school and consequences at home is necessarily long (sometimes 8 or 10 hours), home–school incentive plans can be powerful nonetheless. Fortunately, a reward of video games at home or the chance to do a favorite activity with parents may motivate work completion and good behavior in ways that a school program cannot. Figure 12.2 is an example of a daily report card that is used to convey school performance to a child's parents. A reward menu at home can also be included. Most often, parents sign the form each day so that their child can transport it back to the teacher.

Besides providing motivation, home–school programs keep parents informed. They may also help promote a closer parent–teacher alliance. Shortcomings in the student's education program sometimes are exposed by this type of arrangement. It is easy to see that things are going poorly at school if each day's report indicates unacceptable behavior and/or poor work completion by the child. Obviously, changes can be made more easily when parents and teachers work together. Even schools that are reluctant to provide special services or modify classroom assignments may consent to using home–school incentive plans. For some students with ADHD, a home–school program may be the only adjustments that the school will endorse.

School Suspension

You may be one of the unfortunate parents threatened with suspension of your child. The logic here is self-evident. The child who violates rules too often or too grievously is sent home as a punishment. Beyond the intent of penalizing the

Daily Report Card

Name: Ken

Date: 10-17-99

Following school rules

Good Job | Okay | Try Harder Next Time

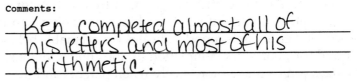

Getting work done

Good Job | Okay | Try Harder Next Time

Comments:

Ken completed almost all of his letters and most of his arithmetic.

Figure 12.2. Daily report card to motivate the child and inform parents of their child's performance.

child, the procedure may be designed to heighten parents' awareness and enlist their cooperation. An unspoken assumption seems to be that if the parents are involved, they are more likely to exert pressure on their child to behave.

Although effective for some students, suspensions fail for many children with ADHD because many children have already been penalized so frequently that a single big penalty has little impact on them. After all, how can one consequence be expected to curtail a variety of potential bad behaviors over the course of an entire school day? Even big penalties such as suspensions may be futile because of the notorious inability of children with ADHD to anticipate consequences. Moreover, there are concerns that this type of exclusion may violate the rights of students with disabilities. The Individuals with Disabilities Education Act (IDEA) Amendments of 1997, which apply to students with documented special education eligibility, provide guidelines for determining whether the behavior prompting suspension was related to the student's disabling condition. Steps to preserve the student's rights may then be required. If school personnel suggest suspension, it is generally wise to try a more thoughtful program involving rewards and response cost or time-out before reverting to the more drastic option.

REVISING EXPECTATIONS TO INCREASE MOTIVATION

Judicious Assignment of Grades

Grades are assigned to inform parents and to motivate students. For the child with ADHD, these purposes may need to be reviewed carefully and grades may need to be adjusted correspondingly. If your child is affected with ADHD of a sufficient magnitude to cause school problems, then you need to have frequent communication with his or her classroom teacher. Daily or weekly reports about level of performance, work productivity and effort, and conduct or deportment are probably required. Because you are already being informed about your child's status in such circumstances, you should expect to find little new from a report card. A report card designed for a student without school problems may be valueless to you. Thus, there is no pressing need for teachers to use low grades to tell you that your child is having trouble, because you already know it.

High grades can motivate achieving students to keep up the good work or spur them toward even greater performance. Low grades can motivate a few students to do better. Unfortunately, too often, students with ADHD receive a report card filled with low grades and indications of "needs improvement" in areas such as effort, cooperation, or following rules. For a student with ADHD, low grades probably do little good. On the contrary, they can do considerable harm to the student's self-esteem and can further erode the student's already depleted level of motivation. The second purpose of grades—to motivate the student—is thus also hard to accomplish for the student with ADHD.

Consequently, teachers should be encouraged to view the grading system flexibly. Each student's unique circumstances and capabilities need to be considered when marks are assigned. Even when grade values are not altered to reflect unique circumstances, teachers and parents may do well to emphasize the student's daily performance—for example, points earned or work completed—rather than dwell on semester report card marks. A report card filled with low marks should generally be avoided.

Expectations for Homework

Homework represents a special pitfall for children with ADHD. Put yourself in your child's position by imagining that you are assigned to do a job at your place of employment that is very difficult for you to do. Try as you may, you can seldom finish the assigned tasks, despite putting in a full work day. Your boss is frequently on your case. Because you have failed to complete your assigned tasks by day's end, you are told you must take your work home to complete it there. How might you feel about your "homework" assignment? Recall, too, that you are an adult, with all the perspective and understanding that only maturity can bring; assume that you possess adult self-control. Most adults in such circumstances, if they were honest with themselves, would admit to approaching their homework with little enthusiasm.

With this perspective in mind, you should encourage your child's teacher to keep homework assignments within reasonable bounds. For some students, setting time limits helps. For example, parents of elementary school children with ADHD may confine each evening's work time to 30 minutes; parents of high school students with ADHD may confine each evening's work time to 60 minutes. If children are unable to complete the necessary material within these time limits, then the length of assignments, their composition, or the student's work productivity in class probably should be checked. Only when all other attempts to improve in-class productivity have been tried and have failed should more homework time be added.

Sometimes overdependence on homework develops. Understandably, this can happen because parents can provide the individual attention and direction lacking in a large classroom. Finding that it is easier to slough off the work at school because help awaits them at home, students with ADHD may complete less and less work in class. The student's parents and teacher must step in if this occurs, often by limiting the amount of work completed at home. The interventions discussed earlier in this chapter probably are needed at these times as well.

Of course, all of the advice that parents hear about homework in general also applies to homework and the student with ADHD. Selecting a quiet environment, a consistent time, and providing encouragement may well boost the student's work completion. Arranging privileges as rewards to be dispensed immediately after the work is completed may help as well. Of course, just as absolute dos and don'ts about homework make no sense for children without ADHD, absolutes have no role for children with ADHD. Each child is an individual, and individual judgment and flexibility are required.

ENSURING CLASSROOM SUPPORT

Selecting an Effective Elementary School Teacher

The patient, encouraging teacher who is filled with energy and willing to accommodate individuals' needs is generally the best choice for your child. Sometimes a general education teacher who possesses these qualities plus coincident training in special education is available. Such an individual should be considered carefully. If your child is in a special education classroom environment, teachers with training in either behavior management or behavior problems or both may be preferred. You may want to ask about the teacher's experience with children with ADHD. Of course, your choice of which teacher is assigned your child in the public schools is probably limited or even nonexistent. Nonetheless, the quality of teaching is so important that you are encouraged to explore the possibilities of selecting a teacher. Alternatives to public school are discussed in Chapter 11. Occasionally, going outside the public education system to secure an exceptional teacher is justified.

Extra Guidance During Transition to Junior High School

For many children, the transition to junior high school is especially difficult. The introduction to departmentalized instruction (i.e., one instructor for English, another for mathematics) presents the most severe challenge. Each teacher may expect something slightly different in terms of work completion, in-class behavior, and homework. In addition to these varying expectations, teachers may not communicate with each other. As a result, homework demands may vary widely, with some evenings being free of assignments and other evenings carrying heavy demands. Organization, such as keeping track of assignments and work materials and budgeting of time, become paramount. Unfortunately, the child with ADHD is apt to be particularly lacking in these skills.

The antidote to the inconsistency of expectations and variable work demands that begin during junior high school (or occasionally earlier) is to find someone capable of adding organization, consistency, and structure to your child's day. Usually, this person is located at the school (as opposed to a parent or a private tutor at the student's home) and is often a school staff member with primary instructional responsibility. For example, a resource teacher may be a liaison to each of the classroom teachers, thereby ensuring that the student is recording work to be completed, consistently taking textbooks home, returning completed assignments, preparing for tests, and generally keeping his or her head above water academically. In some environments, guidance counselors have established methods and procedures to help accomplish these tasks. Among the devices are forms for recording assignments and weekly feedback to parents and guidelines for homework completion. Even for the child who has succeeded in elementary school, this type of support may be necessary. If your child has been identified as having ADHD, you are encouraged to monitor his or her progress closely during the transition from self-contained elementary instruction to departmentalized junior high school instruction.

CONCLUSIONS

In summary, the following techniques have been suggested for use with some children with ADHD:

1. The teacher should establish and maintain eye contact with the child while giving directions to help the child attend to and follow directions.
2. Once directions have been given, the teacher should check with the child to ensure that he or she has understood the directions.
3. Noise and other stimuli can distract the child with ADHD; teachers should avoid seating the child near classroom distractions.
4. Reduce assignment lengths or insert breaks when repetitious or tedious work must be completed, especially if the child can master the skill with a briefer assignment.
5. Concentrate on novel presentations and stimulating subject matter as much as possible.

6. Consider providing the student with reasonable choices about which activities he or she will complete and the order in which they will be completed.
7. Use a classroom computer to enhance work completion and rate of learning.
8. To aid motivation, identify and use a child's strengths while avoiding his or her weaknesses.
9. Use a peer tutor to increase work completion and learning of material.
10. Use programs to monitor a student's behavior, incorporating praise as warranted. Use a system of rewards and incentives to increase work productivity and improve behavior.
11. Use verbal reprimands and redirection to promote on-task behavior, productivity, and suitable classroom behavior. Avoid severe reprimands.
12. Develop a penalty technique involving loss of privileges, rewards, or tokens based on the occurrence of unacceptable behavior, if warranted.
13. Use time-out for children with ADHD but perhaps not in a classroom environment. Modifications of traditional time-out by withholding eligibility for rewards (e.g., a token economy) may be required.
14. Employ a home–school incentive program based on a daily report card to assist classroom teachers in helping children become more productive and learn to control their behavior.
15. Because suspensions fail to influence many children with ADHD, request school personnel to try alternative behavior management techniques first.
16. To help increase motivation, encourage teachers to view the grading system flexibly and consider each student's unique circumstances and capabilities.

17. Work with teachers to improve in-class productivity and to keep homework assignments within reasonable bounds.
18. Explore the possibility of selecting teachers with training in behavior management or behavior problems.
19. Monitor the progress of your child during transition from self-contained elementary instruction to departmentalized junior high instruction, and, if necessary, find someone capable of adding organization, consistency, and structure to your child's day.

You may best champion your child's education if you are aware of some of the special classroom techniques that children with ADHD often require. This chapter enumerates some of those techniques. Developing a working alliance with your child's teacher(s) is essential, however, if any of the plans herein discussed are to receive their fullest and most effective implementation.

Chapter 13

Counseling, Biofeedback, and Other Interventions

ADHD Myths

Most children with ADHD require individual counseling or psychotherapy.

Little can be done about the social problems that many children with ADHD experience.

The more structure present at home, the better.

Specially designed school services, behavior management at home, and medication are the most typically used and most widely accepted interventions for ADHD. This chapter, however, discusses other approaches that exist as well.

PROFESSIONAL COUNSELING AND PSYCHOTHERAPY

Individual Therapy

It is unreasonable to expect that a series of sessions of psychotherapy (i.e., a psychologist or a therapist meeting alone with a child in an office) can "cure" all of your child's ADHD symptoms. As discussed in Chapter 2, the symptoms of ADHD are caused by malfunctions in the central nervous system. They are not caused by internal conflicts, misdirected motives, lack of self-worth, or similar issues that individual therapy addresses.

Simply because individual therapy may fail to "cure" ADHD does not mean that it is valueless, however. Children and teens with ADHD experience the same self-doubts, conflicts, worries, and confusion as anyone else. In fact, they probably experience these emotions more frequently and more harshly than their peers without ADHD because of their histories of failure and because they sense their lack of self-control. Just as individual therapy helps children and teenagers without ADHD when they are experiencing problems, it can also help those with ADHD. When a child is in need of a caring, supportive, or understanding person, a therapist may be extremely helpful. Because of their training and interest in helping, therapists may offer help that is unavailable elsewhere.

Individual therapy may aid specific problems, too. A teenager who is frustrated by recurring peer rejection may gain perspective and learn alternative strategies for interacting with peers. So, too, may a child whose repeated misbehavior has led to feelings of rejection from parents and siblings. Even though therapy is incapable of preventing the child's misbehavior, it may deter further damage to the child's self-esteem if the child understands the causes of the misbehavior and can put others' responses to him or her in their proper light.

Family Therapy

Not surprisingly, family discord often results from the stresses of living with a child with ADHD. Parents may accuse each other of mishandling their child's behavior or of actually promoting problem behavior. They may differ about how to handle discipline. Conflicts about roles may arise. One or both parents may develop an overly close or overly distant relationship with the affected child.

Siblings are likely to be affected, too. Sometimes deeply held feelings of resentment are present among brothers and sisters whose needs have been overlooked in the family's effort to help the most difficult child. Occasionally, these children themselves begin to misbehave as a way to seek attention. This is especially likely when the behavior of the more-difficult-to-manage sibling begins to improve through treatment. A therapeutic approach that works with the entire family may be beneficial at these times.

Cognitive Behavior Therapy

Like the behavioral training for parents discussed in Chapter 8, cognitive behavior therapy can be provided by an individual therapist (and sometimes in group settings, too). Often a psychologist provides the services. Although behavior modification principles are used in both approaches, there are important differences. Cognitive behavior therapy involves working directly with the child or the teenager rather than with a parent or a teacher. The approach attempts to train the child to exercise better self-control or to respond reflectively as opposed to impulsively.

Activities involve changing the cognitions (i.e., thinking) that underlie unacceptable behavior—hence the term *cognitive behavior therapy.* For example, children may be taught the skill of self-monitoring by being provided with feedback about their behavior and then by learning to rate their own behavior accurately. Over time in such a program, rewards are dispensed based on how accurately the child learns to evaluate his or her own behavior. The notion is that children with ADHD fail to monitor their own behavior closely enough, and, when this happens, they are apt to behave in a poorly controlled fashion. If, they were taught to self-appraise and self-monitor better, so the reasoning goes, they would behave better. Thus, impulsive, poorly planned behavior may give way to more-reflective and better-planned behavior.

Children usually participate in a series of training or therapy sessions, perhaps 10–20. The programs are often sequential and may be quite detailed. Training usually moves from simple to complex skills. Some programs teach detailed problem-solving skills in which children are taught to identify problems, plan a strategy, define a solution, and then rate themselves on how effectively the solution worked. As training proceeds, children are taught the necessary steps to solve problems. Early in training, the therapist may guide the child through problem solving with verbal directions. Later, the child is encouraged to guide his or her own behavior with verbal directions spoken aloud. Still later, the child learns to employ internal or "cognitive" directions to lead him- or herself toward engaging in acceptable actions. Throughout training, the therapist uses behavioral principles such as the child's rewarding mastery of the training steps.

Some children appear to learn to slow themselves and exercise better problem-solving skills when using this approach. Yet, proof of the technique's effectiveness is generally lacking. Even when successful training occurs, questions remain about whether the child retains these skills after training stops (i.e., in the months and years to come) or generalizes them to other settings (i.e., on the playground or with friends rather than just in the therapist's office). Skills would appear to be retained and generalized best when parents and teachers are aware of training and are capable of rewarding children when real-world applications are made. Although cognitive behavior therapy is a potential adjunct to traditional treatment such as medication and parent training, it cannot be regarded as a principal treatment for ADHD. Again, there is no evidence that it can "cure" ADHD.

Group Therapy to Teach Social Skills

Many children with ADHD have problems getting along with others their age. It is hardly surprising that the high activity, talkativeness, social intrusiveness, and poor frustration tolerance that characterize many children with ADHD alienates peers. Despite good intentions, many children with ADHD find that they have few consistently functioning friendships. It is unfortunate that, because of impulse and judgment problems, a child with ADHD is likely to be without enduring friendships.

Treatment may help, but many affected children remain isolated even after being treated properly with medicine, special school services, or behavior management at home. Most of these children are not incapable of learning to get along better; they simply find these skills hard to learn. Often a direct teaching approach such as social skills teaching helps.

Using a social skills teaching approach, groups of same-age and same-sex children can function as a laboratory to teach social skills that most children learn naturally—that is, without any particular help. Trained therapists or psychologists can move children through a training curriculum that teaches, step-by-step, how to get along with their age-peers. Unacceptable behaviors can be isolated and reduced by direct feedback. For instance, behavior such as bragging, bossing, belittling peers, and dominating conversations can be addressed directly in the group setting. Candid feedback and negative consequences (e.g., response cost as discussed in Chapter 8) can be dispensed by impartial professionals with an effectiveness unattainable by family members. Feedback from peers themselves can also help. More important, skills that are essential for acquiring and maintaining friendships can be encouraged in a group setting by using rewards, modeling, role-playing, and practice over a period of weeks.

Among the important skills that can be addressed in this fashion are initiating a conversation, sustaining a conversation without dominating, selecting a suitable topic, complimenting peers, taking turns, giving and accepting feedback, and handling teasing and disappointment.

Most social skills development programs are practical and no-nonsense. Group members work together with therapists to develop a list of dos and don'ts. These are tried in contrived role-playing situations within the group and then are tried outside the group. To maximize effectiveness, parents and teachers should be informed of the particular skills being developed and encouraged to reward or prompt skill usage outside the group. Homework assignments and monitoring of skill usage in the real world may be part of the program, too.

Most social skills groups meet for a minimum of 10–15 sessions, usually weekly. Because these skills are expected to develop in relatively slow increments, many children participate in such groups on an ongoing basis. Others are exposed to the basic curriculum only. For the former youngsters, the group may not only help them develop new skills but also offer support, a chance for acceptance, and fraternity. In some multidisciplinary practices that include physicians, social skills groups provide an added advantage in that the therapist is allowed to observe, firsthand, a medication's effectiveness and can make precise reports of the child's behavior to the prescribing physician.

BIOFEEDBACK

Biofeedback refers to a variety of techniques used to teach individuals to control their bodies through the use of feedback. For example, headache patients with extreme tension in the frontalis muscles of the forehead often benefit by learning to relax those muscles. A laboratory apparatus that measures changes in tension can be integrated with a feedback mechanism, such as a light or a tone, so that muscle-tension changes in the desired direction can be signaled to the patient. Over time, individuals can learn to relax their muscles in progressive degrees.

As suggested in Chapter 2, some researchers (e.g., Joel Lubar and colleagues at the University of Tennessee in Knoxville) have speculated that ADHD is associated with underarousal in the brain. Although motorically overactive, individuals with ADHD may lack sufficient nervous system arousal to attend well or to control their impulses. Citing studies accumulated over a period of more than 15 years, Lubar and colleagues presented information suggesting that the underarousal suspected in individuals with ADHD is evident on an electroencephalogram (or "EEG," a graphic record produced by an electroencephalograph, which measures the electrical activity of the brain). More important, it is presumed the underarousal actually causes ADHD symptoms. If more typical arousal levels could be accomplished, it was argued, then ADHD symptoms ought to be diminished or eliminated.

Given this information, some researchers have suggested that biofeedback may play a significant role in treating ADHD. They contend that by using sophisticated EEG devices, patterns of electrical activity can be altered to produce enhanced arousal. For example, individuals may be connected to an EEG device through leads attached at the scalp so that some aspects of the brain's electrical activity can be measured. The individual looks at a computer screen that provides feedback. As waves reflecting higher levels of arousal appear, the computer screen provides an encouraging signal, such as a circle that grows in size, to the individual. Gradually, individuals, including children, reportedly learn to increase the amount of desired brain waves and correspondingly decrease undesirable waves.

Case studies collected over several years, and controlled studies as well, suggest that as EEG changes occur, ADHD symptoms abate. There are also reports of improved academic status, presumably due to the individuals' newly acquired capability to arouse attention and sustain concentration.

Although in relatively narrow use at the time of this writing, the use of EEG biofeedback to treat ADHD is being promoted as a nonpharmacologic (i.e., medicine-free) approach to treating ADHD. Dr. Lubar's writings seem to imply that for some children, a combination of medication and biofeedback may be required, at least at the outset of biofeedback training. It is also noteworthy that the training advocated is quite lengthy, requiring 40–80 sessions spread over several months. The application of this treatment requires considerable time and funding.

How effective this type of biofeedback proves to be in treating ADHD in the long run seems to remain unclear. The professional community will no doubt continue to watch for additional empirical studies or for wider distribution of the studies already conducted.

MARTIAL ARTS TRAINING

Martial arts, such as karate, judo, or tai chi, have been advocated by some as a means of helping children with ADHD. The rationale here seems to be that children benefit by learning to respond to clear expectations (e.g., those that occur during training) and that the self-discipline required to complete training may profit children with ADHD. It is believed by some that by learning to concentrate their attention, follow directions, and exercise restraint, children can learn skills that are potentially generalizable outside of training. If this supposition has been borne out by research, that research is not widely known.

If beneficial at all, it is more likely that martial arts training aids the child or teenager with ADHD in other ways. Perhaps participation in an organized training sequence that builds skills may lead to increased self-confidence—particularly for boys, who are apt to ascribe self-worth to their physical competence and their ability to "take care of themselves." Other advantages may result from the very act of channeling physical activity or by promoting contact with and possibly acceptance from peers with whom such training is done.

Although martial arts training may be worthwhile, uncontrolled rough play such as emulating martial arts heroes in the movies may be harmful. Children with ADHD seem especially prone to act out the roles of heroes (or villains) with martial arts expertise that they have watched in movies or on television. Thus, young boys may insist on demonstrating high kicks or karate chops that they have seen in the movies when friends come to visit. This type of behavior is prone to degenerate into fights and hurt feelings. Children with ADHD are likely to overdo such rough play and alienate peers. It is generally wise to quickly discourage this type of behavior and to avoid allowing children with preexisting tendencies toward rough play and underregulation of impulses to watch excessively violent movies or television shows.

MATCHING EXPECTATIONS TO CAPABILITIES

Admittedly, matching expectations to capabilities is a general notion rather than a specific treatment, but the idea is so important to your child's long-term adjustment and happiness that it merits mention. This book stresses repeatedly that children with ADHD have characteristic, constitutional differences that distinguish them from other children and that these differences are usually longstanding and resistant to easy change. No one knows your child better than you do; you have the best vantage point from which to discern your child's temperament. Study your child. You will know how long and under what circumstances your child can maintain attention, what frustrates or discourages him or her, what precipitates conflict with peers or siblings, and when impulsivity is likely to result in problem behavior. At the same time, you can recognize your child's strengths and those instances in which success is most probable.

This information is essential because it provides a basis for guiding your child toward success and away from failure. Many children with ADHD become demoralized because they fail repeatedly. To the extent that repeated failure can be avoided, your child is likely to feel happier and more successful. Some situations are so destined to produce failure that they should be avoided. Still, well-intentioned parents often expect their child with ADHD to attend a church service, sit quietly with absolutely no diversions during a long car ride, exercise self-control in a room filled with rambunctious children (e.g., at a poorly structured outing), or play a frustrating video game without temper outbursts. If these situations are a sure bet for failure, consider avoiding them altogether. If the situation is unavoidable, try simplifying the task or adding structure to the activity (see Chapter 8).

If your child does participate (total avoidance of frustration wouldn't be acceptable anyway), then don't be surprised if failure, discouragement, and anger ensue. Try to avoid your own overreaction to these occurrences. To place a child with ADHD in a difficult situation without revising expectations for focused and well-controlled behavior would be terribly unfair. Learn to match your expectations with your child's capabilities. He or she is not equally as capable as siblings or friends in all situations; learn to protect your child from pointless frustration.

At the same time, recognize your child's talents and find ways that he or she can use them. The failure-plagued child often has a crucial need for success. Thus, parents can help the sports-minded child feel good about his or her ability by signing up the child to play in a local soccer or baseball league. Indeed, trips to the ballpark may afford chances for your child to exhibit knowledge about baseball facts. Alternatively, a baseball card collection may give your child a sense of pride in being able to marshal substantial amounts of information as well as or better than peers, at least in some situations. Similarly, the child who loves animals and is good with them may benefit from assisting in a veterinarian's office or volunteering at an animal shelter. Activities such as these that do not require intensive focusing of attention or capability to inhibit impulses enhance success as they promote feelings of self-worth.

PROVIDING A PREDICTABLE HOME ROUTINE

Perhaps the suggestion given most often to parents of children with ADHD is to make their children's schedules predictable. To the extent possible, children with ADHD should arise, eat, complete chores, tackle homework, recreate, and sleep at regular times and places. The reasoning behind this is obvious. The external structure provided by a rote system means that fewer demands are placed on the child's impairments in coping skills. Regular expectations successfully met can turn into good habits. This general recommendation makes sense, especially if parents avoid going overboard and resist the temptation to become too rigid. A generally understood routine is probably even more helpful if coupled with frequent, parent-imposed structure in the form of clear directions and immediate consequences (as discussed in Chapter 8).

AVOIDING OVERDOING HOME TREATMENT

For the minority of parents who tend to overdo their youngsters' treatment, it is important to emphasize that although structure and routine are generally wise, when taken to extremes, they can become counterproductive. No child tolerates a schedule in which there is no room for spontaneity. Few children can remain resentment-free in the face of unrelenting parental suggestions to "slow down" and "think over your options and then make a plan." The extremely overcoached child may come to view him- or herself as incapable of independent action or as peculiar and different from his or her peers. Sometimes the ADHD is so highlighted that it becomes the parents'—at times, even the entire family's—central concern. For the child with ADHD in such circumstances, home ceases to be a home and becomes a 24-hour treatment center.

Children with ADHD are first and foremost children and are likely to manifest all the unique interests, talents, hopes, and frustrations of other children. Parents need to strike a balance between concern and assistance on the one hand and tolerance and perspective on the other. Many parents do this wonderfully. All parents are encouraged to examine their own outlook and, if need be, back off a little and relax.

CONCLUSIONS

Devising a comprehensive intervention plan for your child is accomplished best by working with a professional who is knowledgeable about ADHD. Aside from considering the most conventional interventions—medication, training in behavior management for parents, and educational modifications—your child's professional (e.g., psychologist, pediatrician, psychiatrist) can help determine which, if any, additional services may be worthwhile. For some children, individual or family counseling, cognitive behavior therapy, or social skills training may be advisable. Less frequently, martial arts training or biofeedback may be suggested. A professional who knows your child and family can also help establish suitable expectations and determine ways to maximize your child's successes.

Chapter 14

Case Examples in Treatment

ADHD Myths

All children with ADHD benefit from the same types of services.

Several different types of treatment are rarely required for children with ADHD.

Chapters 8–13 outline a variety of potentially helpful methods for treating children with ADHD. One or several of these suggestions may be applied with any particular youngster. The following case studies may help you appreciate the specifics regarding how children with ADHD can be assisted.

HUGH: ADHD AND SPECIAL SCHOOL SERVICES

Hugh's family met with the school psychologist for the first time when Hugh was 6 years old and already manifesting significant behavior problems. His mother and stepfather were unsure why he was so hard to discipline at home. They were hardly surprised that his behavior was equally troublesome at school, but they remained baffled about the cause of his problems. They had heard of ADHD but doubted that Hugh had such a disorder.

Although Hugh was strong-willed and active at home, his behavior was worse at school. He seldom sat for an activity, laughed wildly at minor provocations of his classmates, and sometimes stubbornly refused his teacher's requests. As his first-grade year proceeded and he found himself in trouble more frequently, his behavior worsened. By the end of October, he was often sent to the time-out square (see Chapter 12), yet he frequently refused to go. When prompted by his teacher, he became angry and had to be escorted to the principal's office. This sequence occurred twice, then Hugh was suspended from school for 3 days.

The relationship between Hugh and his teacher and that between Hugh and his classmates suffered. He was shunned or teased on the playground. A common insult that one of his classmates might hurl at another was, "You're acting just like Hugh!" His teacher's patience had also worn thin. Although she recognized her anger and its source ("It's unfair to 25 other students when 1 takes so much time"), she felt powerless to refrain from snapping at Hugh. She ultimately came to dread his morning arrival.

Some school officials were convinced that Hugh's behavior was entirely willful and purposely defiant. Despite the failure of a simple point system for in-class cooperation (happy face for a good day, frowning face for a bad day with accompanying loss of privileges at home) and the use of suspension for disruption, Hugh's teacher and principal rejected the idea that he had an emotional or behavior problem. Although sympathetic, the school psychologist believed that the door for special services through a learning disabilities designation was closed. When she administered screening tests to Hugh, he read, spelled, and computed arithmetic problems about as well as other first graders.

The school psychologist asked for a consultation from a child psychologist in private practice and also sought guidance from the state department of education. The psychologist quickly noted that Hugh's in-office behavior and history were compatible with ADHD. The diagnosis was soon confirmed by a variety of parent- and teacher-completed rating forms. Although the start of therapy with the psychologist and the use of behavior management techniques at home resulted in some improvement, Hugh's school behavior remained unacceptable. Increasingly frustrated, school officials again threatened Hugh with school suspension unless his defiance and disruption stopped.

At this time, the school psychologist was encouraged to conduct a more detailed evaluation. Hugh's pediatrician was also consulted to rule out any physical problems. The school psychologist's evaluation found Hugh to be a bright child and free of any memory, perceptual, or fine motor impairments that would hinder learning. His academic skills were found to be solidly average. Personality testing, interviews, and rating forms showed no obvious problems with depression, anxiety, or disturbed thinking. Problems with attention, impulse control, cooperation, and interpersonal relationships were documented, however.

Because of Hugh's uninhibited, underregulated, and inattentive behavior and his conduct problems, perhaps resulting from impaired anticipation of consequences, Hugh obviously required altered educational services. First, Hugh's parents and local public school personnel advocated reduction of assignment length, a reward system that provided feedback for success every 5 minutes, and an immediate consequence of time-out in an isolated classroom corner (followed by more-stringent isolation if required). To implement this plan, additional personnel in Hugh's classroom (e.g., a teacher's aide), and a staff member to monitor the plan's effectiveness (e.g., school psychologist, counselor, special education teacher) would be required. The option of placing Hugh in a self-contained class composed of 10 students, a teacher, and a teacher's aide, and operating on a strict reward system was held in abeyance in case the less-restrictive approach failed. Unfortunately, school personnel—and most adamantly the school principal—contended that there was no basis for providing Hugh with these special services. He was said to be ineligible for special education, and his teacher was said to be unable to check his behavior every 5 minutes or to dispense rewards and punishment without assistance.

The team concluded in an oral summary to his parents that Hugh was not eligible for serious emotional disturbance designation either. They argued that his problems resulted from his intentional defiance of authority. A dissenting opinion, offered by the school psychologist, was that although Hugh chose his actions and must be held accountable for them, he nonetheless was operating at a disadvantage compared with his classmates. Among these were severe problems with sitting and remaining on task during seatwork and impaired ability to inhibit his impulses or weigh the consequences of his behavior. Although it was grudgingly agreed that Hugh indeed had ADHD and that this disorder was affecting him in school, the team believed that they were left with no options for providing him with the individualized services he required.

Assistance came from the state department of education, however, when experts from the department encouraged the team to think more broadly regarding Hugh's options. After recognizing that Hugh's behavior was affecting him in school, the school team considered two possible ways to acquire services. The first was to designate him as a seriously emotionally disturbed student (see Chapter 10). The team focused on one emotional characteristic from the federal definition that permits identification if there exists "an inability to build or maintain satisfactory relationships with peers and teachers." The team unanimously agreed that this was true of Hugh. In fact, they concurred that his interpersonal status was deteriorating daily. Clearly, Hugh's ADHD symptoms were having a severe impact on his interpersonal relationships. An additional element of the criteria for receiving services as a student with serious emotional disturbance calls for the emotional problem to "adversely affect educational performance." In Hugh's case, there was little doubt that his performance was suffering. In fact, his emotional problem was so significant that he was excluded from class (i.e., sent home or to the principal's office) for extended time periods.

A second option for securing services was to suggest that Hugh's disorder (ADHD) was exerting a significant negative impact on an important aspect of his life (i.e., school learning) and to seek protection under Section 504 of the Rehabilitation Act of 1973 (see Chapter 10). As such, Hugh's ADHD and associated failure meant that Hugh was being discriminated against when he was excluded from school. The necessary steps to rectify this discrimination were to implement the plan mentioned earlier. To do so, the school could either use an already-available special education aide or provide an additional (non–special education) aide in Hugh's classroom. Because this approach resulted in less-obvious labeling, it was preferred by Hugh's parents and by some school officials.

Ultimately, Hugh was provided services as a student with serious emotional disturbance. The combination of behavior management and therapy services with the family and the in-class management or reward plan resulted in a drastic reduction in problems. After an initial period of resistance to the sit-out consequence, Hugh began to respond in a more controlled fashion. He came to recognize when he was about to receive a consequence, a recognition that helped deter some of his impulsive behavior. Equally important, the relationship between Hugh and his teacher improved. He was especially responsive to the 5-minute reward program; but he did poorly if the teacher or the classroom aide failed to stick closely to the 5-minute time line. With better control, Hugh came to anticipate rewards that he was about to receive for completing work and following rules. Once he stopped disrupting class, his classmates were more accepting of him. Eventually, Hugh had a reasonably successful first-grade year.

JAMES: SPECIAL EDUCATION, MEDICATION, AND BEHAVIOR MANAGEMENT

Ten-year-old James had been identified as having learning disabilities when he was in the third grade. As a fifth grader, he was continuing to struggle in school despite a daily hour of resource tutoring in reading and language arts. James's classroom teacher reported that he failed to complete classwork and was disorganized and forgetful. His grades were mostly F's. James also displayed many ADHD symptoms, including a short attention span, distractibility, and social intrusiveness; impulsivity seemed to underlie many of his problems.

At the encouragement of his teacher, James was taken to his pediatrician. The pediatrician collected a medical and developmental history, which revealed a healthy child whose developmental rate was slightly delayed linguistically but advanced motorically. James had always been overactive. His exuberance had been noted as early as age 8 months. His play had tended to be rough, and he never tolerated sedentary activities. Peers accepted him, although he was often too talkative. An informal teacher assessment reported inattention, impulsivity, and academic failure. These were confirmed in a telephone conversation between James's teacher and his pediatrician.

In a meeting with his mother in the pediatrician's office, James was initially well focused. After he became more comfortable, his impulsivity was clear as he investigated items in the examining room while his mother and the physician talked. He was restless, sitting only briefly on the examining table. He asked questions with increasing impertinence, although good-naturedly. The pediatrician noted several facial scrapes, which had been caused by James's rough, careless, high-energy style of play.

Based on the history and observation, the pediatrician concluded that James indeed experienced ADHD–Combined Type and was a candidate for treatment with medication. The pediatrician decided to proceed with Ritalin, and the family concurred. The initial dosage was 5 milligrams each morning and at noon. Possible side effects were explained. The pediatrician inquired and recorded the fact that James had difficulty with falling asleep even without medication, a potentially important finding in case sleep problems were noted after the medication was started. James's appetite was good. He had no tics or complaints of headache or stomachache before the medicine was started.

The pediatrician suggested that James start taking the medicine on a Saturday morning. This start day, she suggested, allowed two advantages. First, James's parents would be able to observe therapeutic and side effects, should they occur. Second, in the unlikely event that severe side effects should arise, the medicine could be stopped quickly. James's parents were encouraged to keep a log of observations—an informal summary of any unusual events, either positive or negative—following the start of medication. She asked that James's parents talk with his teacher by telephone on Wednesday afternoon to identify any changes in James's behavior at school. After that call was completed, the parents were to speak with the pediatrician by telephone to apprise her of the child's status.

James took his first dose of Ritalin at 8:30 on Saturday morning. By 9:30 A.M., his mother noted an important change: James was actually watching television with his younger siblings. There was no fighting or arguing. The parents conferred, but they could not reach a consensus about whether James was sitting stiller. They did both agree that he was getting along better with his brother and sister throughout the morning. James subsequently ate a large midday meal.

A second 5-milligram tablet was administered at 12:30 P.M., and again James's parents noted changes in his behavior. From approximately 2:00 P.M. until 4:00 P.M. he watched his father work on a model airplane. Although he left several times, he always returned, sat attentively, and talked in a polite fashion. There were no signs of intrusion, nor did he attempt to dominate the conversation. Soon after 4:00 P.M., however, he seemed to be back to his old behavior. He fought with his younger brother, repeatedly taking the younger child's toy even though his mother had warned him to keep his hands to himself. James ate a large dinner at 6:00 P.M.; there were no complaints about lack of hunger. He went to bed at his normal weekend bedtime of 10:00 P.M. without any problems. Improvement in James's behavior was evident, but his parents believed the improvement to be less than dramatic.

By the time of the parent-to-teacher telephone call on Wednesday, James's teacher had noticed he was completing more work. James's teacher volunteered that she had noticed fewer trips to the pencil sharpener. James had remained too talkative, however, and he had had two playground incidents.

When James's mother spoke to the pediatrician, she assured the doctor that James was experiencing no severe side effects from the medicine; however, she also thought that the therapeutic effects were inadequate. The pediatrician pointed out that 5 milligrams was a beginning dose, and she suggested an increase to 10 milligrams each morning and at midday, and a 5-milligram dose at 4:00 P.M. She pointed out that the afternoon dose is often important to ensure that some therapeutic effects exist during crucial social and homework times. The afternoon dose was also designed to lessen any potential rebound effect. This time there was an even more obvious improvement of symptoms, especially at school. James's teacher commented that he was completing substantially more work and appeared to be "better focused." Fewer playground problems had occurred as well. At home, he was "paying better attention and sitting still for quiet activities, which he never did before," according to his mother.

James's appetite, however, became a slight problem. His parents were uncomfortable with his occasional picking at lunch, and they disliked his snacking late in the evening. They backed off from demanding that he clean his plate, however, and acquiesced to the high-calorie evening snacks suggested by his pediatrician.

At a 3-month follow-up, James's mother reported that he was making outstanding school progress. Not only was he better able to complete work in class but his resource teacher reported that he was more attentive and better able to profit from their time together. She commented that the overly fast pace that had previously characterized James's approach to reading had changed. With coaching, he now slowed down and sounded out words syllable by syllable. In addition, he seemed to pay better attention to the nature of stories he read aloud for his resource teacher. This allowed him to focus more on comprehension and to use the context of the story to help figure out unknown words.

James's mother told the pediatrician, however, that she was frustrated that his behavior at home was still a problem. Her comments were, "It seems like the Ritalin has solved many of his school problems, but he still talks back too much and there are too many times that he won't cooperate. Maybe I notice these now more that we are less worried about school, but it is still a problem." In response to these concerns, the pediatrician suggested that the family visit a psychologist who was knowledgeable about ADHD. The goal was to examine James's home behavior and the ways in which his parents coped with his behavior to determine whether alternative discipline methods might help.

The psychologist met with James only briefly during the first office visit. Subsequently, he met with the parents alone: James did not come to this appointment. Each of the first few sessions consisted of the parents' outlining their areas of greatest conflict with their son, such as refusal to follow directions, rough play in the house, and dawdling on chores. Next, the parents discussed their traditional method of handling the problem: discussion, threats, and grounding. Each problem was then reviewed by the psychologist, with an attempt to understand the behavior in terms of behavior and consequences. Using steps similar to those outlined in Chapter 8, James's parents and the psychologist worked out alternative discipline methods together. James's parents found that using clearer directives helped them tremendously. They also discovered that when they reduced their discussion with James and used the time-out consequence more promptly, James responded much more quickly. Although there was a brief period of resistance and complaints by James, he ultimately became more manageable.

James's parents met with the psychologist for six weekly sessions. To promote independent problem solving, the psychologist asked the parents to describe how they might solve various hypothetical problems. At the conclusion of the sixth session, the parents believed that they had mastered the basic ideas of defining problems, targeting behaviors, and applying consequences promptly. They were fast learners. A 1-month follow-up appointment was scheduled to reappraise progress. A 6-month appointment was also scheduled. James's parents were encouraged to return sooner if they found that the techniques were losing effectiveness or if they had specific questions about discipline or behavior.

With regard to medication, James remained on the 10 milligrams of Ritalin each morning and midday and 5 milligrams each afternoon for 2 years; thereafter the morning and midday doses were increased to 15 milligrams. His weight was monitored twice yearly, and there were no changes from his prior rate of growth.

MICHELLE: MEDICATION AND SOCIAL SKILLS TRAINING

Few children with ADHD are treated in specialized settings such as university-affiliated medical schools or children's hospitals. Centers such as these that treat large numbers of children with ADHD offer advantages of specialization. Michelle's case exemplifies two of these advantages.

Michelle was an 8-year-old girl referred to the ADHD clinic at a regional children's hospital at the encouragement of her school. At school, she showed the classic array of ADHD symptoms: incomplete work, classroom disruptiveness, impulsivity, poor regard for danger on the playground, and alienation of peers because of her intrusiveness and nonstop action.

Michelle and her family underwent a thorough assessment by a child psychiatrist and psychologist. Michelle's history was consistent with ADHD, as was her presentation when observed in the office. General teacher- and parent-completed rating forms were in accord with the observation and history. After initial data were collected, the tentative impression was that Michelle probably was affected by ADHD. Consequently, she underwent a more-detailed evaluation specifically designed to assess ADHD and ultimately a carefully controlled Ritalin trial.

First, Michelle was brought to a specially arranged observation room and presented with a set of simple arithmetic problems. Her mother was seated beside her with a set of ADHD rating forms to complete while Michelle worked to solve the arithmetic problems. Michelle was instructed to work without looking around, to remain seated, and to refrain from talking to her mother. She was told that she would be observed by the psychologist, who would be stationed behind a one-way mirror. Using the observation procedure discussed in Chapter 3, Michelle was monitored for a 10-minute period. She was found to be "off task" during 12.5% of that time. This is substantial off-task behavior for such a short observation in a largely distraction-free environment.

Second, rating forms specific to ADHD were completed by Michelle's mother and her classroom teacher. This ADHD clinic used both the ADHD Rating Scale (one form completed by the parents, another completed by the teacher) and the Home and School Situations Questionnaires (see Chapter 5). Michelle was found to have extremely high scores on each of these rating forms. That is, not only was she evidencing severe symptoms but also her problems were apparent in many different settings, both at home and in school. Her mother also completed the Personality Inventory for Children, which resulted in a single elevation, on the hyperactivity scale. These pretreatment observations and ratings of behavior are considered to be crucial to a careful appraisal of medication effects; they document the presence and severity of ADHD symptoms before treatment begins.

Third, Michelle's mother completed the Side Effects Rating Scale questionnaire. This form (see Figure 14.1) lists the most common signs and symptoms that may be reported as side effects of stimulant medication, such as Ritalin. Parents are asked to rate whether any of these are present before medication is prescribed and, if so, how severe they are. Collecting ratings of possible side effects while the child is medication-free is important. For example, many children have preexisting problems with appetite or insomnia. When their medication-free existence is documented, mistaken beliefs that the medicine caused these problems can be avoided. Michelle's mother rated her as having minor problems with headaches (a rating of 3 on a scale of 1–9) prior to treatment. No other symptoms on the side effects questionnaire were checked.

After physical data were collected and the child psychiatrist explained the medication to Michelle's mother, Michelle was ready for the medication trial. She was initially given a 3-week supply of medication. Each week Michelle was to receive a different dosage of Ritalin. One week the dosage would be 5 milligrams twice per day, another week the dosage would be 15 milligrams twice per day, and a third week the dosage would be a placebo (i.e., an empty capsule disguised to look like the Ritalin-filled capsules) twice per day. Michelle, her mother, her teacher, and the psychologist who performed the observation-room-derived ratings of on-task behavior were unaware of which dosage was being consumed each week. They were thus "blinded" to the procedure.

At the conclusion of each week, Michelle returned to the ADHD clinic. As part of each visit, she again worked at arithmetic problems in the observation room, and on-task/off-task ratings were calculated. These ratings helped the professional team to evaluate her attention levels as the medication dosages changed. Likewise, Michelle's mother returned completed rating forms (ADHD Rating Scale and Home Situations Questionnaire) describing the status of her ADHD symptoms for that week (i.e., for that particular dosage of medication). Equivalent forms (ADHD Rating Scale and School Situations Questionnaire) were completed by Michelle's classroom teacher. Finally, her mother completed the Side Effects Rating Scale (see Figure 14.1) each week.

At the end of the 3-week trial, the dosages used each week were revealed, and information was summarized so that decisions about continuing medication and selecting an ongoing treatment dosage, if any, could be made. The results of Michelle's trial are shown in Figure 14.2, allowing a quick appraisal of whether improvement had occurred and which dosage was most effective. The use of various observations and ratings—some more sensitive to attention, others more sensitive to conduct and behavior, others more sensitive to the broad array of ADHD symptoms—helped ensure a thorough investigation of Michelle's symptoms. Michelle responded well to the 15-milligram dose and less well but still favorably to the 5-milligram dose when com-

SIDE EFFECTS RATING SCALE

Name ___Michelle Smith___ Date ___7-10-99___

Person Completing This Form ___Mrs. Smith___

Instructions: Please rate each behavior from 0 (absent) to 9 (serious). Circle only one number beside each item. A zero means that you have not seen the behavior in this child during the past week, and a 9 means that you have noticed it and believe it either to be very serious or to occur very frequently.

Behavior	Absent									Serious
Insomnia or trouble sleeping	(0)	1	2	3	4	5	6	7	8	9
Nightmares	(0)	1	2	3	4	5	6	7	8	9
Stares a lot or daydreams	(0)	1	2	3	4	5	6	7	8	9
Talks less with others	(0)	1	2	3	4	5	6	7	8	9
Uninterested in others	(0)	1	2	3	4	5	6	7	8	9
Decreased appetite	(0)	1	2	3	4	5	6	7	8	9

Irritable	0	1	2	3	4	5	6	7	8	9
Stomachaches	0	1	2	3	4	5	6	7	8	9
Headaches	0	1	2	3	4	5	6	7	8	9
Drowsiness	0	1	2	3	4	5	6	7	8	9
Sad/unhappy	0	1	2	3	4	5	6	7	8	9
Prone to crying	0	1	2	3	4	5	6	7	8	9
Anxious	0	1	2	3	4	5	6	7	8	9
Bites fingernails	0	1	2	3	4	5	6	7	8	9
Euphoric/unusually happy	0	1	2	3	4	5	6	7	8	9
Dizziness	0	1	2	3	4	5	6	7	8	9
Tics or nervous movements	0	1	2	3	4	5	6	7	8	9

Figure 14.1. Michelle's pretreatment ratings on the Side Effects Rating Scale. (From Barkley, R.A., & Murphy, K.R. [1998]. *Attention-deficit hyperactivity disorder: A clinical workbook* [2nd ed., p. 133]. New York: Guilford Press; reprinted by permission.)

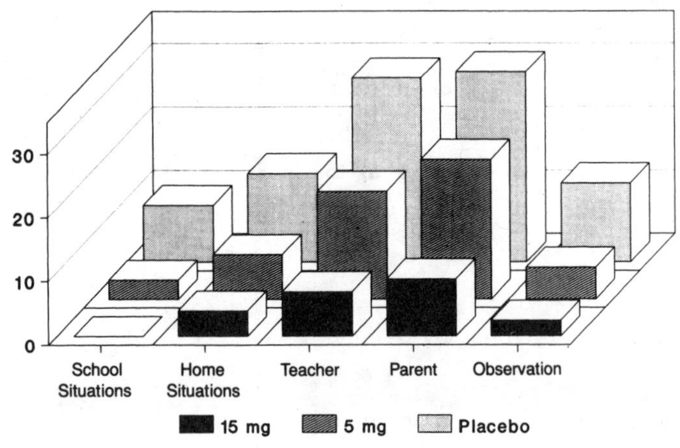

Figure 14.2. Summary of 3-week trial of Michelle's response to controlled Ritalin trial. The lower the ratings on each form, the fewer and less severe the symptoms noted. (School Situations = School Situations Questionnaire; Home Situations = Home Situations Questionnaire; Teacher = Teacher-Completed ADHD Rating Scale; Parent = Parent-Completed ADHD Rating Scale; Observation = in-office observation.)

pared with the placebo. She had only slight problems with insomnia, as reflected by the side effects questionnaire ratings, at the two Ritalin dosages. Her headaches did not worsen after medication was started.

Ongoing treatment with 15 milligrams twice per day was agreed to by the child psychiatrist and Michelle's mother. She was scheduled for follow-up visits with the child psychiatrist. Michelle's social problems also received treatment. She was enrolled in a fall and spring sequence (15 sessions each) of group therapy with other girls her age, most of whom had social problems, too. Michelle's tendencies to dominate conversations, make disparaging comments, argue abruptly, and flit rapidly from topic to topic were addressed. This group, which was designed to reduce the problems just listed through behavioral techniques, offered important advantages. First, it approximated a natural environment of peers. Immediate feedback and, if necessary, negative consequences could follow inappropriate behavior in this setting. Second, acceptable alternative behavior could be taught by using shaping techniques, modeling, and positive feedback (these general techniques are discussed in Chapter 8). Third, Michelle's parents were enlisted as allies. By noting the behaviors embraced within the group and using similar consequences outside the group, treatment changes could be built on and their appearance outside the group could be encouraged.

The combined intervention of medication and social skills training helped Michelle's overall behavior and improved her interaction with her peers. More important, her feelings of self-control and self-satisfaction were strengthened.

CONCLUSIONS

Numerous intervention options are available for children with ADHD. Any individual child may require one or more types of intervention. The most frequently used options include the following:

1. Modification of education services or changes in classroom approach
2. Medication
3. Alternation of techniques of home discipline with increased emphasis on behavior management
4. Development of social skills in a group therapy format

Parents of children with ADHD should be encouraged by the range of interventions that do exist. Most important is that parents, health practitioners, and school personnel work together closely to ensure that the intervention plans they develop are finely tuned to the child's individual needs and circumstances.

Chapter 15

Financing Help for Your Child

ADHD Myths

Parent advocacy has little or no impact on the services that your child receives.

There are few services that parents can secure for their child with ADHD without spending a lot of money.

Because recognizing your child's needs is pointless if you are unable to meet them, you need to be able to finance the services that your child requires. What is the best way to accomplish this task? There is no universally correct answer. Your own family's particular circumstances and differences in service networks in different areas prevent pat formulas. Nevertheless, this chapter provides some general ideas about the cost of services for your child as well as approaches for financing them.

PUBLIC SCHOOL SERVICES

As stated in Chapter 10, services are provided free to parents under the Individuals with Disabilities Education Act (IDEA) of 1990 or Section 504 of the Rehabilitation Act of 1973. Arranging a meeting with school personnel, usually a special education administrator or the school psychologist assigned to your child's school, is usually the first step. Such a meeting may provide you with a sense of the services your child's school is willing to offer. Suspicions that your child has ADHD should generally be shared during this meeting, or an already-established diagnosis should be conveyed. Recall also that the school team must itself establish a diagnosis, or at least concur with a diagnosis from a nonschool professional, before services can be provided. A diagnosis rendered by an outside professional alone is insufficient.

Many schools confine their help for eligible students to classroom adjustments and assistance with academics; that is, they may modify teaching methods or offer tutoring but nothing more. Some schools, however, do offer more and, in rare instances, much more. Social skills training, individual counseling, and/or parent training are offered by some schools. It is not unheard of for school personnel to arrange for medical consultations or perhaps even to pay for such services. Some full-service schools have introduced teams of health services providers, such as pediatricians, on school campuses. Even if the school assumes no financial responsibility for nonacademic services, sharing your concerns with school personnel is still wise. School personnel may know the location of free or sliding-scale services or which services have good reputations and which don't. Again, situational factors vary, but seeking help from the school is a viable strategy, especially when financial resources are limited.

PUBLIC SECTOR MENTAL HEALTH SERVICES

Community mental health centers or other facilities committed to the public's mental health are located at many sites in the United States. These facilities generally render services on a sliding-fee basis that is indexed according to a family's ability to pay. Accordingly, fees may be less—sometimes far less—than those charged by a private practitioner. If insurance benefits capable of covering services related to ADHD are unavailable for your child, then it may make sense to inquire about community-based mental health programs.

Community-based mental health programs are not principally concerned with ADHD, nor do they necessarily concern themselves with the education-related problems that children with ADHD often experience. Nonetheless, both ADHD and conduct disorders are common enough that most mental health programs develop some expertise in diagnosing and treating these conditions. Many of these programs stress outpatient counseling and psychotherapy, with groups of individuals, with whole families, or with the identified individuals themselves. Some programs also offer psychiatric diagnostic services and medication management. A school liaison may be provided as well so that a comprehensive plan can be implemented. Again, individual circumstances vary. You are encouraged to ask school personnel, your child's primary care physician, clergy, and/or friends about this category of services.

PRIVATE SECTOR MEDICAL AND BEHAVIOR HEALTH CARE

Private sector medical and behavior health care encompasses private practitioners and facilities that charge for services, either directly to the family or to the family's health insurance company.

ADHD Clinics and Programs

ADHD clinics and programs are specialized programs that tend to be rare and are often confined to medical schools, children's hospitals, or large medical facilities. In these settings, extremely specialized medical professionals such as child psychiatrists or child neurologists team with professionals from the field of either psychology or education to create the intricate diagnostic and treatment services that a condition such as ADHD requires.

Evaluations in these settings may involve one or more professionals. Typically, rating forms and observation are used, the child and the parents are interviewed, and a medical assessment occurs. Depending on the initial reports of the child's school status, a detailed psychoeducational evaluation may or may not be performed. Similarly, a neuropsychological evaluation or even laboratory neurological tests may be conducted for some children. These programs often charge a basic assessment fee, with additional charges being incurred only if supplemental testing or laboratory studies are needed. An estimated cost range for this basic evaluation is $200–$1,000.

Treatment services vary according to the needs of the child. Of course, large, more-specialized centers are most apt to provide a full array of services, including services that may be required by only a small percentage of the children whom they treat. For example, several centers in the United States offer controlled medication trials. This is a precisely controlled procedure consisting of several weeks' trial on various dosages of medication and the use of a placebo. Observations are made as medication dosages are changed. Fees for this type of service may range from $300 to $500. Some services and fee ranges of ADHD clinics might include group therapy and social skills training, $25–$80 per session; individual or family therapy, $75–$150 per session;

school visits and consultation, $75–$150 per hour; medication review and physical examination, $25–$60 per quarter hour; and parent training, $25–$70 per group session.

Generally, fees reflect the complexity of the service provided, the level and specialization of the service providers, and the amount of time required to perform the service. Thus, specialized centers that perform complicated procedures with highly trained professionals are likely to be somewhat more expensive than nonspecialized programs. Moreover, some procedures at specialized centers are time-consuming (e.g., tabulating ratings, structured observation of the child while he or she works, collaboration among several diagnosticians to formulate a treatment plan). Understandably, these types of service are costly.

Psychiatrists and Psychologists

Most child psychiatrists and child psychologists encounter large numbers of children with ADHD and most are quite accustomed to diagnosing ADHD. A child psychiatrist (i.e., a psychologist with an M.D. or a D.O. [Doctor of Osteopathy] degree) working alone may charge between $125 and $500 for a complete assessment. He or she may need to make a referral to a psychologist if a psychoeducational evaluation is required.

A child psychologist working alone may charge between $100 and $400 for a basic evaluation to determine your child's ADHD status. If the child is not under the care of a primary care physician (i.e., a pediatrician or a family physician), then an additional referral to rule out medical causes may be required. Both psychiatrists and psychologists, of course, diagnose all sorts of behavior and emotional problems. Their examinations tend to be detailed in order to rule out other possible mental or behavioral disorders. Follow-up services may range from approximately $80 to $200 per hour for psychiatrists and from $65 to $150 per hour for psychologists.

Pediatricians, Family Practitioners, and Neurologists

Although not universally true, pediatricians and family practitioners tend to offer less-expensive diagnostic services than specialists. This is true simply because a primary care physician cannot allocate 1 or 2 hours for a single patient. The demands of caring for individuals who are ill preclude this kind or lengthy examination. Less time spent diagnosing your child means smaller charges. Evaluations may range from $40 to $120 for a diagnostic visit. Briefer follow-up visits to discuss medication or discipline usually range from $25 to $80. Some pediatricians schedule blocks of time devoted to behavior or developmental problems. For those who do, appointments tend to be longer, with corresponding increases in fees.

Neurologists are specialists rather than primary care physicians, and their fees tend to be higher. A basic evaluation for ADHD by a neurologist is likely to range from approximately $150 to $300.

Medication Costs

Medication costs range widely. For the most commonly used medication, Ritalin, children receiving small doses (e.g., 5 milligrams twice per day) may accumulate bills as low as approximately $20 per month. For children who require larger doses (e.g., 45 milligrams per day) costs are typically in the $50–$90 per month range. Generic medications appear to cost a bit less than name brands, and time-release preparations tend to be a bit more expensive than tablets.

Prices vary among the less frequently used medications, too (e.g., Cylert, clonidine). Some medications are difficult to obtain without advance notice to your pharmacist. Parents generally find it helpful to shop around or inquire of parents whose children have required medicine for some time. Their experience can be informative.

Health Insurance

The extent to which the services described in the previous section are paid for by health insurance varies greatly. Coverage seems to vary even more for mental health or behavioral health services than for other types of services. Some plans pay a percentage, such as 80%, of "usual and customary" charges. Thus, if a psychiatric consultation is assumed to have a "usual and customary" charge of $200, then the plan will pay $160 and patients will shoulder the difference. Families are free to select any provider they choose under this arrangement.

Increasingly common is the managed-care option, whereby plan enrollees are directed to specific service providers. Under this arrangement, enrollees typically receive services at fixed (often reduced) rates, or they may make a set copayment (e.g., $15).

Parents seem to encounter three main frustrations with their insurance companies. First, the fee limits can be extremely low. Thus, a company may allow for a psychiatric evaluation but agree to pay only $55 regardless of the charge; alternatively, authorizations for outpatient counseling sessions have caps of $15 per hour. Obviously, such plans leave parents with a large financial burden. Second, some policies exclude ADHD from coverage. No matter how good the coverage may otherwise be, services to diagnose or treat ADHD are not reimbursed. The rationale is that ADHD is a developmental or learning problem, not a psychiatric or medical condition. Third, some managed-care plans do not include practitioners who are expert in ADHD or in behavior or developmental problems. For example, none of the available psychiatrists and psychologists in a plan may specialize in treating children.

You are encouraged to consult your company's benefits manual and/or to speak directly to personnel from your company to determine precisely the scope and limitations of benefits relating to ADHD. The need to seek exact information about your particular coverage cannot be overstated. If no acceptable practitioners are listed under your managed-care program, it may be worthwhile to discuss this with officials from your insurance company. Sometimes modifications can be made.

SUPPORT AND ADVOCACY GROUPS

Many communities have support groups, which are often created and maintained by parents. Although these groups cannot provide funding for ADHD services, they do help by directing parents to affordable services. They may also assist by advocating for individual children's educational needs. Moreover, problems common to parents of children with ADHD, such as how to discipline, may be examined in meetings of the support group, through invited speakers, or by distribution of written material. Parents who create their own support network may find that this lessens the need for professional support or advocacy services. Participation in such a group typically involves little or no cost to parents.

Following are the addresses of two national support groups for ADHD. Parents may inquire about local chapters by contacting the national offices.

Children and Adults with Attention Deficit Disorders (CHADD)
National Headquarters
8181 Professional Place
Suite 201
Landover, Maryland 20785
(301) 306-7070
(800) 233-4050
Email: national@chadd.org
Web site: http://www.chadd.org/

National Attention Deficit Disorders Association (ADDA)
Post Office Box 1303
Northbrook, Illinois 60065
Email: mail@add.org
Web site: http://www.add.org/

CONCLUSIONS

Ensuring that your child receives proper services often depends on your knowledge of funding sources and your insistence that he or she gets the services to which he or she is entitled. Hard work and dogged determination may thus be required. Indeed, many parents find that their efforts ultimately pay off and that their children's long-term success is enhanced because proper services are secured.

References

Abramowitz, A.J., & O'Leary, S.G. (1991). Behavioral interventions for the classroom: Implications for students with ADHD. *School Psychology Review, 20,* 220–234.

Achenbach, T.M., & Edelbrock, C.S. (1983). *Manual for the Child Behavior Checklist and Revised Child Behavior Profile.* Burlington: University of Vermont, Department of Psychiatry.

Acker, M.M., & O'Leary, S.G. (1987). Effects of reprimands and praise on appropriate behavior in the classroom. *Journal of Abnormal Child Psychology, 15,* 549–557.

Ambrosini, P.J. (1987). Pharmacotherapy in child and adolescent major depressive disorder. In H.Y. Meltzer (Ed.), *Psychopharmacology: The third generation of progress* (pp. 1247–1254). Philadelphia: Lippincott Williams & Wilkins.

Amen, D.G., & Carmichael, B.D. (1997). High-resolution brain SPECT imaging in ADHD. *Annals of Clinical Psychiatry, 9,* 81–86.

American Psychiatric Association. (1968). *Diagnostic and statistical manual of mental disorders* (2nd ed.). Washington, DC: Author.

American Psychiatric Association. (1980). *Diagnostic and statistical manual of mental disorders* (3rd ed.). Washington, DC: Author.

American Psychiatric Association. (1987). *Diagnostic and statistical manual of mental disorders* (3rd. ed. rev.). Washington, DC: Author.

American Psychiatric Association. (1994). *Diagnostic and statistical manual of mental disorders* (4th ed.). Washington, DC: Author.

Arky, R., et al. (1999). *Physicians' desk reference* (53rd ed.). Montvale, NJ: Medical Economics Co.

August, G.J., & Garfinkel, B.D. (1990). Comorbidity of ADHD and reading disability among clinic-referred children. *Journal of Abnormal Child Psychology, 18,* 29–45.

Barkley, R.A. (1987). *Defiant children: A clinician's manual for parent training* (1st ed.). New York: Guilford Press.

Barkley, R.A. (1990). *Attention deficit hyperactivity disorder: A handbook for diagnosis and treatment.* New York: Guilford Press.

Barkley, R.A. (1991). Diagnosis and assessment of attention deficit-hyperactivity disorder. *Comprehensive Mental Health Care, 1,* 27–43.

Barkley, R.A. (1997). Behavioral inhibition, sustained attention, and executive functions: Constructing a unifying theory of ADHD. *Psychological Bulletin, 121,* 65–94.

Barkley, R.A. (1997). *Defiant children: A clinician's manual for assessment and parent training* (2nd ed.). New York: Guilford Press.

Barkley, R.A., & Biederman, J. (1997). Toward a broader definition of the age-of-onset criterion for attention-deficit-hyperactivity disorder. *Journal of the American Academy of Child and Adolescent Psychiatry, 36,* 1204–1210.

Barkley, R.A., DuPaul, G.J., & McMurray, M.B. (1991). Attention deficit disorder with and without hyperactivity: Clinical response to three dose levels of methylphenidate. *Pediatrics, 87,* 519–531.

Barkley, R.A., & Edelbrock, C.S. (1987). Assessing situation variation in children's behavior problems: The Home and School Situations Questionnaires. In R. Prinz (Ed.), *Advances in behavioral assessment of children and families* (Vol. 3, pp. 157–176). Greenwich, CT: JAI Press.

Barkley, R.A., Fischer, M., Edelbrock, C.S., & Smallish, L. (1990). The adolescent outcome of hyperactive children diagnosed by research criteria: I. An 8-year prospective follow-up study. *Journal of the American Academy of Child and Adolescent Psychiatry, 29,* 546–557.

Barkley, R.A., & Grodzinsky, G.M. (1994). Are tests of frontal lobe functions useful in the diagnosis of attention deficit disorder? *Clinical Neuropsychologist, 8,* 121–139.

Barkley, R.A., & Murphy, K.R. (1998). *Attention-deficit hyperactivity disorder: A clinical workbook* (2nd ed.). New York: Guilford Press.

Burns, G.L., Walsh, J.A., Owen, S.M, & Snell, J. (1997). Internal validity of attention deficit hyperactivity disorder, oppositional defiant disorder, and overt conduct disorder symptoms in young children: Implications for teacher ratings for a dimensional approach to symptom validity. *Journal of Clinical Child Psychology, 26,* 266–275.

Cantwell, D.P. (1972). Psychiatric illness in the families of hyperactive children. *Archives of General Psychiatry, 27*, 414–417.

Conners, C.K. (1973). Conners' Rating Scales for use in drug studies with children. *Psychopharmacology Bulletin [Special issue: Pharmacotherapy with children], 9*, 24–84.

Conners, C.K. (1994). *Conners' Continuous Performance Test.* North Tonawanda, NY: Multi-Health Systems.

Dulcan, M.K. (1990). Using psychostimulants to treat behavioral disorders of children and adolescents. *Journal of Child and Adolescent Psychopharmacology, 1*, 7–21.

Dulcan, M.K., & Benson, R.S. (1997). Summary of the practice parameters for the assessment and treatment of children, adolescents, and adults with ADHD. *Journal of American Academy of Child and Adolescent Psychiatry, 36*, 1311–1317.

DuPaul, G.J. (1990). *The ADHD Rating Scale: Normative data, reliability, and validity.* Unpublished manuscript, University of Massachusetts Medical Center, Worcester.

DuPaul, G.J., & Barkley, R.A. (1992). Situational variability in attentional problems: Psychometric properties of the Revised Home and School Situations Questionnaires. *Journal of Clinical Child Psychology, 21*, 187–188.

DuPaul, G.J., & Ekert, T.L. (1998). Academic interventions for students with attention-deficit hyperactivity disorder: A review of the literature. *Reading and Writing Quarterly: Overcoming Learning Difficulties, 14*, 59–82.

DuPaul, G.J., Power, T.J., Anastopoulous, A.D., Reid, R., McGoey, K.E., & Ikeda, M.J. (1997). Teacher ratings of attention deficit hyperactivity disorder symptoms: Factor structure and normative data. *Psychological Assessment, 4*, 436–444.

Ernst, M., Zametkin, A.J., Phillips, R.L., Cohen, R.M. (1998, Spring). Age-related changes in brain glucose metabolism in adults with attention-deficit/hyperactivity disorder and control subjects. *Journal of Neuropsychiatry and Clinical Neurosciences, 10*(2), 168–177.

Fergusson, D.M., Lynskey, M.T., & Horwood, L.J. (1997). Attentional difficulties in middle childhood and psychosocial outcomes in young adulthood. *Journal of Child Psychology and Psychiatry and Allied Disciplines, 38*, 633–644.

Findling, R., Schwartz, M., Flannery, D., & Manos, M. (1996). Venlafaxine in adults with ADHD: An open trial. *Journal of Clinical Psychiatry, 57*, 184–189.

Frick, P.J., Kamphaus, R.W., Lahey, B.B., Loeber, R., Christ, M.G., Hart, E.L., & Tannenbaum, L.E. (1991). Academic underachievement and the disruptive behavior disorders. *Journal of Consulting and Clinical Psychology, 59,* 289–294.

Frick, P.J., & Lahey, B.B. (1991). The nature and characteristics of attention-deficit hyperactivity disorder. *School Psychology Review, 20,* 163–173.

Garfinkel, B.D. (n.d.). *Structured ADHD interview: Child version.* Unpublished report, University of Minnesota Medical School, Minneapolis.

Garland, E.J. (1996). Clonidine: Finding its place in child psychiatry. *Child and Adolescent Psychopharmacology News, 1,* 8–9.

Gaub, M., & Carlson, C.L. (1997). Behavioral characteristics of DSM-IV ADHD subtypes in a school-based population. *Journal of Abnormal Child Psychology, 25,* 103–111.

Gennaro, A.R. (Ed.). (1990). *Remington's pharmaceutical sciences* (18th ed., 6 vols.). Easton, PA: Mack Publishing Co.

Gittelman, R., Mannuzza, S., Shenker, R., & Bonagura, N. (1985). Hyperactive boys almost grown up. *Archives of General Psychiatry, 42,* 937–947.

Gordon, M. (1983). *The Gordon Diagnostic System.* DeWitt, NY: Gordon Systems.

Green, W.H. (1991). *Child and adolescent clinical psychopharmacology.* Philadelphia: Lippincott Williams & Wilkins.

Green, W.H. (1995). *Child and adolescent clinical psychopharmacology* (2nd ed.). Philadelphia: Lippincott Williams & Wilkins.

Greenberg, L.M. (1992). *Test of Variables of Attention.* Los Alamitos, CA: Universal Attention Disorders.

Greenhill, L.L. (1990). Attention-deficit hyperactivity disorder. In B.D. Garfinkel, G.A. Carlson, & E.B. Weller (Eds.), *Psychiatric disorders in children and adolescents* (pp. 149–182). Philadelphia: W.B. Saunders.

Hakola, S.R. (1992). Legal rights of students with attention deficit disorder. *School Psychology Quarterly, 7,* 285–297.

Halperin, J.M., Gittelman, R., Klein, D.F., & Rudel, R.G. (1984). Reading-disabled hyperactive children: A distinct subgroup of attention deficit disorder with hyperactivity? *Journal of Abnormal Child Psychology, 12,* 1–14.

Hartsough, C.S., & Lambert, N.M. (1985). Medical factors in hyperactive and normal children: Prenatal, developmental, and health history factors findings. *American Journal of Orthopsychiatry, 55,* 190–210.

Hauser, P., Soler, R., Brucker-Davis, F., & Weintraub, B.D. (1997). Thyroid hormones correlated with symptoms of hyperactvity but not inattention in attention deficit hyperactivity disorder. *Psychoneuroendocrinology, 22,* 107–114.

Hinshaw, S.P., Henker, B., & Whalen, C.K. (1984). Cognitive-behavioral and pharmacologic interventions for hyperactive boys: Comparative and combined effects. *Journal of Consulting and Clinical Psychology, 52,* 739–749.

Individuals with Disabilities Education Act (IDEA) Amendments of 1991, PL 102-119, 20 U.S.C. §§ 1400 *et seq.*

Individuals with Disabilities Education Act (IDEA) Amendments of 1997, PL 105-17, 20 U.S.C. §§ 1400 *et seq.*

Individuals with Disabilities Education Act (IDEA) of 1990, PL 101-476, 20 U.S.C. §§ 1400 *et seq.*

Jacobvitz, D., & Sroufe, L.A. (1987). The early caregiver-child relationship and attention-deficit disorder with hyperactivity in kindergarten: A prospective study. *Child Development, 58,* 1496–1504.

Jacobvitz, D., Sroufe, L.A., Stewart, M., & Leffert, N. (1990). Treatment of attentional and hyperactivity problems in children with sympathomimetic drugs: A comprehensive review. *American Journal of Child and Adolescent Psychiatry, 29,* 677–688.

Kendall, P.C. (1985). Toward a cognitive-behavioral model of child psychopathology and a critique of related interventions. *Journal of Abnormal Child Psychology, 13,* 357–372.

Kline, R.G. (1987). Pharmacotherapy of childhood hyperactivity: An update. In H.Y. Meltzer (Ed.), *Psychopharmacology: The third generation of progress* (pp. 1215–1224). Philadelphia: Lippincott Williams & Wilkins.

Lachar, D. (1982). *Personality Inventory for Children (PIC): Revised format manual supplement.* Los Angeles: Western Psychological Services.

Lahey, B.B., Pelham, W.E., Schaughency, E.A., Atkins, M.S., Murphy, A., Hynd, G.W., Russo, M., Hartdagen, S., & Lorys-Vernon, A. (1988). Dimensions and types of attention deficit disorder. *Journal of the American Academy of Child and Adolescent Psychiatry, 27,* 330–335.

Lambert, N.M., Hartsough, C.S., Sassone, D., & Sandoval, J. (1987). Persistence of hyperactivity symptoms from childhood to adolescence and associated outcomes. *American Journal of Orthopsychiatry, 57,* 22–32.

Leo, R.J., Khin, N.A., & Cohen, G.N. (1996). ADHD and thyroid dysfunction. *Journal of the American Academy of Child and Adolescent Psychiatry, 35,* 1572–1573.

Lubar, J.F. (1991). Discourse on the development of EEG diagnostics and biofeedback for attention-deficit/hyperactivity disorder. *Biofeedback and Self-Regulation, 16,* 202–225.

Mannuzza, S., Klein, R.G., Bessler, A, Malloy, P., & Hynes, M.E. (1997). Educational and occupational outcome of hyperactive boys grown up. *Journal of the American Academy of Child and Adolescent Psychiatry, 36,* 122–1227.

Mannuzza, S., Klein, R.G., Bonagura, N., Malloy, P., Giampino, T.L., & Addalli, K.A. (1991, January). Hyperactive boys almost grown up: V. Replication of psychiatric status. *Archives of General Psychiatry, 48*(1), 77–83.

Mariani, M.A., & Barkley, R.A. (1997). Neuropsychological and academic functioning in preschool boys with attention deficit hyperactivity disorder. *Developmental Neuropsychology, 13,* 111–129.

Mash, E.J., & Johnson, C. (1983). Parental perceptions of child behavior problems, parenting self-esteem, and mothers' reported stress in younger and older hyperactive and normal children. *Journal of Consulting and Clinical Psychology, 51,* 68–99.

McCurry, L., & Cronquist, S. (1997, May). Pemoline and hepatotoxicity. *American Journal of Psychiatry, 154*(5), 713–714.

Methylphenidate (Ritalin) revisited. (1988). *Medical Letter, 26,* 97–98.

Milberger, S., Biederman, J., Faraone, S.V., Guite, J., et al. (1997). Pregnancy, delivery, and infancy complications and attention deficit hyperactivity disorder: Issues of gene-environment interactions. *Biological Psychiatry, 41,* 65–75.

Millichap, J.G. (1997). Temporal lobe arachnoid cyst-attention deficit disorder syndrome: Role of the electroencephalogram in diagnosis. *Neurology, 48,* 1435–1439.

Miller, L.S., Koplewicz, H.S., & Klein, R.G. (1997). Teacher ratings of hyperactivity, inattention, and conduct problems in preschoolers. *Journal of Abnormal Child Psychology, 25,* 113–119.

Nichols, P.L., & Chen, T.-C. (1981). *Minimal brain dysfunction: A prospective study.* Mahwah, NJ: Lawrence Erlbaum Associates.

Rapport, M.D., & Gordon, M. (1987). *Attention Training System.* DeWitt, NY: Gordon Systems.

Rasey, H.W., Lubar, J. F., McIntyre, A., Zoffuto, A.C., & Abbott, P.L. (1996). EEG neurofeedback for the enhancement of attentional processing in normal college students. *Journal of Neurotherapy, 1,* 15–21.

Reeder, G.D., Maccow, G.C., Shaw, S.R., Swerdlik, M.E., Horton, C.B., & Foster, P. (1997). School psychologists and full-service schools: Partnerships with medical, mental health, and social services. *School Psychology Review, 26,* 603–621.

Reid, R., Maag, J.W., Vasa, S.F., & Wright, G. (1994). Who are the children with attention deficit-hyperactivity disorder? A school-based survey. *Journal of Special Education, 28,* 117–137.

Remington, J.P. (1995). *The science and practice of pharmacy* (19th ed., 6 vols.). Easton, PA: Mack Publishing Co. (Original work published 1936)

Reynolds, C.R., & Kamphaus, R.W. (1992). *BASC: Behavior Assessment System for Children: Manual.* Circle Pines, MN: American Guidance Service.

Rosen, L.A., O'Leary, S.G., Joyce, S.A., Conway, G., & Pfiffner, L.J. (1984). The importance of prudent negative consequences for maintaining the appropriate behavior of hyperactive students. *Journal of Abnormal Child Psychology, 12,* 581–604.

Ross, D.M., & Ross, S.A. (1976). *Hyperactivity: Research, theory, and action.* New York: John Wiley & Sons.

Shaywitz, B.A, Fletcher, J.M., Holahan, J.M., Schneider, A.E., Marchione, K.E., Stuebing, K.K., Francis, D.J., Shankweiler, D.P., Katz, L., Liberman, I.Y., & Shaywitz, S.E. (1995). Interrelationship between reading disability and attention-deficit/hyperactivity disorder. *Child Neuropsychology, 1,* 170–186.

Shea, K.M., Rahmani, C.H., & Morris, P.J. (1996). Diagnosing children with attention deficit disorders through a health department-public school partnership. *American Journal of Public Health, 86,* 1168–1169.

Teeter, P.A. (1991). Attention-deficit hyperactivity disorder: A psychoeducational paradigm. *School Psychology Review, 20,* 266–280.

Ullmann, R.K., Sleator, E.K., & Sprague, R. (1984). A new rating scale for diagnosing and monitoring ADD in children. *Psychopharmacology Bulletin, 20,* 160–164.

Velting, O.N., & Whitehurst, G.J. (1997). Inattention-hyperactivity and reading achievement in children from low-income families: A longitudinal model. *Journal of Abnormal Child Psychology, 25,* 321–331.

Voelker, S.L., Lachar, D., & Gdowski, C.L. (1983). The Personality Inventory for Children and response to methylphenidate: Preliminary evidence for predictive validity. *Journal of Pediatric Psychology, 8,* 161–169.

Weiner, J.M. (Ed.). (1985). *Diagnosis in psychopharmacology of childhood and adolescent disorders* (1st ed.). New York: John Wiley & Sons.

Weiner, J.M. (Ed.). (1996). *Diagnosis in psychopharmacology of childhood and adolescent disorders* (2nd ed.). New York: John Wiley & Sons.

Weiss, G. (1991). Attention deficit hyperactivity disorder. In M. Lewis (Ed.), *Child and adolescent psychiatry: A comprehensive textbook* (1st ed., pp. 544–561). Philadelphia: Lippincott Williams & Wilkins.

Weiss, G., & Hechtman, L.T. (1986). *Hyperactive children grown up: Empirical findings and theoretical considerations* (1st ed.). New York: Guilford Press.

Weiss, G., & Hechtman, L.T. (1993). *Hyperactive children grown up: ADHD in children, adolescents, and adults* (2nd ed.). New York: Guilford Press.

Whalen, C.K., & Henker, B. (1991). Therapies for hyperactive children: Comparisons, combinations, and compromises. *Journal of Consulting and Clinical Psychology, 59,* 126–137.

Wilens, T.E., Biederman, J., Mick, E., Faraone, S.V., et al. (1997). Attention deficit hyperactivity disorder (ADHD) is associated with early onset substance abuse. *Journal of Nervous and Mental Disease, 185,* 475–482.

Wodrich, D.L., & Kush, J.C. (1998). The effect of methylphenidate on teachers' behavioral ratings in specific school situations. *Psychology in the Schools, 35,* 81–88.

Zametkin, A.J., Nordahl, T.E., Gross, M., King, A.C., Semple, W.E., Rumsey, J., Hamburger, S., & Cohen, R.M. (1990). Cerebral glucose metabolism in adults with hyperactivity of childhood onset. *New England Journal of Medicine, 323,* 1361–1366.

Zentall, S.S. (1989). Attentional cueing in spelling tasks for hyperactive and comparison regular class children. *Journal of Special Education, 23,* 83–93.

Zentall, S.S., & Dwyer, A.M. (1989). Color effects on the impulsivity and activity of hyperactive children. *Journal of School Psychology, 27,* 165–173.

Index

Page references followed by *t* or *f* indicate tables or figures, respectively.